HISTORY OF EARLY IRAN

HISTORY OF EARLY IRAN

BY GEORGE G. CAMERON

INSTRUCTOR IN ORIENTAL LANGUAGES
THE UNIVERSITY OF CHICAGO

GREENWOOD PRESS, PUBLISHERS
NEW YORK

TO MY WIFE

PREFACE

HISTORIES of Iran regularly begin with Cyrus the Persian and generally conclude with Alexander the Great. At present there is no single work which describes in a comprehensive fashion the history of the Iranian plateau *before* Cyrus attained mastery. This is the more regrettable since the history of a section of the plateau, Elam, cannot be neglected by any serious student of the ancient Near East. The present study endeavors to present the facts about early Elamite and Iranian history in a manner which will be at the same time useful to the scholar and intelligible to the layman.

Some years ago the writer became interested in the origin and history of the Iranian Medes. After a brief period of research it became obvious that the empire of the Medes fitted into a wider historical perspective than hitherto assumed, and that Median as well as Persian origins could not be disassociated from the history of the Iranian plateau before Iranians appeared on the scene. The attempt to unravel the mystery of that broader history led naturally to an examination of the languages which were first, to our knowledge, spoken in that land. Since the Old Persian kings had composed their inscriptions in three

languages—Old Persian, Babylonian, and Elamite—
the first step was the preparation of a concordance of
Old Persian words. Through an intimate knowledge
of this language and by a comparison with the Akkadian, late Elamite could be made intelligible. Next
followed the compilation of an Elamite dictionary
which included every published text. Finally, the
pertinent data from the Land of the Two Rivers were
scrutinized for information, previously overlooked or
disregarded, which might illuminate the picture.

The writer cannot claim full satisfaction with the
results obtained. Until recent years there have been
few excavations in Iran, and the scarcity of archeological investigations has greatly hampered historical
understanding. The researches undertaken in the tell
of Susa in Elam have been remarkably productive,
and there is little question but that other and even
more attractive sites on the plateau will add ma-
terially to our knowledge. Until archeology has assumed a larger share of the burden, much of the history of greater Iran must lie buried in the tells and
ruined city-mounds which dot the country. It is,
however, safe to say that future investigations will
and must be fitted into the historical picture to the
degree that they tie their results into the history of
Elam. The chronology of Elamite history is now, we
may assume, assured within close limits, and will provide a solid foundation for all subsequent history of
the plateau, until the first millennium B.C.

This work in its inception was inspired by Professor Albert Ten Eyck Olmstead, Oriental Institute Professor of Oriental History in the University of Chicago. From what seemed at times an inexhaustible store of knowledge, he has often pieced together the scattered threads of historical data into a perfect whole. From his unrivaled ability to see each isolated fact in its relationship to the entire picture he has given to this study a perspective it could never otherwise have achieved. From his unpublished notes and manuscripts, and, more than these, from his discussions, criticisms, and suggestions at every stage of the progress, I have obtained more than words can say. From him I have secured encouragement in hours of perplexity; his aid, given unstintingly, has enormously lightened my labors.

Professor Arno Poebel and Professor F. W. Geers have often confided to me, as student and friend, their opinions on historical questions and their improved translations of historical documents. Professor Geers and Dr. I. J. Gelb have done me the great service of reading the manuscript and offering their suggestions. The unwavering enthusiasm and vitality of Professor M. Sprengling have often heartened me in moments of despair. Other members of the Oriental Institute staff and of the Department of Oriental Languages and Literatures have been no less kind. To the Oriental Institute and its director, Professor James H. Breasted, as well as to the University of

Chicago Press, I owe my thanks for making possible the adequate publication of results. Dr. T. G. Allen, associate editor of the Institute's publications, has my sincere thanks for his careful editing. Beyond all these is the contribution acknowledged by the dedication.

GEORGE G. CAMERON

UNIVERSITY OF CHICAGO
October 1, 1935

TABLE OF CONTENTS

xi

ABBREVIATIONS

AJSL	American Journal of Semitic Languages and Literatures (Chicago, etc., 1884———).
AMI	Archäologische Mitteilungen aus Iran (Berlin, 1929———).
AOF	Archiv für Orientforschung. Band III——— (Berlin, 1926———).
BA	Beiträge zur Assyriologie und semitischen Sprachwissenschaft (Leipzig, 1890———).
Barton, *RISA*	BARTON, G. A. The Royal Inscriptions of Sumer and Akkad (New Haven, Conn., 1929).
BE	Pennsylvania. University. The Babylonian Expedition. Ser. A: Cuneiform Texts. Ser. D: Researches and Treatises. Ed. by H. V. HILPRECHT (Philadelphia, 1893———).
CT	Cuneiform Texts from Babylonian Tablets, etc., in the British Museum (London, 1896———).
Harper, *ABL*	HARPER, ROBERT FRANCIS. Assyrian and Babylonian Letters Belonging to the Kouyunjik Collections of the British Museum (14 vols.; London, 1892–1914).
Hüsing, *Quellen*	HÜSING, GEORG. Die einheimischen Quellen zur Geschichte Elams. 1. Teil. Altelamische Texte (Leipzig, 1916).

JAOS   American Oriental Society. Journal (Boston, etc., 1849———).

JRAS   Royal Asiatic Society of Great Britain and Ireland, *London*. Journal (London, 1834———).

KB   Keilinschriftliche Bibliothek, hrsg. von EBERHARD SCHRADER (6 vols.; Berlin, 1889–1915).

Klauber, *Texte*   Politisch-religiöse Texte aus der Sargonidenzeit, hrsg. von E. G. KLAUBER (Leipzig, 1913).

Knudtzon, *Gebete*   Assyrische Gebete an den Sonnengott für Staat und königliches Haus aus der Zeit Asarhaddons und Asurbanipals, hrsg. von J. A. KNUDTZON (Leipzig, 1893).

König, *Älteste Geschichte*   KÖNIG, F. W. Älteste Geschichte der Meder und Perser (Der Alte Orient, Band XXXIII, Heft 3/4 [Leipzig, 1934]).

König, *Geschichte Elams*   KÖNIG, F. W. Geschichte Elams (Der Alte Orient, Band XXIX, Heft 4 [Leipzig, 1931]).

LAR   LUCKENBILL, D. D. Ancient Records of Assyria and Babylonia (2 vols.; Chicago, 1926–27).

MAOG   Altorientalische Gesellschaft, *Berlin*. Mitteilungen (Leipzig, 1925———).

Mém.   France. Délégation en Perse. Mémoires. Tome I–XIII (Paris, 1900–1912).
France. Mission archéologique de Susiane. Mémoires. Tome XIV (Paris, 1913).
France. Mission archéologique de Perse. Publications. Tome XV (Paris, 1914).

ABBREVIATIONS

SAK   THUREAU-DANGIN, FR. Die sumerischen und akkadischen Königsinschriften (Vorderasiatische Bibliothek, 1. Stück [Leipzig, 1907]).

SAOC   Chicago. University. The Oriental Institute. Studies in Ancient Oriental Civilization (Chicago, 1931——).

Waterman, RCAE   WATERMAN, LEROY. Royal Correspondence of the Assyrian Empire (University of Michigan Studies, Humanistic Series, Vols. XVII–XIX; Ann Arbor, 1930–31).

WZKM   Wiener Zeitschrift für die Kunde des Morgenlandes (Wien, 1887——).

ZA   Zeitschrift für Assyriologie und verwandte Gebiete (Leipzig, 1886——).

ZDMG   Deutsche morgenländische Gesellschaft. Zeitschrift (Leipzig, 1847——).

CHAPTER I

THE LAND AND ITS PEOPLE

IRAN, a plateau with numerous large depressions, is cradled between two mountain ranges sweeping majestically from the knotted heights of Armenia north of the Fertile Crescent. One wing, a lofty ridge known as the Elburz, advances eastward along the south of the Caspian, where it reaches its climax in the towering peak of the Demavend. Continuing eastward, it dwindles away in the steppes of Khurasan, where it meets the line of the Hindu Kush coming from the opposite direction, from the Pamirs, the "roof of the world." The second wing, called the Zagros ranges, curves gently southeastward, then still more south. In numerous parallel folds it skirts the eastern edge of fertile Babylonia, forms a glittering and almost impassable barrier on the eastern shore of the Persian Gulf, and, after advancing over the desolate regions along the Indian Ocean, turns sharply northward through Baluchistan and Afghanistan to join other mountains spreading, like the Hindu Kush, fanlike from the Pamirs.

These mountain ranges on either side of the plateau have been from time immemorial Iran's strength—and weakness. From them came treasured metals and stones, gold and silver, lead and copper, lapis lazuli and carnelian. From them also, thrust up in the wake of the volcanic activity of late Pliocene times, came diorite and obsidian, both highly prized in antiquity. Finally, the rivers of Iran, racing swiftly through tremendous defiles from the heights to level land, brought fertility to many thousand square miles of barren soil, and desolation to other thousands. Silt carried by these streams during the glacial or pluvial periods was deposited in an inner basin and covered with water which evaporated as the winds swept together the sandy gravel. Thus, what was once a mighty sea became only sandy wastes and salt deserts. By far the greater portion of Iran is desert throughout the year, while, as summer advances, large tracts which in the spring were green are burned up and the whole plateau becomes dry and parched.

Judged on this basis, the land might truly be thought forbidding and uninviting to foreigners. Nevertheless, it is the connecting link between the Far East and the Near East. Migratory movements and warriors' campaigns have frequently swept across its borders in historic times, and these surely began in the dark past of prehistory. Consequently, the routes which lead without great difficulty into the land are worthy of special consideration.

Two passes across the Caucasus lead through Armenia into Anatolia, but a third permits entry to the coastal region south of the Caspian or to the mountain valleys of the Zagros. This was the route followed, for example, by some of the Scythians in the seventh century before our era, when they penetrated into Media and Persia and for a time threatened to upset the political arrangement of Western Asia.

On the part of the dwellers in Mesopotamia, there was a constant need to hold in check the highlanders from the Zagros Mountains and the Iranian plateau and to maintain an open trade route with the east. Accordingly, warriors of the lowlands succeeded from time to time in following a few of the arduous paths across the Zagros; then as now, however, for conquest or for commerce, the most frequently traveled route was the Baghdad–Kirmanshah–Hamadan trail. It seemed an irony of fate that this path, favored by the Assyrians, was used by their enemies, the Medes, when they descended from the highlands and subdued the worshipers of Ashur.

On the northeastern frontier, in spite of numerous parallel mountain ranges, entrance to Iran is comparatively unobstructed. Across this frontier, to and from Turkestan and Central Asia, roamed Mousterian man; and the Indo-Iranian peoples who swarmed over it in the second millennium B.C. ultimately brought into being the first of the Indo-Iranian empires, namely, the kingdoms of the Medes and the Persians. In contrast with this frontier the eastern and southeastern borders are almost impassable; yet cultural relationships between Iran and India even in prehistoric times can be pointed out, and Darius the Persian controlled the Indus Valley and the Punjab for a time.

The southern border of Iran faces so abruptly on the Indian Ocean that inhabitants of this region are denied the enjoyment of maritime pursuits. Northwest of this district the mountain ranges which are a continuation of the Zagros chain trend with remarkable regularity from northwest to southeast. These ranges are separated by regular valleys and intersected by enormous defiles, so that passage is difficult and commerce seriously impaired.

One district alone in this region gave easy access to the plateau of Iran itself, to the Persian Gulf, and to the fertile and early civilized Babylonia. This district, the plain of Susa, geographically bade fair to be called a part of Babylonia. However, an encircling arm of the Zagros, added to the marshes which in early days surrounded the head of the Persian Gulf, protected this level basin. In the north and northeast other snow-topped ranges of the Zagros furnished abundant water for several rivers which irrigated the land. Two of these approach each other at right angles in the center of the plain. When but a few miles apart they again recede, the Karkhah turning southwest toward Babylonia, the river Diz flowing southeast into a third river, the Karun. At the point where the Karkhah and Diz most nearly approach, there grew up in antiquity a city to be famous in Babylonian as in Elamite and Iranian history— Susa. This city, today but a "tell," still speaks eloquently of its one-time grandeur. It measures almost 3,000 feet on a side, and its highest point is well over 120 feet above the surrounding plain. Since the winter of 1897 the Ministère de l'instruction publique et des beaux-arts, by authority of the French government, has excavated at this site; and each year has seen some striking revelation of the history of the ancient Orient or some beautiful addition to the magnificent collection in the Louvre. Though much still remains to be excavated, we must emphasize the fact that Susa alone, in her fertile lowland, can never reveal the deeper secrets of Elamite history. For the Elamites were primarily highlanders, and during many periods of their history Susa played but a minor part, while a leading character in the drama was Anshan, not yet certainly located. Doubtless one reason for this relative political unimportance was the climate of the Susa basin. During nine months of the year the whole plain is burned up by the sun's heat, whose intensity affords some credence to Strabo's tale that lizards and serpents could not crawl across the streets at midday without being burned. Susa must nevertheless provide most of our available material for a political history of early Iran, since no other Elamite site has been excavated.

Iran, as thus described, gave little geographical

promise of great things to come in history. It was far more suited to "food-gatherers" than to "food-producers," for it was a land adapted to the grazing of animals rather than to the tilling of the soil. Nevertheless, its influence goes back to prehistory, and this influence demands present consideration.

Flint implements of Middle Paleolithic types have been found in central Iran, northeast of modern Shiraz, near the shores of what may have been a large sweet-water lake in those times. It has been suggested that Paleolithic man passed through the valleys of southern Iran in a general northwesterly direction and entered Kurdistan through the gorges at Sulaimaniyah, Rowandiz, and points north.[1] Artifacts of Mousterian man, very similar to others discovered in Palestine, have been found in caves near Sulaimaniyah.[2] Although the evidence is incomplete, it is sufficient to suggest that occupation of the caves was contemporaneous with the last glacial advance. It can be only an accident that other Mousterian implements have not been reported from diverse sites in Iran, for they have been discovered throughout all Europe in the west, through Africa, Palestine, India, even to Manchuria. Aurignacian man, successor to the declining Mousterian, seems also to have found a home in the Zagros, as he did in other parts of the

[1] Henry Field in *AJSL*, LI (1934/35), 208 f.

[2] D. A. E. Garrod, "The Palaeolithic of Southern Kurdistan," *Bulletin of the American School of Prehistoric Research*, No. 6 (March, 1930).

ancient Orient. There is no evidence, however, for other types of flints of Paleolithic manufacture.

It is possible that Iran passed through the Neolithic stage of development, although it is not until the very latest subperiod, the so-called "Chalcolithic," when copper was being introduced for ornaments, that we can obtain clarity of vision. Professor Herzfeld recently announced the discovery of a village near Persepolis which must be assigned to this stage of man's development.[3] The village, with its single-story mud-brick dwellings on either side of a narrow street, remains today almost as early Chalcolithic man left it millenniums ago. His stone implements and stone bowls are a lasting memento of his life at this site; and his wheelmade pottery, carefully fashioned and magnificently painted, is a permanent tribute to his craftsmanship. Two ornaments of copper, presumably hammered, are trifles among the thousands of stone objects; but they show that this man lived at the very dawn of the Metal Age.

While Europe was still in the later stages of Paleolithic culture, Iran, like the rest of the Near East, advanced rapidly into the Copper Age. Man, having made the acquaintance of metals, used them freely in his everyday life, although stone implements were still widely employed. At the same time he began to domesticate plants and animals. At Jemdet Nasr in

[3] E. Herzfeld in the *Illustrated London News*, May 25, 1929, pp. 892 f., and *Iranische Denkmäler*, Lfgn. 1 and 2 (Berlin, 1932), pp. 3–18, Pls. 1–30.

Babylonia the excavators found kernels of true wheat
and six-rowed barley,[4] a discovery equaling that of
wheat and barley chaff in the lowest stratum of Anau,
just beyond the northeastern border of Iran in
Russian Turkestan.[5] Wild emmer, long considered
the ancestor of cultivated wheat, has been revealed
near the city of Karind on the Baghdad-Kirmanshah
road in the Zagros Mountains.[6] Sheep and long-
horned cattle are portrayed on sherds of painted
pottery from every section of Iran. This ware, the
most notable contribution of Copper Age man, was a
direct descendant of the Iranian early Chalcolithic
painted pottery. It appears at Susa, where it is
known as Susa I,[7] and, in successively later develop-
ments, at Nihavend[8] and Kirmanshah[9] in the Zagros;
at Bushire in the south;[10] near the cities of Teheran,[11]

[4] H. Field in the *American Anthropologist*, XXXIV (1932), 303–9.

[5] Pumpelly, *Explorations in Turkestan, Expedition of 1904* (Washing-
ton, D.C., 1908), pp. 38 f., 67, and 72; cf. Schellenberg, *ibid.*, pp. 469–73.

[6] A. Schulz in *Berichte der deutschen botanischen Gesellschaft*, XXXI
(1913), 226–30, and *Die Geschichte der kultivierten Getreide* (Halle, 1913),
pp. 13 f.

[7] De Morgan, *Mém.*, I, 184–88; De Morgan, Pottier, and De Mecquenem, *Mém.*, Vol. XIII.

[8] Herzfeld in the *Illustrated London News*, June 1, 1929, pp. 942–45;
AMI, I (1929–30), 65–71; *Iranische Denkmäler*, Lfg. 3/4 (Berlin, 1933),
pp. 19–26, Pls. 1–27. See also Contenau and Ghirshman in *Syria*, XIV
(1933), 1–11.

[9] De Mecquenem, *Mém.*, XX, 126 f.

[10] Pézard, *Mém.*, XV, 13–19.

[11] De Mecquenem, *Mém.*, XX, 115–25.

Shiraz,[12] and Kashan[13] in the central part of the plateau; and in Seistan[14] and Baluchistan[15] in the east.

All the available evidence indicates that the painted-pottery culture persisted steadfastly within Iran while Mesopotamia was undergoing a gradual and distinct evolution. Susa alone on the border of the plateau felt the impact of the development on the west, and recent excavations have revealed the presence at this site of the typically Mesopotamian wares. Thus superimposed upon the pottery of Susa I are sherds which belong to the earliest period of Mesopotamian archeology, namely, the al-ʿUbaid period; and above these again are fragments which can be assigned in turn to the Uruk and to the Jemdet Nasr periods.[16] One group of pottery vases does not, however, belong with the Mesopotamian objects but has its closest parallels in far-off Seistan and Baluchistan.[17] This is the generally monochrome

[12] H. Field in *AJSL*, LI (1934/35), 208.

[13] A. U. Pope in the *Illustrated London News*, December 15, 1934, p. 1005; R. Ghirshman, *ibid.*, March 16, 1935, pp. 416 f.

[14] Aurel Stein, *An Archaeological Tour in Gedrosia*, "Memoirs of the Archaeological Survey of India," No. 43 (Calcutta, 1931); *Innermost Asia* (Oxford, 1928), II, 949–58, and Vol. III, Pls. 113 f.; "The Indo-Iranian Borderlands" (Huxley Memorial Lecture for 1934), *Journal of the Royal Anthropological Institute*, LXIV (1934), 179–202.

[15] Aurel Stein, *An Archaeological Tour in Waziristān and Northern Balūchistān*, "Memoirs of the Archaeological Survey of India," No. 37 (Calcutta, 1929).

[16] De Mecquenem, *Mém.*, XX, 99–112 and 128–32.

[17] With some of the pottery published by Aurel Stein in "Memoirs of the Archaeological Survey of India," Nos. 37 and 43.

pottery known as Susa II; although it may be contemporary with Jemdet Nasr wares, its occurrence
has unfortunately never been stratigraphically determined. It has recently been suggested that Susa
II represents an intrusion of a peculiar phase of the
late Iranian painted-pottery culture,[18] but nothing
definite can be asserted at present.

We are doubly unfortunate in lacking a precise.
dating for the ware, since the earliest writing on clay
tablets in Elam was contemporary with its manufacture.[19] In Mesopotamia clay tablets have been
discovered in strata which belong to the Uruk period;[20]
by the Jemdet Nasr period tablets with pictographic
inscriptions show words and names that are indubitably Sumerian. The signs are no longer linear; and
the primary numerical system, perhaps of these texts
and certainly of the Sumerian, is sexagesimal.[21] Our
Susa documents,[22] as well as those from central Iran,[23]

[18] H. Frankfort, *Archeology and the Sumerian Problem* (*SAOC*, No. 4
[1932]), pp. 65–72.

[19] De Mecquenem, *Mém.*, XXV, 189–91 and 205.

[20] See now A. Nöldeke, E. Heinrich, and E. Schott, "Fünfter vorläu-
figer Bericht über die von der Notgemeinschaft der deutschen Wissen-
schaft in Uruk unternommenen Ausgrabungen," *Abhandlungen der
Preussischen Akademie der Wissenschaften*, phil.-hist. Klasse, 1933, No. 5,
esp. pp. 9 and 14.

[21] Langdon, *Pictographic Inscriptions from Jemdet Nasr* ("Oxford Editions of Cuneiform Texts," Vol. VII [Oxford, 1928]); cf. Meissner in
AOF, VI (1930–31), 303 f.

[22] Scheil, *Mém.*, VI, 59 ff., and Vol. XVII.

[23] Ghirshman, "Une tablette proto-élamite du plateau iranien," *RA*,
XXXI (1934), 115–19.

are written in what is commonly known as proto-Elamite and are comparable with those from Babylonia in shape only. The signs retain the linear design and are seemingly to be read as pure ideographs. The numerical system appears to be decimal.[24] A common origin for the two scripts is possible; nevertheless, it is also conceivable that proto-Elamite was independent. Eventually the inhabitants of Elam adopted the Sumerian script and employed it to write their own language. Period by period their signs followed those in current use in Babylonia; judged on this basis, an inscription from the island Bushire, known as Liyan (*li-ia-an*) to the Elamites, in the Persian Gulf shows that Sumerian script was already in use for Elamite at a period somewhat antecedent to that of Sargon of Agade and hints at a widespread culture, if not empire.[25] Thereafter, particularly in the twelfth century B.C., numerous inscriptions reveal the main essentials of the Elamite language.[26]

To clarify these main essentials, and thereby to make possible a more accurate translation of the

[24] For discussions of the proto-Elamite texts see Scheil, *loc. cit.;* Weidner, *AOF*, III (1926), 84; Langdon in *JRAS*, 1925, pp. 169–73.

[25] François Lenormant, *Choix de textes cunéiformes* (Paris, 1873), p. 127, No. 41; cf. Hüsing, *Quellen*, No. 1.

[26] For discussions on Elamite phonetics and grammar see F. Bork, "Elam. B. Sprache," *Reallexikon der Vorgeschichte*, III (1925), 70–83, with the bibliography there cited; R. Bleichsteiner, "Beiträge zur Kenntnis der elamischen Sprache," *Anthropos*, XXIII (1928), 167–98; Th. Kluge, "Das Elamische," *Le Muséon*, XLVI (1933), 111–56; Bork, "Elamische Studien," *MAOG*, VII, Heft 3 (1933), 3–31.

Elamite texts for historical purposes, the writer undertook some years ago the compilation of an Elamite dictionary. The facilities furnished by the great Assyrian Dictionary of the Oriental Institute were at his disposal; and his dictionary, since completed, in the manner of its Assyrian predecessor permits the examination and comparison of every word in the published Elamite inscriptions with full context. Without the revised translations made possible by the dictionary, this history could never have been prepared, nor would many important details of Elamite grammatical structure have become clear. Only the essential features of the Elamite language need, however, be indicated in this study.

In matters of phonology there is marked disagreement between the spoken word and the written script. The Elamites rarely made clear distinction in writing between voiced and voiceless consonants; their *b* and *p*, *d* and *t*, *g* and *k*, and *z* and *s* were seldom differentiated.[27] Individual vowels were frequently nasalized in the spoken language, but in the written word an overhanging *m*, *n*, or *ng* was often omitted. Further, the cuneiform script made no provision for a few of the sounds which could be heard in the spoken language; thus, for example, a sound variously heard as *t*, *l*, or *lt* led to diverse methods of spelling

---

[27] Thus arose such dual forms as *kudur* and *kutur* or *kutir*, as in Kudur-Nahhunte; Lagamar and Lakamar, the name of a deity; Anzan and Anshan, the name of a land. Throughout this work, attempt has been made to adhere to the Elamite usage customary in the period in question.

the native name for Elam, *Haltamti*, by the Elamites themselves.

As in English, the noun does not distinguish between masculine and feminine, though the difference between person and thing, as "king" and "kingdom," is usually marked. One remarkable characteristic of the language is a double genitive construction in which the suffix of a noun is repeated at the close of the genitival phrase, together with all its modifying elements. Thus such a phrase as "in the temple of Shimutta, the god of Elam," is expressed in this order: "temple, Shimutta, the god, Elam, of, of, in."

The verbal forms are by far the most troublesome elements. In addition to the fact that the root meaning of the verb has often been unknown, failure to identify a subordinate verb as such, even when the root meaning of the verb was clear, frequently has led students of the language to an impossible translation or to a hopeless *impasse*. Fortunately, the subordinate verb is, almost without exception, clearly recognizable; our main problem now is a more accurate definition of the meanings of the verbal roots.

Many of the elements characteristic of Elamite seem common to those of a linguistic group found today in the Caucasus area only and referred to as the "Caucasian" family of languages, although certain phonetic and grammatical parallels with the Tamil dialect of Dravidian in southern India have been noted.[28]

[28] Cf. G. W. Brown, "The Possibility of a Connection between Mitanni and the Dravidian Languages," *JAOS*, L (1930), 273–305.

Many of these elements seem to have ancient counter-
parts in the languages spoken by the Kassites,[29] the
Lullubi,[30] and the Guti[31] in the central Zagros; by the
Haldians in the mountains of Armenia;[32] by the
Hurrians in the great bend of the Euphrates;[33] by a
few peoples of Asia Minor, such as the Protohattians[34]

[29] Friedrich Delitzsch, *Die Sprache der Kossäer* (Leipzig, 1884); T. G.
Pinches, "The Language of the Kassites," *JRAS*, 1917, pp. 101–14.

[30] Cf. E. A. Speiser, *Mesopotamian Origins* (Philadelphia, 1930),
pp. 88–96.

[31] *Ibid.*, pp. 96–119.

[32] A. H. Sayce, "The Cuneiform Inscriptions of Van, Deciphered and
Translated," *JRAS*, 1882, pp. 377–732; Tseretheli, "Die neuen ḫaldischen
Inschriften König Sardurs von Urarṭu," *Sitzungsberichte der Heidelberger
Akademie der Wissenschaften*, phil.-hist. Klasse, Vol. XVIII (1927/28),
No. 5; J. Friedrich, "Beiträge zu Grammatik und Lexikon des Chaldi-
schen," *Caucasica*, VII (1931), 53–86, and VIII (1931), 114–50; "Zur
urartäischen Nominalflexion," *ZA*, XL (1931), 264–88; cf. also Th.
Kluge, "Die Sprache der urartäischen Inschriften und ihre Stellung im
kaukasischen Sprachenkreise," *MVAG*, XII, Heft 5 (1907), 176–224.

[33] L. Messerschmidt, "Mitanni-Studien," *MVAG*, IV, Heft 4 (1899),
175–308; Bork, "Die Mitannisprache," *MVAG*, XIV, Heft 1/2 (1909),
1–126; A. Gustavs, "Verbindungs-Linien zwischen dem Mitannischen,
dem Elamischen, und dem Lykischen," *Memnon*, VII (1915), 228–32;
A. Gustavs, "Mitanni. *B.* Sprache," *Reallexikon der Vorgeschichte*, VIII
(1926), 218–26; E. Forrer, "Die Inschriften und Sprachen des Ḫatti-
Reiches," *ZDMG*, LXXVI (1922), 224–28; Bork, "Studien zum Mitani,"
AOF, VIII (1932/33), 308–14.

[34] Forrer, "Die acht Sprachen der Boghazköi-Inschriften," *Sitzungsberichte der Preussischen Akademie der Wissenschaften*, phil.-hist. Klasse,
1919, pp. 1032–34, and "Die Inschriften und Sprachen des Ḫatti-
Reiches," *ZDMG*, LXXVI (1922), 228–41; Bleichsteiner, "Zum Proto-
chattischen," *Berichte des Forschungs-Institutes für Osten und Orient*, III
(Wien, 1923), 102–6.

and the later Lycians[35] and Lydians;[36] possibly also by the Etruscans in Italy.[37] Such analogues as may be found between Elamite and any of these other languages naturally point only to linguistic affinities and not to a linguistic unity; with due caution, however, they may indicate ethnic relationships.

For a modern anthropologist it is difficult, if not impossible, to imagine that the present-day inhabitants of Iran could make up a single ethnological family. From time immemorial the plateau has been subjected to invasion and counter-invasion, for, in spite of the difficulties its borders present, it must be remembered that Iran is as much a bridge between the Far East and the Land of the Two Rivers as is Palestine between Asia and Africa. Consequently, peoples of highly diverse origin have sheltered themselves under a single linguistic roof in Iran; and the

[35] Kluge, "Die lykischen Inschriften," *MVAG*, XV, Heft 1 (1910), 1–135; Bork, *Skizze des Lükischen* (Königsberg i. Pr., 1926); Deeters, "Lykia. *VII*. Sprache," Pauly-Wissowa, *Real Encyclopädie der classischen Altertumswissenschaft*, XXVI (1927), 2282–91; P. Meriggi, "Über einige lykische Pronominal- und Verbalformen," *Indogermanische Forschungen*, XLVI (1928), 151–82, and "Beiträge zur lykischen Syntax," *Kleinasiatische Forschungen*, I, Heft 3 (1930), 414–61.

[36] Deeters, "Lydia. Sprache und Schrift," Pauly-Wissowa, *op. cit.*, XXVI (1927), 2153–61; W. Brandenstein, "Die lydische Sprache," *WZKM*, XXXVI (1929), 263–304, and XXXVIII (1932), 1–67; "Die Nominalformen des Lydischen," *Caucasica*, IX (1931), 25–40; "Die lydische Nominalflexion," *ibid.*, X (1932), 67–94.

[37] G. Herbig, "Etrusker. *B*. Sprache," *Reallexikon der Vorgeschichte*, III (1925), 138–47; cf. F. Sommer, "Das lydische und etruskische F-Zeichen," *Sitzungsberichte der Bayerischen Akademie der Wissenschaften*, phil.-hist. Abt., 1930, Heft 1, pp. 1–23.

southern part of the land today, as it must have been in ancient times, is pronouncedly piebald in an ethnic sense.

The paucity of archeological and anthropological data has given rise to innumerable speculations concerning the people who dwelt in Iran at the dawn of written history. Some of these are based on philology alone—a dangerous and often misleading guide. Others are derived from cultural features and frequently disregard the effects of borrowing by peoples on the outer fringes of a cultural area, or the changes resulting when new immigrants adopt the cultural advances of indigenous populations. The best we can hope is to avoid the more obvious pitfalls while we state what appear to be the ascertainable facts.

Physical anthropologists are certain that Mesopotamia was the eastern borderline for Semitic types of individuals and that the Semites, whom we know as the brown Mediterranean peoples who invaded Mesopotamia from Arabia, did not inhabit Iran at an early date. When, therefore, the author of the tenth chapter of Genesis calls Elam a son of Shem, that is, a Semite, he is speaking not in anthropological but in geographical and cultural terms. Nor did Nordic peoples speaking an Indo-Iranian language dwell in Iran in early times; the earliest evidence indicating their entry is dated to the beginning of the second millennium B.C. and is based on the mention of Indo-Iranian deities among Kassite gods.

There is some evidence leading to the belief that a protonegroid population once extended westward from India along the shores of the Persian Gulf. Individuals of that group seem to be portrayed on seventh century B.C. reliefs of an Assyrian king.[38] Greek authors speak of "Ethiopians" in the southeast of the land;[39] their modern descendants possess copper skins, straight hair, and round skulls.[40] It is, however, safe to say that these peoples never constituted an important or a large element in the population.

So far as it is possible to determine, in ancient times there were longheaded races in Iran preceding the Nordic peoples. The basis for this belief is found in the appearance, in Mesopotamia, of a brown Eurafrican type of man. Our present evidence concerning him is indeed scanty, but seems to suggest a remote physical connection with India.[41] It is possible that these longheads themselves were Sumerians, or were related to them, for it has been said that one can still

[38] Cf. the upper register of the Ashurbanipal relief in E. Pottier, *Les Antiquités assyriennes* (du Musée du Louvre) (Paris, 1917), Pl. 23; for details cf. Victor Place, *Ninive et l'Assyrie*, Vol. III (Paris, 1867), Pl. 59, No. 1. Or see H. R. Hall, *Babylonian and Assyrian Sculpture in the British Museum* (Paris and Brussels, 1928), Pl. XLIV. Finally, cf. the Achaemenian reliefs from Susa in M. Dieulafoy, *L'acropole de Suse* (Paris, 1893), Pls. V and VI.

[39] Herodotus vii. 70; Strabo xv, 1, 13, and 24.

[40] Dieulafoy, *L'acropole de Suse*, p. 28.

[41] Buxton in L. H. Dudley Buxton and D. Talbot Rice, "Report on the Human Remains Found at Kish," *Journal of the Royal Anthropological Institute*, LXI (1931), 57–119, esp. pp. 84 ff.

trace the ancient Sumerian face eastward among the
peoples of Afghanistan and Baluchistan, even to the
valley of the Indus.[42]

The most important element, however, appears to
have been roundheaded. In the present population
of the plateau, at least in the eastern portion, there
is a very striking group of roundheads, who are more
numerous in the uplands than on the plain.[43] Some
may be related to the Dravidians of India, in particular to the Tamil-speaking peoples, among whom there
is a marked brachycephalic element.[44] The stature of
others is often rather tall, with frequently a marked
correlation between this stature and fairness of skin.
Such features might argue for an admixture with
Nordics; but recalling the fairness of some European
Alpines, we might also conjecture that these present-
day peoples are the remnant of a proto-Alpine race.
If the daring suggestion[45] that the so-called "Arme-
noids" originated in Turkestan be accepted, the
hypothesis that the early inhabitants of Iran were
primarily of this stock would be strengthened. Philol-

[42] Sir Arthur Keith in Hall and Woolley, *Al-ᶜUbaid* ("Ur Excavations," Vol. I [Oxford, 1927]), p. 216. On this question cf. H. Frankfort,
Archeology and the Sumerian Problem (*SAOC*, No. 4), pp. 40–47.

[43] Cf. Buxton, *The Peoples of Asia* (New York, 1925), pp. 112 f.;
W. Z. Ripley, *The Races of Europe* (New York, 1919), pp. 450 f.; R. B.
Dixon, *The Racial History of Man* (New York, 1923), pp. 309–12.

[44] Cf. Dixon, *op. cit.*, p. 263.

[45] G. Elliot Smith, *Human History* (London, 1930), pp. 167 f., and
The Ancient Egyptians (new and rev. ed.; London, 1923), pp. 102–5;
Buxton, *op. cit.*, pp. 107–13.

ogy, dangerous as its evidence may be, concurs with this "Alpine" theory and tentatively suggests that the extension of "Caucasian" linguistic elements from far-away India on the east through Elam and the Zagros into Anatolia on the west is perhaps not without significance.

Nevertheless, this view conflicts with the theory already stated and commonly held, that the brown Eurafrican variety of longheads in Mesopotamia was also the chief block of the earliest population in Iran. If this be accepted, we must assume, as indeed would not be difficult, that the "Caucasian" linguistic affinities have transcended race and people, being spoken both by the *supposed* original roundheads of Asia Minor and by the dolichocephalic peoples of Iran.

The present state of our knowledge leaves us at a complete stalemate. No theory, enticing as it may be, is acceptable; only with the help of physical anthropology shall we solve the problem.

Where we possess written records the social customs are much less difficult to describe. Such documentation for Iran is found only in Elam and only after the twenty-fifth century B.C.; even then we must read between the lines of a few inscriptions to obtain the maximum amount of evidence.

In Elam, as elsewhere throughout the Orient in early times, woman's sphere of activity was not limited to the home. Like man, she signed documents, carried on business, inherited and willed fortunes, brought suits in the law courts, and owned slaves. Her importance increased with the passing years. In early Elamite documents we notice the frequent mention of the ruler's mother, sister, or daughter. The available evidence in the so-called "classical" period points to the matrilinear character of the royal succession; that is, right to the throne was traceable through the mother. Instances of brother-sister marriages occur, and presumably this was a general practice. It is even possible that this type of marriage practiced by Achaemenian Persian kings should be traced back to an Elamite origin, for to Aryan minds union of full brother and sister was repulsive.

Peculiarities of the Elamite royal succession will be pointed out from time to time as they occur. Particularly noteworthy is a curious system by which a prince in a relatively minor position could advance step by step to one of great importance, sometimes even to sovereignty. On other occasions the kingship descended, not from father to son, but from brother to brother. In many parts of the ancient East the kings were considered as gods; in Elam not the king alone but the entire ruling family was deified.

Elamite religion was naturally polytheistic in character. Unfortunately, some of the divine names were written only by means of the Akkadian ideograms. This does not mean that the name of the sun-god, Shamash in Semitic, for example, was so pronounced

in Elam; there his name had doubtless a wholly
different pronunciation, perhaps Nahhunte. Two
deities were all-important in the royal and official
literature: Huban and Inshushinak. The name of the
former was often written by means of the Akkadian
ideogram which proclaimed him "the Great One."
Inshushinak was, quite literally, "the Lord of Susa."[46]
Nevertheless, although the rulers might proclaim the
supremacy of these gods, many passages referring to
Kiririsha, a form of the mother-goddess, and hundreds of clay statuettes of this deity found in the
course of the Susa excavations, bespeak her whom the
common people of Elam really and sincerely worshiped.

Thus briefly we may conclude our survey of the
land and its prehistory, language, and people. Re-
strictions of time and space will prevent the presentation in the following pages of many subjects which are
largely cultural in aspect. Much that follows will be
concerned with names, dates, and synchronisms with
Babylonian events, for this study is primarily a political history. Even thus limited, a history is not
without value, for to comprehend fully the contributions of early man in Iran and in Elam we must first
understand his relationship to his immediate neighbors. For that purpose a political history is essential.

[46] The Elamite name form Inshushinak (also spelled Insushnak and
Inshushnak) developed from the Sumerian name Nin-shushin-ak. The
Akkadian form is Shushinak. Cf. Poebel in *AJSL*, XLIX (1932/33), 136,
and LI (1934/35), 171.

CHAPTER II

HISTORICAL BEGINNINGS

WHEN Babylonian scribes reduced to written word the myths and legends of antiquity, they told of the world's creation, of kings enthroned for reigns of fabulous length, and of a mighty flood which threatened entirely to depopulate the earth. They told how kingship, after the waters had receded, descended from heaven upon the city Kish in northern Babylonia, where ruled a dynasty of long-lived sovereigns. Their lists make dry reading, for the names of the kings with their lengths of rule alone are given. Of the twenty-first ruler of this dynasty, however, a significant fact is related, a fact which to the scribes was the first political event after the Flood. Enmenbaragesi, we are informed, subdued Elam.[1] Eventually the sovereignty of Kish yielded to that of Uruk in southern Babylonia, but Elam had still to be dealt with. It is reported that Mesken-gasher, founder of the new dynasty, descended to the sea and ascended the mountain, statements which may refer to the Persian Gulf and the Elamite high-

[1] S. Langdon, "Oxford Editions of Cuneiform Texts," II (Oxford, 1923), 11.

lands.[2] Traditions other than those preserved in the
king lists declared that in the times of Lugalbanda
and Dumuzi, the third and fourth kings of this dynasty, the Elamites invaded Babylonia from their
mountains.[3] With sad hearts the scribes were forced
to record the fact that considerably later the kingship
deserted Uruk for Awan, definitely an Elamite city.
For a time a second dynasty at Kish restored the
sovereignty to Babylonia, but the succeeding rule in
the city Hamazi suggests a return of power to the
highlands north of Elam.[4] Finally, when the kingship
once more returned to grace the city Kish under the
ruler Utug, omitted from the scribal lists,[5] reverbera-
tions of the struggles between Elamite highlanders
and Babylonians may be referred to in an inscription
of Lugal-anne-mundu of Adab, who warred with
Elam, Marhashi, and Gutium.[6]

[2] *Ibid.;* P. Dhorme in *Revue biblique,* XXXV (1926), 72 n., interprets
the phrase to mean the death of Meskengasher.

[3] A. Poebel, *Historical and Grammatical Texts (PBS,* Vol. V), No. 20
rev. 14 ff.; cf. Poebel, *Historical Texts (PBS,* Vol. IV, Part 1), pp. 117
and 122.

[4] Langdon, *op. cit.,* pp. 13 f.; cf. Poebel, *Historical Texts,* p. 128; E. A.
Speiser, *Mesopotamian Origins* (Philadelphia, 1930), pp. 35 f. and 43.

[5] H. V. Hilprecht, *Old Babylonian Inscriptions (BE,* Series A, Vol. I),
Part 2, Nos. 108 f.; cf. F. Thureau-Dangin, *Die sumerischen und akkadischen Königsinschriften* (Leipzig, 1907; hereafter abbreviated *SAK),*
pp. 160 f.

[6] Poebel, *Historical and Grammatical Texts,* No. 75 iii 29 ff., and
iv 27 ff. See H.-G. Güterbock in *ZA,* XLII (1934), 42 ff. Marhashi (in
its Akkadian form, Barahshi) is doubtless to be located north of Elam;
cf. W. F. Albright in *JAOS,* XLV (1925), 232; Speiser, *op. cit.,* p. 31.

So far we have been dealing with legends, or with shadowy figures who stand on the borderline between legend and history. Discoveries of recent years have transferred several other supposedly legendary characters to the realm of actual history, and some lucky chance may do the same for the individuals mentioned above. For the present we can only quote the statements about them as they have come down to us, and indicate possible solutions.

Fortunately for the historian, from this time forward contemporary royal inscriptions verify and supplement the traditions or separate from them the actual events. Our most complete records for a short time emanate from the Babylonian city-state Lagash, where a dynasty was begun by Ur-Nanshe. Although the founder brought down objects from the mountains,[7] he may have had no significant contacts with the Elamites. One of his successors, Eannatum, was a far more energetic ruler, or so his inscriptions would have us believe. These tell us that he vanquished the marvelous mountain Elam and heaped up mounds of the slain; he defeated the *ishakku*'s, or princes, of two Elamite cities;[8] when Elam and all the other coun-

[7] *SAK*, pp. 2 ff.

[8] The names of these cities are written URU+A and URU.AZ. The former is mentioned in Susian documents of the Agade period, *Mém.*, Vol. XIV, Nos. 19 and 21; it is named by Sargon, and together with URU.AZ appears in Third Ur Dynasty texts from Babylonia; see below, pp. 28 and 52 ff. A city Uruaz appears in documents of the Hammurabi period from Susa, *Mém.*, Vol. XXII, No. 144.

tries revolted, he drove the Elamite back to his land, which he conquered.[9] These are great claims. Though we may wonder whether the Elamites were not invaders rather than rebels, there is also proof that the wars of Eannatum were not wholly defensive; a support for a battle mace brought, doubtless as booty, from the first Elamite city to be made subject was inscribed in Lagash by Dudu, priest of the city's deity Ningirsu.[10] Nevertheless, it is certain that Elamite raiding parties subsequently penetrated deep into Babylonia, for in the time of Enetarzi, third *ishakku* after Eannatum, a band of six hundred Elamites actually plundered Lagash.[11]

The Elamite royal city from which such sorties descended into Babylonia was Awan. The Sumerian scribes, by recording in their lists a postdiluvian dynasty in this city, preserved for posterity their knowledge that throughout the early periods of history Awan was pre-eminent in the eastern land. They also recognized the fact that Susa at this time was only commercially important. We ourselves learn from the baked-clay documents found at Susa, written in the proto-Elamite language, that this metropolis al-

[9] *SAK*, pp. 20 ff.

[10] E. de Sarzec, *Découvertes en Chaldée* (Paris, 1884–1912), Vol. II, Pl. 5 *bis*; cf. *SAK*, pp. 34 f.

[11] Thureau-Dangin, "Une incursion élamite en territoire sumérien," *RA*, VI (1907), 139–42, now in Barton, *RISA*, pp. 66 ff.

ready had a local history;[12] but its political fate was inextricably bound up with the city Awan, where there now (*ca.* 2670 B.C.) began to rule a dynasty of kings, twelve in number.[13]

Peli founded the dynasty; and, if names are to be trusted, his immediate successors were all pure Elamites. To us these rulers—Tata,[14] Ukku-tahesh, Hishur, Shushun-tarana, Napi-ilhush, and Kikku-simetemti—are no more than names, though we might, with some degree of probability, ascribe to one of them an inscription since found on Liyan, modern Bushire, an island in the Persian Gulf. Fragmentary though it is, this text with its archaic signs is yet proof that by the time of Sargon of Agade the Elamites had adopted the Sumerian script to write their own language.[15] With the eighth member of the dynasty, Luhhi-ishshan, and his successor, Hishep-

[12] Scheil, *Mém.*, VI, 59 ff., and Vol. XVII. For the seal imprints cf. L. Legrain, *Mém.*, Vol. XVI.

[13] Scheil, "Dynasties élamites d'Awan et de Simaš," *RA*, XXVIII (1931), 1–8, now definitive in *Mém.*, XXIII, iv. In an old Hurrian text discovered at Boghazköy a certain Autalummash is named as a king of kings of Elam preceding Manishtusu; cf. E. Forrer, *Die Boghazköi-Texte in Umschrift*, Band II, Heft 2 ("Wissenschaftliche Veröffentlichungen der Deutschen Orient-Gesellschaft," Band XLII, Heft 2 [Leipzig, 1926]), 25*, now in Brandenstein, *Keilschrifturkunden aus Boghazköi*, Vol. XXVIII (Berlin, 1934), No. 38 iv 8 ff. From our present data we are unable to verify or to deny the truth of this statement.

[14] The last signs of the names Peli and Tata are doubtful.

[15] Text from the papers of L. K. Tavernier, published by François Lenormant, *Choix de textes cunéiformes*, p. 127, No. 41; cf. Hüsing, *Quellen*, No. 1.

ratep, we step for the first time into the full light of
history, for they were contemporary with one of the
most colorful figures of ancient times, Sargon, king
of Agade (*ca.* 2530–2475 B.C.).

Shortly after his accession to the throne, Sargon
laid plans to overthrow the power of the eastern
mountaineers. He presaged an attack upon them by
a conquest of the district Kazallu east of the Tigris.[16]
Slightly beyond Kazallu was Der, modern Badrah,
important as commanding an outlet from the mountains and not yet accounted a really Babylonian city.[17]
Its capture led him to more truly Elamite territory;
and, in an inscription which does not attempt to be a
topographical description of his march, he lists the
individuals whom he has encountered and the cities
from which he has obtained booty.[18] Here are enumerated various rulers of Barahshi: Ul . . . . and
Sidgau, both *shakkanakku*'s or governors; Kunduba,

[16] Omens in L. W. King, *Chronicles Concerning Early Babylonian Kings*
(London, 1907), I, 41 f.; cf. the chronicle, *ibid.*, II, 5.

[17] Conquest of Der by Sargon is mentioned only in the geographical
treatise which may describe his empire, published by O. Schroeder,
Keilschrifttexte aus Assur verschiedenen Inhalts, No. 92; cf. W. F. Albright,
"A Babylonian Geographical Treatise on Sargon of Akkad's Empire,"
JAOS, XLV (1925), 193–245, and XLVI (1926), 220–30. For the loca-
tion of Der see E. Forrer, *Die Provinzeinteilung des assyrischen Reiches*
(Leipzig, 1920), p. 97; Sidney Smith in *Journal of Egyptian Archaeology*,
XVIII (1932), 28–32.

[18] The text is a composite of L. Legrain, *Royal Inscriptions and Fragments from Nippur and Babylon* (*PBS*, Vol. XV), No. 41 and pp. 12 ff.,
and Poebel, *Historical and Grammatical Texts*, No. 34 (cf. Poebel, *Historical Texts*, pp. 184 ff.); both now complete in Barton, *RISA*, pp. 110 ff.

a judge; and Dagu, a brother of the king of Barahshi. Zina, the *ishakku* or prince of Huhunuri,[19] and Hidarida . . ,[20] the *ishakku* of Gunilaha, are both mentioned, as are the cities Saliamu, Karne . . . . , Heni, and Bunban(?).[21] These were but lesser figures in the contest; the list now proceeds to mention the chief actors in the drama, Sanam-Shimut, an *ishakku* of Elam, and Luh-ishan, whom Sargon's ill-informed scribes called the son of Hiship-rashir and king of Elam. We know him better as Luhhi-ishshan, the eighth king of Awan, who was the successor, if not the son, of Kikku-sime-temti, and whose own son was Hiship-rashir or, rather, Hishep-ratep.[22] Sargon's scribes did know, however, of Awan, for it together with Susa closes the enumeration.

Somewhat later another venture into the east proved even more successful. Once more Sargon engaged with Sidgau and Kunduba of Barahshi, who were now joined by an *ishakku* of Shirihum, and with Sanam-Shimut and Luhhi-ishshan. The latter may have been killed, for shortly afterward "Hiship-rashir, king of Elam," in whom we recognize Hishep-ratep, sent tribute to the warrior of Agade through

[19] So perhaps with sign traces.

[20] Two dots are used to indicate loss of a single sign; four dots represent loss of more than one or of an uncertain number of signs.

[21] Also URU+A.

[22] Text cited above, p. 26, n. 13. For Legrain's Hisibrasini read Hiship-rashir; the *si* may be read *ši* in this period, and the ending -*r* is the Elamite masculine singular, while -*p* (as in *ratep*) is plural.

the hand of Hibabri; and, if we may judge from the fact that a stele of Sargon has been found at Susa, this city itself appears to have been captured.[23]

By this achievement Sargon was free to undertake additional conquests in the lands north of Elam. A geographical treatise on his empire furnishes the names of many districts in this region which later scribes alleged he had subdued. There we find Lubdu in the land of Arrapha, which is the district surrounding the modern town Kirkuk, besides "the way of the upper and lower Zab" and the lands Lullubium and Gutium. These lay north of the present Diyala River, whose place of exit from the mountains was eventually known by the Elamites as Ialman and which here appears as the land Arman. In addition to these, the lands Nikkum and Der to the south of this river are mentioned; and in a final summary Marhashi (better known as Barahshi), Tukrish, Elam, and Anshan are named. We may accept as fact Sargon's conquest of the majority of the lands enumerated, but we must ask for further evidence before including in his empire Lullubium, Gutium, and Tukrish, all of which, like Anshan, lay within the Zagros boundary range.[24]

[23] Scheil, *Mém.*, X, 4 ff.; J.-Et. Gautier, "Note sur une stèle de Sargon l'ancien," *RT*, XXVII (1905), 176–79; Essad Nassouhi, "La stèle de Sargon l'ancien," *RA*, XXI (1924), 65–74.

[24] Text cited above, p. 27, n. 17. In the old Hurrian text from Boghaz-köy referred to above, an Immashkush as king of kings of Lullubium and a Kiklipatallish of Tukrish are included among predecessors of Manish-tusu.

Like so many empires which expand too rapidly, Sargon's crumbled at the first sign of revolt; and he himself was its victim. Arrayed against his successor, Rimush, were even Babylonian princes, among them the *ishakku* of Kazallu, Asharid, and the king, the *ishakku*, and the great *sukkal* or "messenger" of Der. But Rimush, like Sargon, bore the stamp of the conqueror. Quickly he brought all Babylonia under control; then he too looked eastward. In that direction Elam, or rather Awan, was naturally his chief opponent; and Awan had asked and received support from the *shakkanakku* of the land Zahara and from Barahshi, where Sidgau was still *shakkanakku* under his king Abalgamash.[25] Valiant as their resistance may have been, the cause of the highlanders was a lost one. Rimush himself proudly claims the victory; the modern excavator proves his claim by unearthing in Babylonia booty from the conquest of Elam and Barahshi: vases at Nippur, once presented to Enlil, and vases and a macehead at Ur, formerly offered to Sin.[26]

Susa fell to the warriors of Rimush; and when Rimush was succeeded by Manishtusu it was in this city that an Elamite, Uba, dedicated a bust of his new suzerain to Narute, a local deity. Cylinder seals in-

[25] This inscription is a continuation of that cited above, p. 27, n. 18; on the name Abalgamash cf. Speiser, *op. cit.*, p. 44, n. 66.

[26] Hilprecht, *Old Babylonian Inscriptions*, Part 1, Nos. 5 and 10, and cf. pp. 20 f.; Gadd and Legrain, *Royal Inscriptions*, Nos. 9 f. and 273.

form us that Uba was actually the *ishakku* of Elam.[27]
No more is heard of the kings of Awan, though Elam-
ite antiquaries named Helu as the successor to
Hishep-ratep. Perhaps he was active in Anshan and
Shirihum, the mountains north and northeast of
Elam, where the Assyrians were to find the land
Parsumash and into which the Iranian Chishpish or
Teispes entered about 675 B.C. For Manishtusu divided his troops and sent one army into this region;
successful, his warriors brought the defeated king
back to Babylonia and led him in triumph before
Shamash in Sippar. The other army crossed the
Persian Gulf to the Persian coast, where it defeated
the warriors from thirty-two cities; the whole region
was devastated up to the mines of precious metals,
and the way was opened for the transportation of
diorite and valuable ores from the Persian coast of
the Gulf to Babylonia.[28]

[27] *Mém.*, X, 1, and XIV, 4; the reading of the name Uba is doubtful.

[28] For the division of troops see the Constantinople inscription published by Thureau-Dangin in "Notes assyriologiques," *RA*, VII (1910),
179–84; see also the "Cruciform Monument" in *CT*, Vol. XXXII, Pls.
1–4; cf. L. W. King, "The Cruciform Monument of Manishtusu," *RA*, IX
(1912), 91–105. For claims of wider conquest cf. the broken statue from
Susa published by Scheil, "Inscription de Manistusu," *RA*, VII, 103–6,
now in *Mém.*, XIV, 1–3; the Nippur text, Poebel, *Historical Texts*, pp.
205 ff.; and the document from Ur, Gadd and Legrain, *Royal Inscriptions*,
No. 274.

The location of Anshan is still a moot point. So long as the *homeland*
of the Achaemenian Persians was believed to lie around Pasargadae,
scholars were agreed that Anshan must be located far to the southeast of
Elam in the later Persis at no great distance from the Persian Gulf; cf.
Prášek *Geschichte*, I, 189, n. 1, for a summary of the views expressed on

Mountaineers do not, however, yield up their freedom without a struggle. The Zagros highlanders, grown hardy from attempting to eke out an existence in the scarped mountains, might be expected to revolt more than once against foreign domination. This actually happened at the death of Manishtusu. Their attempt to break away from or to avoid subservience to the new ruler, Naram-Sin, had its ramifications in the nearby lowlands of Babylonia, where Kazallu, Timtab, and Awak rebelled. Being nearer to Agade,

---

this location. In recent years, however, students of Elamite have protested against this opinion and have suggested that the Karkhah River valley northwest of Susa may have been the center of the land and that the city Anshan itself may lie beneath the ruins near Derre-i-Shahr in the Saimarreh plain; cf. G. Hüsing in *Mitteilungen der Anthropologischen Gesellschaft in Wien*, LX (1930), 263; F. Bork in M. Ebert, *Reallexikon der Vorgeschichte*, III, 72 (*s.v.* "Elam. *B.* Sprache"); F. W. König in *Reallexikon der Assyriologie, s.v.* "Anšan," and again in *Geschichte Elams*, p. 6. Unfortunately, the Elamite texts themselves give but little light on the question.

New data on the origin of the Achaemenian empire enable us to avoid some of the earlier difficulties. It is now clear that Anshan was the Elamite name of a city and district near Parsumash. The latter land, according to Assyrian letters and texts, lay northeast of Elam proper; over it the Iranian Chishpish or Teispes ruled about 675 B.C. When the neo-Elamite kingdom ceased to lay claim to Anshan, it had good reason for so doing; Teispes, now king in Anshan, had already begun true Iranian expansion. At his death Ariaramnes, one of his two sons, ruled the district which included the later city Pasargadae and which was properly known as Parsa. The second son, Kurash or Cyrus I, inherited the original domain Parsumash, of which the chief city, after the absorption of the land Anshan, was the city Anshan itself. Thus Cyrus II, or Cyrus the Great, as a descendant of the latter line, spoke correctly when he proclaimed himself and his progenitors "kings of the city Anshan." These facts are dealt with more fully on pp. 179 f. and 212 f. They are treated here only for the purpose of assisting us to locate the land Anshan.

they were perhaps the more easily subdued; but the opposition presented to Naram-Sin by peoples to the north and east may well have been more ominous. Near modern Altun Köprü a little kingdom known as Shimurrum,[29] now ruled by Puttimadal, was actively hostile. In the land Namar, later known as Namri, in the central Zagros, Arisen, son of Sadarmat, had only recently declared himself king of Urkish and Namar;[30] the present ruler, Inbir, had no desire to lose his independence. Another enemy was to be found in Hubshumkibi, the king of Marhashi or Barahshi.[31] It is even possible that Hita, named by the Elamite scribes as the eleventh king of Awan, had induced some of these rulers to join him in one last desperate effort against Agade. Naram-Sin was more than a match for them; the lands to the north came definitely under his control, and even Elam and Barahshi were subdued.[32]

The new master was not, however, merely a destroyer. Susa, constantly under the impact of Baby-

[29] Known from texts of the Third Ur Dynasty and located at Zaban, modern Altun Köprü; cf. A. H. Sayce in *PSBA*, XXI (1899), 20 n.

[30] Thureau-Dangin, "Tablette de Samarra," *RA*, IX (1912), 1–4.

[31] List of opponents in text published by Boissier, "Inscription de Naram-Sin," *RA*, XVI (1919), 157–64; cf. now Barton, *RISA*, pp. 138 ff.; the historicity of this text has been doubted by Landsberger in *ZA*, XXXV (1924), 215 f. I. J. Gelb has shown that Apirak (Apishal?), long considered an eastern city, is to be located in the northwest; cf. *OIP*, XXVII, 6.

[32] Gadd and Legrain, *Royal Inscriptions*, No. 274.

lonian civilization, was rapidly becoming Akkadianized; there Naram-Sin with his inscribed bricks
erected buildings in which he placed his own statues,
as well as vases from the spoil of Magan.[33] There he
installed his own *ishakku*, Enammune, that the
region might be held constantly loyal.[34]

The language of the Susa documents of this period,
no less than the personal names, illustrates clearly
the effects of such a benevolent policy upon the district. The Akkadian language largely supplants the
Elamite, and even the names are mostly Semitic.
These documents, among which there are letters,
syllabaries, and lists of armor in addition to the usual
sales, exchanges, and salary payments, throw a vivid
light on the commercial relationships of the period,
for the cities Shuruppak and Awal and the land
Barahshi are all mentioned, as is Umma, whose
ishakku is known by name.[35]

In other regions of greater Elam the native language and culture remained unaffected, in proof of
which there is a treaty between a native king, most
probably Hita, and Naram-Sin, written in Elamite.
This begins with an invocation to numerous gods; of
the Elamite deities mentioned, those best known from
later texts are Pinikir, Huban, Nahiti or Nahhunte,
Inshushinak, Shimut, Hurbi, Hutran, and Narude or

[33] Bricks: *Mém.*, II, 56; vase: *Mém.*, IV, 1; statues: *Mém.*, VI, 2–6.

[34] *Mém.*, XIV, 5 f.; personal names show that Documents 17, 20, 45,
and 73 also belong to the time of this *ishakku*.

[35] *Mém.*, Vol. XIV.

Narute. Amal, Ninkarak, and perhaps Ninurta appear to be the only foreign gods invoked, and even these may have borne Elamite names. The invocation is followed by an oath: "The enemy of Naram-Sin is my enemy, the friend of Naram-Sin is my friend." The Elamite is obviously admitting his vassalage to the ruler of Agade.[36]

By his defeat of the kings of Shimurrum and Namar, Naram-Sin came into direct contact with the inhabitants of the northern and central Zagros. These were the peoples of Lullubium and Gutium, of whom Sargon before him may have heard, who spoke Caucasian languages related to, but distinct from, Elamite.[37] The Lullubi were secure in their possession of a fertile plain within the mountains, the Shehrizor, administered in modern times from the town of Sulaimaniyah.[38] Their marauding bands could easily interfere with the customary traffic along the Babylonian road now marked by the towns of Kifri, Kirkuk, and Altun Köprü. Tradition knew of a king of the Lullubi named Immashkush preceding Sargon;[39] their ruler in the days of Naram-Sin offered battle to the Babylonian in a gorge of the "Black

[36] Scheil, *Mém.*, XI, 1 ff.; cf. Hüsing, *Quellen*, pp. 7 f. and No. 3.

[37] Cf. Speiser, *op. cit.*, chap. iv, "The Lullu and the Guti," pp. 87–119, Hüsing, *Der Zagros und seine Völker* (*Der alte Orient*, IX, Heft 3/4 [1908]), pp. 19 ff.

[38] Cf. A. Billerbeck, *Das Sandschak Suleimania*, pp. 6–11; Speiser, "Southern Kurdistan . . . .," *Annual of the American Schools of Oriental Research*, VIII (1926–27), 1–41.

[39] See reference above, p. 26, n. 13.

Mountain," called today the "Pagan's Pass," south of the Shehrizor. The Lullubian was hopelessly defeated, and to commemorate the victory the king of Agade carved on the walls of the gorge a relief,[40] the prototype of the better-known "Stele of Victory."[41] A wholly different outcome resulted from Naram-Sin's attack on the Guti, for these barbarians, soon to overrun all Babylonia and to bring an end to his dynasty, inflicted upon him a crushing defeat.[42]

In Elam proper, Naram-Sin knew how to reward long years of faithful service; Enammune, once merely the *ishakku* of Elam, became *shakkanakku*, or governor, of the land, and as such made a new official seal.[43] Perhaps the post he relinquished fell to a deserving Elamite, Puzur-Inshushinak, son of Shimbi-ishhuk, who first appears as the *ishakku* of Susa. Eager to please his masters, this prince at first wrote his inscriptions in Akkadian only,[44] but soon he was putting alongside of this language his own proto-Elamite.[45] Perhaps with the death or removal of

[40] Described by C. J. Edmonds, "Two Ancient Monuments in Southern Kurdistan," *Geographical Journal*, LXV (1925), 63 f., reproduced in Sidney Smith, *Early History of Assyria*, p. 97; the exact site in the Darband-i-Gawr gorge of the Qara Dagh is near Seosenan on the route between Sulaimaniyah and Rubat.

[41] *Mém.*, I, 144 ff., and II, 53 ff., Pl. 11; cf. *SAK*, pp. 166 f.

[42] Weidner Chronicle from Ashur; see Güterbock in *ZA*, XLII (1934), 47 ff.

[43] *Mém.*, XIV, 6.   [44] Door socket in Scheil, *Mém.*, VI, 7.

[45] Statuette of a goddess in Scheil, *Mém.*, XIV, 17 ff. The latest attempt to decipher all the proto-Elamite texts of this ruler, with references

Enammune, he too became *shakkanakku* of Elam; but
if the new office implied an increase of power, it
meant also an extension of his sphere of activities, for
we find him embarking upon foreign conquest. Not
improbably he declared to Naram-Sin that he was
merely subjecting vassals who had been disobedient
to the lord of Agade. On a statue presented to his
god he states that when Kimash and Hurtum made
war against him, he conquered them and ravaged
Hupshana. Since Kimash was far up in the Zagros
at a point opposite Kirkuk,[46] and Hurtum is possibly
that Humurtum so familiar from Third Ur Dynasty
date formulas, Naram-Sin might well have been wary,
for it was into territory at least nominally his that
Puzur-Inshushinak was entering. The Elamite also
claims that he conquered over sixty other sites. Although these are enumerated apparently without
topographical order, we may still gain some history
from their names. Possible mention of Kashshen may
be our earliest reference to the land from which the
Kassites took their name. Gutu surely attests contact with the Gutians or with the land whence their

---

to the previous literature, has been made by F. Bork, *Die Strichinschriften
von Susa* (Königsberg i. Pr., 1924). Unfortunately, there is no proof that
these texts are duplicates of the Akkadian.

[46] On its location cf. Poebel in *ZA*, XXXIX (1930), 137 f.; on Hupshana cf. the Hupshan of Shilhak-Inshushinak, *Mém.*, XI, 21 ff. (No. 92),
obv. i 95 and rev. ii 34, and *Mém.*, V, 39 ff. (No. 77), iv 10, and of the neo-
Elamite Shutruk-Nahhunte, *Mém.*, V, 67 (No. 85*a*), l. 9. Cf. the place
Hupshan and the god Aiahupshan in Rawlinson, *Cuneiform Inscriptions
of Western Asia*, Vol. II, Pl. 60, No. 1 i 7 f.

hordes descended upon Babylonia. Shilwan suggests
the mountainous country east of ancient Der near
modern Sirwan. The land Huhunuri was soon to be
familiar from date formulas of the Third Dynasty of
Ur, and Mu Turran[47] may be the *Mê Turnat* of the
Assyrian annals, a city on the modern Diyala River.
Separate mention is made of the king of Simash,
who came from afar to seize the feet of Puzur-Inshushinak.[48]

Booty from the humbled cities enriched Susa, and
a new temple to Inshushinak crowned the acropolis.
For its foundation deposit Puzur-Inshushinak decreed four *magi* of silver, emblems of silver and gold,
a long dagger, and a great ax whose sides were over-
laid with silver. With magnificent ceremony a fine
new statue of the deity was brought to the site on a
new canal leading from the city Sidari. In his honor
two sheep were sacrificed daily, and at his gate musicians sang morning and evening. We are told all
this by a stele with an Akkadian inscription, which
further declares that Puzur-Inshushinak gave righteous judgment to the city.[49] From the wreck of the
temple a lion-headed block, inscribed in Akkadian
and in the still undecipherable proto-Elamite,[50] has

[47] Read by Scheil as *Mu-i-um?-an.*

[48] Scheil, *Mém.*, XIV, 9 ff., supplemented by the cities mentioned on
the fragment *Mém.*, VI, 14 f. Many names are almost illegible; others are
at present unknown.

[49] Scheil, *Mém.*, IV, 4 ff.; cf. *SAK*, pp. 178 ff.

[50] Scheil, *Mém.*, VI, 8; cf. *SAK*, pp. 178 f.; drawing and description by
Lampre, *Mém.*, VIII, 162 ff. To this period also belongs a bas-relief with
proto-Elamite text, *Mém.*, Vol. VI, Pl. 2.

survived to our day. Clay cones commemorated the erection of a dwelling for the god Shugu on behalf of Inshushinak;[51] but alabaster statuettes, fashioned with the boast that they were neither of silver nor of copper, were dedicated to deities other than the local god, and on some of these the Akkadian inscription is supplemented by a proto-Elamite text.[52] In the curses which he invokes against those who would damage his monuments, Puzur-Inshushinak calls upon Inshushinak, Narite or Narute, and Nati of the Elamite deities, and upon Shamash, Nergal, Ishtar and Sin, Enlil and Ea, and Ninhursag of the Babylonian gods. Some of the latter may have had Elamite epithets, for the proto-Elamite texts themselves indicate that the ruler was attempting to revive the national feeling of his subjects.

If this were indeed his purpose, he was wise to wait until the death of his nominal lord in Babylonia. When Naram-Sin gave place to Sharkalisharri, the Elamite declared his independence with a vengeance. Allied with Zahara, the land which had previously aided Elam and Barahshi against Rimush, he invaded Babylonia early in the reign of the new sovereign; his troops were driven back only after they had penetrated to the territory of Opis in the very center of

[51] Scheil, *Mém.*, II, 58–62; cf. *SAK*, pp. 176 f.; notice of discovery in Jéquier, *Mém.*, I, 117.

[52] (1) *Mém.*, II, 63–65; *SAK*, pp. 178 f.; (2) *Mém.*, X, 11 (No. III), bearing a proto-Elamite text; (3) *Mém.*, XIV, 20 f.; details of discovery, Jéquier, *Mém.*, I, 128 f., and VII, 27. Other proto-Elamite texts are given in *Mém.*, Vol. X, Pls. 4 f.

Akkad.[53] Fortified by this success—for safe return
from an invasion into the land of the king of Agade,
the king of the "Four World-Quarters," could be considered nothing less than a triumph—Puzur-Inshushinak was at once crowned king of Awan, as successor of Hita.[54] As for Sharkalisharri, it is no wonder
that he was thereafter merely "King of Agade,"
while the Elamite Puzur-Inshushinak tells how in one
year Inshushinak looked with favor upon him, the
mighty king of Awan, and granted to him the "Four
World-Regions."[55]

Meanwhile the peoples of the central Zagros had
become restless. To highlanders such as themselves
the lowlands of Babylonia seemed always most desir-
able. From afar they watched the fertile plain teem-
ing with activity, until desire or need became too
strong, or new peoples appeared from their rear to
drive them forward. Then irresistibly they poured
into the rich land which lay before them. For a time
they obtained control; more and more, however, they
themselves became subject to the higher civilization
which they found in the new habitat, and succumbed
to its inexorable influences.

So it was with the people of Lullubium. From their
central point, the Shehrizor, they advanced southeastward to the district Holwan, where a relief of
their king Anubanini has been found at Zohab near

[53] Date formula of Sharkalisharri; cf. *Reallexikon der Assyriologie*,
II, 133.

[54] *Mém.*, XXIII, iv.   [55] Stele, published by Scheil, *Mém.*, X, 9 f.

Sar-i-Pul. His inscription is in the Akkadian script and language; as the mighty king, king of Lullubium, he declares that he has set up his own image and that of Ishtar on Mount Batir, and with a good Babylonian curse he calls upon Anu and Antum, Enlil and Ninlil, Adad and Ishtar, Sin and Shamash, and other deities to preserve his monument.[56] In later times tradition assigned him to the ranks of the kings of Gutium and finally made him a king of the city Kutha. As a horrible monster he figured in a legend which illustrates the impression made by Guti barbarians upon the inhabitants of Babylonia.[57] Not far distant from his relief is the stele of Tardunni, son of Ikki, also bearing an Akkadian inscription which invokes Shamash and Adad.[58] Tardunni must be placed in the same period and may likewise have been a king of Lullubium.

Perhaps the Guti, who seem to have lived north of the Shehrizor, were responsible for this advance of the Lullubi. They too longed for possession of the

[56] J. de Morgan, *Mission scientifique en Perse*, IV, 160–71, Pl. 11; cf. De Morgan and Scheil in "Les deux stèles de Zohab," *RT*, XIV (1893), 100–105; *Mém.*, II, 67 f.; cf. *SAK*, pp. 172 f. For recent photographs and drawings cf. Herzfeld, *Am Tor von Asien*, pp. 3 ff.

[57] *CT*, Vol. XIII, Pls. 39 ff.; cf. L. W. King, *Seven Tablets of Creation*, I, 140 ff. On the identity of the Anubanini of the inscription cf. Hommel in "Assyriological Notes," *PSBA*, XXI (1899), 115–17; P. Jensen in *KB*, VI, Heft 1, 552, objected to this identification on grounds which seem insufficient to the writer.

[58] Stele at Sheikhan; cf. Scheil in *RT*, XIV (1893), 105 f.; cf. *SAK*, pp. 172 f. Only a preliminary notice of a copy made recently by Herzfeld has appeared in *ZDMG*, LXXX (1926), 228.

Land of the Two Rivers, and their victory over
Naram-Sin some years before had given them con-
fidence. Their masses poured into Babylonia, striking a glancing blow at their southern neighbors, but
never pausing in their headlong dash for the region
most to be desired. Sharkalisharri valiantly attempted to stem the tide; one of his year formulas
records an expedition against them, another the capture of Sharlak, their king.[59] But his efforts were useless, and he himself became their prey. Shortly after
his death, even the ghost of independent rule in the
cities disappeared; and the period following his reign
was one of such anarchy that it became known under
the suggestive designation: "Who was king? Who
was not king?"[60]

About the same time, the Elamites and their dynasty of Awan disappear from the stage of oriental
history. Puzur-Inshushinak was the twelfth and last
king of Awan, and with his sudden eclipse the land is
enshrouded in darkness. Babylonia and Elam alike
appear to have been inundated by the Gutian tide.

[59] *SAK*, pp. 225 f.; *Reallexikon der Assyriologie*, II, 133. Sharlak, like
Anubanini, was for a time with some misgivings considered a king of
Kutha; cf. Hommel, *Ethnologie und Geographie des alten Orients* (Mün-
chen, 1926), p. 1017; see, however, Speiser, *Mesopotamian Origins*, p. 98,
n. 44.

[60] King lists, as in Langdon, "Oxford Editions of Cuneiform Texts,"
II, 17. The confusion within Babylonia throughout this period is illustrated by a letter and a lament published by S. Smith in *JRAS*, 1932,
pp. 295 ff.; the lament was first published by Pinches in "Assyriological
Gleanings," *PSBA*, XXIII (1901), 196–99.

CHAPTER III

BABYLONIAN DYNASTS AND KINGS OF SIMASH

THE peoples of Gutium who overwhelmed Babylonia in the twenty-fifth century B.C. appear indeed to have been barbarians. Later authors hurl fierce invectives against them, and apparently these were not altogether unwarranted. It was said that they antagonized the gods, carried off the sovereignty of Sumer to the mountains, and established enmity and wickedness in the land.[1] From the viewpoint of the Babylonian, schooled in the virtues of law and order, no greater accusation could be brought against any people than that they lacked the firm hand of a rightful sovereign. Yet it was said of the Guti that they had no ruler before they entered the lowlands.[2] We may attribute this state-

[1] Utuhegal inscription; cf. Thureau-Dangin, "La fin de la domination gutienne," *RA*, IX (1912), 111–20, and X, 98–100; M. Witzel in *Babyloniaca*, VII (1913), 51–62.

[2] King lists, as in Langdon, "Oxford Editions of Cuneiform Texts," II, 18. The assumption that the Guti capital was Arrapha because they carried off to this city the statue of Anunit of Sippar (apparently first stated by Scheil in *RT*, XXXIII [1911], 216, and recently by Langdon in *Cambridge Ancient History*, I, 423) is based on a misinterpretation of the "Constantinople" text of Nabu-naid, which is No. 8 in Langdon, *Die neubabylonischen Königsinschriften*, pp. 276 f.

43

ment to the fact that Sharkalisharri captured their king, Sharlak, and excuse it on that account; but we cannot pardon their overthrow of the administrative and economic order, which is indicated by the dearth of Babylonian records.

Little is known about the Gutian rule in Babylonia save the names of their kings in two dynastic lists. A few scattered inscriptions of sovereigns who do not appear in those records tell us but little of their makers. The lists themselves disagree; and, although the brief reigns which are given to the individual kings indicate a period of intense unrest and inner combat, these figures are all suspiciously alike and arouse distrust.[3] One record says that the invaders controlled the land for 124 years; another insists that

---

[3] The main list as published by Langdon in "Oxford Editions of Cuneiform Texts," II, 18 f., gives the following names with their lengths of rule:

Imta (error for Imbia)	3 years	Kurum	1 year
Ingishu	6	....nedin	3 years
Nikillagab	6	....rabum	2
Shulme	6	Irarum	2
Elulumesh	6	Ibranum	1 year
Ilimabakesh	5	Hablum	2 years
Igeshaush (?)	6	Puzur-Sin, son of Hablum	7
Iarlagab	15	Iarlaganda	7
Ibate	3	[....]	7
Iarla	3	Tiriga[n]	40 days

The second list is incomplete; it has been published in part by Poebel, *Historical and Grammatical Texts*, No. 4 (cf. Poebel, *Historical Texts*, p. 80), and in part by L. Legrain, *Historical Fragments* (*PBS*, Vol. XIII), No. 1, p. 27. It gives only the following names:

Imbia	5 (or 3) years	Warlagaba	6 years
Ingishu	7	Iarlagash	3

the correct total is 125 years and 40 days. It is impossible to doubt the proven ability of Babylonian mathematicians; yet our addition of the separate reigns totals only 91 years and 40 days, leaving an unexplained balance of 34 years. From these facts it should be clear that there is much yet to be learned concerning the period of Gutian domination.

Toward the end of the period the barbarians appear to have come under the persistent and prevailing influence of Babylonian culture. Perhaps we may assign to this time those kings who have left their own inscriptions but whose names do not appear in the king lists of the native scribes. Lasirab, king of Gutium, called upon the god of Gutium as well as Ishtar and Sin to guard a macehead upon which he inscribed an Akkadian text.[4] To his title another ruler, named Erridupizir, added "King of the Four World-Regions" when he dedicated an object to Enlil of Nippur.[5]

Strange as it may appear, some of the Babylonian cities seem to have enjoyed a renewal of prosperity under the foreign rule. In these the *ishakku*'s of the older races apparently retained control, though they fully acknowledged the sovereignty of the invaders. One of these cities was Umma, whose *ishakku* Lugal-annadu tells us that while Sium was king of Gutium

[4] H. Winckler in *ZA*, IV (1889), 406; cf. *SAK*, pp. 170 ff.

[5] Hilprecht, *BE*, Ser. D, V, Part 1, 20–24; cf. Poebel, *Historical Texts*, p. 134.

there was welfare in the land for thirty-five years.[6] Nammahni, another *ishakku* of the same place, rebuilt an old temple of Ninurra at the time Arlagan was his ruler;[7] and a scribe of Umma dedicated a votive plaque to his king, Saratigubisin.[8]

Tirigan, a Gutian king whose name was given to several cities within the empire,[9] reigned but forty days before he fell a prey to the hate and violence of a native prince.[10] The rule of Gutium was over. Immediately whatever unity had existed within the kingdom disappeared, and tiny independent states arose in the Zagros regions and in Elam as well as in Babylonia. To us some of these principalities are old friends known from the days of Sargon or of Puzur-Inshushinak of Awan. Others are new, to whom the fall of Gutium for the first time gave freedom.

Far to the north, near the foothills of the Zagros, was Urbillum, more famous as Arbela, whose name

[6] Scheil, "Une nouvelle dynastie suméro-accadienne," *Comptes rendus de l'Académie des inscriptions et belles-lettres*, 1911, pp. 318–27; cf. Poebel, *Historical Texts*, pp. 134 f.

[7] Clay, *Miscellaneous Inscriptions* ("Yale Oriental Series," *Babylonian Texts*, Vol. I), No. 13, pp. 11 f., corrected by C. H. W. Johns, "The Dynasty of Gutium," *PSBA*, XXXVIII (1916), 199 f.

[8] Thureau-Dangin in "Notes assyriologiques," *RA*, IX (1912), 73–76; cf. Poebel, *Historical Texts*, p. 135.

[9] Cf. Sidney Smith, "The Three Cities Called Tirqan," *JRAS*, 1928, pp. 868–75. One city is described as lying "in front of Gutium" and is equated with Harhar; for a location of Harhar south of the Zeribor Sea on the upper Diyala cf. Billerbeck, *Das Sandschak Suleimania*, p. 63.

[10] Utuhegal of Uruk, whose text was cited above, p. 43.

still lingers as Erbil.[11] South of this was Shimurrum, at modern Altun Köprü, the main crossing of the Lower Zab River.[12] South of this again was Harshe, perhaps the Hurshitum of the Babylonians, at the village known today as Tuz Khurmatli.[13] In the mountains east of Kirkuk, Kimash once more became turbulent. Remnants of the Lullubi banded together within the central Zagros, and the adjacent land Ganhar proved that it too could be troublesome. Farther south Marhashi, known in Akkadian as Barahshi, began once more to rear its head; and in her low plain it would seem that even Susa declared for independence. Northeast of Elam a self-reliant state arose in Anshan; and in Simash, a land perhaps not far distant, which had sent tribute to Puzur-Inshushinak, the ruler Girnamme founded a new dynasty.[14] Any Babylonian sovereign who would bring unity to the Near East must subdue many of these city-states; the effort would demand constant warfare and recourse to numerous political intrigues.

The Babylonian ruler who overthrew the Guti was himself subjected by Ur-Nammu (2290 B.C.),[15] who founded the Third Dynasty of Ur. His successor,

[11] Sayce in *PSBA*, XXI (1899), 21, n. 2.

[12] See above, p. 33.   [13] See below, p. 60.

[14] Named on the same tablet which lists the kings of Awan, published by Scheil in *RA*, XXVIII (1931), 1–8, now in *Mém.*, XXIII, iv.

[15] In an unpublished study Professor Olmstead has solved many of the chronological difficulties in the periods which follow. I am greatly indebted to him for permission to employ the new dates in this manuscript.

Shulgi (2272–2226 B.C.), began that policy of expansion which brought under the control of Ur many of the states just enumerated.[16] In his seventh year Shulgi restored the god Sataran[17] to the temple at Der, and in his eighth he returned Numushda to the shrine in Kazallu. The reason is obvious: the dominance of Ur was so universally recognized by the cities within Babylonia proper that local deities could be established in their own dwellings without danger of revolt by the separate districts.

Now began a determined effort to explore the east and the north. From Der it was an easy march to Marhashi, to whose *ishakku* Shulgi married his own daughter in the fourteenth year. The ravaging of Ganhar in the twenty-second year initiated a series of raids against the Lullubi. Shimurrum on the Lower Zab was attacked in the twenty-third and twenty-fourth years, and Harshe in the twenty-fifth.

By this time Shulgi felt capable of bringing the states which lay beyond the Zagros boundary range under his control; in his twenty-eighth year he married a daughter to the *ishakku* of Anshan, perhaps

[16] Shulgi date formulas best in *Reallexikon der Assyriologie*, Vol. II, *s.v.* "Datenlisten"; cf. also Myhrman, *Sumerian Administrative Documents* (*BE*, Ser. A, Vol. III, Part 1), pp. 34–39, and *SAK*, pp. 229 ff. List of Ur III *ishakku*'s conveniently gathered by C. E. Keiser, *Patesis of the Ur Dynasty* ("Yale Oriental Series," *Researches*, Vol. IV, Part 2).

[17] For the reading ^{d}KA.DI = ^{d}Sataran see Weidner in *AOF*, IX (1933–34), 99; for earlier readings see Poebel in *MVAG*, XXVI, Heft 1 (1921), 2, n. 3; R. Scholtz in *ZA*, XLI (1933), 304; cf., however, the name *Awîl-Qadi* in *Mém.*, Vol. XVIII, No. 159, l. 4.

Libum or Shalabum—an act which should imply the latter's vassalage. The kingdom of Simash, now ruled by Tazitta I,[18] was apparently untouched. Returning to the north, Shulgi ravaged Shimurrum for the third time in his thirtieth year, and Ganhar for the second and third times in the twenty-ninth and thirty-first, respectively. In the interim Anshan, possibly supported by Tazitta of Simash, revolted and had to be won back in the thirty-second. In the attempt to preserve control of this region Shalhuni was established as *shakkanakku* of Zabum; but a little later we hear of a second devastation of Anshan,[19] the war against which was apparently a failure.

In the latter years of the reign, attack was concentrated on the restless northern districts. Far from Ur, and belonging to a hostile race, the peoples of these regions were unwilling to accept domination by the south, and their determined resistance finds its echo in the date formulas. Shashrum was entered in the fortieth year; Shimurrum and Lullubium were ravaged for the ninth time in the forty-second. In the forty-third, Shimurrum, Lullubium, Ganhar, and Urbillum felt the hand of the conqueror; while Kimash and Humurtum, probably the Hurtum of earlier fame, were penetrated in the forty-fourth. As the most important border fortress guarding the

[18] Scheil, *Mém.*, XXIII, iv.

[19] C. E. Keiser, *Selected Temple Documents of the Ur Dynasty* ("Yale Oriental Series," *Babylonian Texts*, Vol. IV), No. 286 and p. 18.

eastern mountains, Der received a *shakkanakku* by
the forty-sixth year,[20] in which we hear once more of
a devastation of Harshe, Kimash, and Humurtum.

While all these raids into foreign lands were being
carried out, Susa and her lowlands appear to have
been completely under Shulgi's control. The city may
have been won at the time he first entered Anshan,
that is, in his twenty-eighth year, for we first hear
of an *ishakku* of Susa, Urkium, in the thirty-first.
Thereafter the story is more easily told from Shulgi's
own texts in the city. He erected a new temple for
Inshushinak, the god of Susa, and a new dwelling for
the goddess Ninhursag, known to Elamites since the
days of the last king of Awan. His bricks, inscribed
bronze statuettes, and stone tablets were still to be
found on the Susian acropolis a millennium later
when Shilhak-Inshushinak used them for foundation
deposits, and again after another five hundred years
when the neo-Elamite rulers employed them for the
same purpose;[21] even Shulgi himself can hardly have
expected such honor. To the great lady Ningal he

[20] Seals mentioning Ur-Sin, *shakkanakku* of Uruk and Der, published
by Scheil in *RA*, XIII (1916), 20 f.

[21] All these objects were found in the neo-Elamite temple foundations;
cf. De Mecquenem, *Mém.*, VII, 63; XII, 67–72. Objects dedicated to
Inshushinak include bricks: *Mém.*, IV, 8, and VI, 20; statuettes: De
Mecquenem, *Mém.*, Vol. VII, Pl. 11; tablets: *Mém.*, VI, 21; for the inscriptions cf. also *SAK*, pp. 190 ff. Other inscriptions of Shulgi have only
recently been uncovered in the "Villa royale"; cf. De Mecquenem, *Mém.*,
XXV, 236. The texts of the objects dedicated to Ninhursag have not
yet been published; cf. De Mecquenem, *Mém.*, XII, 70–72.

inscribed a precious pearl,[22] while two of his subordinates in the city, Ur-niginmu and Nin-kisalshu, presented to the "Lady of the City" a macehead for his life.[23]

From this time forward, almost to the exclusion of the more truly Elamite regions such as Anshan and Simash, the influence of Ur reigned supreme in Susa and the adjacent districts. As "Elam," this territory became the province of Ur par excellence. Multitudes of men-at-arms for the protection of caravans, couriers bearing royal messages, *ishakku*'s, and occasionally men of even higher rank such as *sukkallu*'s or plenipotentiaries, traversed Babylonia between the royal capital and this land, receiving at the various cities en route the provisions necessary for their journey; the records of their transit are found in hundreds of contemporary clay documents.[24] The Elamites, not to be outdone, entered actively into the comparatively new but wealth-producing commerce; and hundreds entered Babylonia to take part in numerous business ventures. Thus the same documents mention Elamites from Susa, Anshan, Simash or Shimash, Huhunuri, Marhashi, and many other

[22] Scheil, *Mém.*, VI, 22; cf. *SAK*, pp. 194 f.; on details of discovery cf. De Mecquenem, *Mém.*, VII, 94.

[23] Scheil in *RT*, XXXI (1909), 135, now in *Mém.*, XIV, 22.

[24] Cf. C.-F. Jean, "L'Elam sous la dynastie d'Ur," *RA*, XIX (1922), 1–44.

cities,[25] while Zabum and Adamdun[26] figure no less prominently. Of Adamdun, the name of which is possibly derived from the Elamite name for Elam,[27] we even know of two *ishakku*'s in the reign of Shulgi. These are Uba in the forty-first year and Riba in the forty-fourth. We may never know how far Ur's control extended beyond this low plain into Iran, but we may be perfectly certain that its influence was keenly felt deep within the hinterland.

The death of a ruler is always the signal for an outbreak of restless peoples; it was a striking tribute to Shulgi's administrative ability that this region accepted without a struggle his successor Bur-Sin (2225–2217). For three years the new sovereign allowed the officials of Shulgi to remain unmolested;

[25] Including Siri, Gizili, Gisha, Siu, Zaul, Ulum (doubtless somewhere on the Ulai River), Kinunir, and Mahili; cf. Thureau-Dangin in *Comptes rendus de l'Académie des inscriptions et belles-lettres*, 1902, pp. 88 f.

[26] Also URU+A and URU.AZ.

[27] Adamdun equated with Ha(l)tamti by Scheil, *Mém.*, X, 3. The objections to this equation have been based largely on the erroneous reading *Hapirti* for *Hatamti*, but Professor Poebel's demonstration that Sumerian and Akkadian *Elam* were derived from the Elamite *Ha(l)tamti* now definitely proves the latter reading; cf. his article "The Name of Elam in Sumerian, Akkadian, and Hebrew," *AJSL*, XLVIII (1931/32), 20–26. Objections to the equation of Adamdun with Hatamti are still in order, however, for in the Sumerian texts Adamdun is obviously a city, while Hatamti in the Elamite texts is the land. For a solution of the problem two other documents must be considered. The first is Thureau-Dangin, *Recueil de tablettes chaldéennes* (Paris, 1903), No. 351, rev. 2 ff., where occurs the mention of Elamites from Siri coming from Adamdun. The other is an inscription of Ibi-Sin published by Gadd and Legrain, *Royal Inscriptions*, Nos. 210 f. and 289, in which it is stated that Susa, Adamdun, and the land Awan were subjected.

then he began to replace them with men of his own choosing. In his fourth year a new *ishakku* of Susa, Zariqum, was inducted into office with great ceremony in the presence of ten important witnesses;[28] his contemporary Nagidda was already the *ishakku* of Adamdun.[29] From the fourth year onward Libanug-shabash was to be found in Marhashi, with Busham in Simanum by the sixth year. An individual with the Semitic name Sharrum-bani, established in Awak by the fifth year, remained there till the second year of Ibi-Sin, a period of sixteen years, while Ur-ishkur likewise was retained in Hamazi from Bur-Sin's seventh year to the second of Gimil-Sin. Such long tenures of office bespeak peace and quiet in the land.

This was not true of the central and northern Zagros, where a series of revolts and suppressions harried the country. Bur-Sin plundered Urbillum in the second year, Shashrum in the sixth, and Huhunuri and Iaprum in the seventh.[30] Perhaps after

[28] Scheil, "Diplomatica," *Hilprecht Anniversary Volume*, pp. 152 f.; text recopied by Dossin, *Mém.*, Vol. XVIII, No. 219; on the dating cf. Scheil in *RT*, XXXVII (1915), 133–35. Documents from Susa dated the fourth and fifth years of Bur-Sin, *Mém.*, Vol. X, Nos. 125 f.

[29] Thureau-Dangin, *Receuil de tablettes chaldéennes*, No. 325; cf. Ch.-G. Janneau, *Une dynastie chaldéenne: Les rois d'Ur* (Paris, 1911), p. 42, n. 2.

[30] For the latter year cf. Scheil in *RT*, XXXVII (1915), 135–37, where, however, the equation of *bitum rabium* with a postulated Elamite *hal risha* and hence Harshe must be denied. Booty from Shashrum received in Drehem already in the fourth year suggests that its "devastation" in the sixth came as the result of a revolt; cf. Olmstead in *AJSL*, XXXV (1918/19), 77.

this frightful lesson, Huhunuri received Simhuzia as *ishakku*, with definite instructions to remain loyal. Farther north, in the region east and south of modern Kirkuk, Hunnini carried on as the *ishakku* of Kimash and *shakkanakku* of Madga; to him Ugugu dedicated a cylinder seal.[31]

Our sources become fewer with the reign of Gimil-Sin (2216–2208), although one cannot on that account say that the kingdom was already in decline. To be sure, Simanum had to be invaded in the third year; and Zabshalu, within Babylonia proper at no great distance from the capital, appears to have revolted in the seventh, for it too was plundered. But we hear of an *ishakku* of Humurtum, Hubamersili, in the first year; and a daughter of the king was sent, apparently in marriage, to the *ishakku* of Zabshalu after its subjection. These events assume the maintenance of law and order. As early as the second year we learn of supplies which the daughter of the king took into Anshan, doubtless as part of her marriage dowry.[32] Anshan, then, had been attacked; we hear of this war from another source than the date formulas, namely, from the well-known inscriptions of Gudea, *ishakku* of Lagash from perhaps the eighth year of Bur-Sin to at least the sixth year of Gimil-Sin.

[31] Sayce, "Babylonian Cylinders in the Hermitage at St. Petersburg," *ZA*, VI (1891), 161–63; Poebel, "Eine neue sumerische Mundart," *ZA*, XXXIX (1930), 129–39. On the location of Madga at Kifri or Tuz Khurmatli see, besides Poebel, C. J. Gadd in *RA*, XXIII (1926), 65.

[32] Virolleaud in *ZA*, XIX (1905–6), 384.

Curiously enough, Gudea fails to acknowledge any superior; in the document which mentions his only war, this very conquest of Anshan in Elam, there is no hint that the campaign was carried out in the train of Gimil-Sin.[33] He does inform us that Elamites came from Elam and Susians from Susa to aid him in reconstructing the temple of his god.[34] We have, therefore, definite evidence that in the time of Gudea and Gimil-Sin Anshan, the Elamite highlands, and the Susian plain were all under Babylonian overlordship.

Further proof comes from the names of cities which paid allegiance. By the seventh year Shulgi-admu was recognized in one Elamite city,[35] while in Susa itself Beliarik replaced Zariqum a year or two later. Gimil-Sin wisely ordered the restoration of the temple to Ninhursag on the Susian acropolis, and his own bricks commemorated its rebuilding.[36]

The uplands to the north of Elam in territory for which Shulgi had so valiantly fought were likewise obedient to the new lord of Ur. Gudea, again without reference to his master, describes his operations

[33] Statue B, vi 64 ff.; cf. *SAK*, pp. 70 f.; cf. also Olmstead in *AJSL*, XXXV, 67 f.

[34] Cylinder A, xv 6 ff.; cf. I. M. Price, *The Great Cylinder Inscriptions .... of Gudea*, Part I (Leipzig, 1899), p. 25; translation *ibid.*, Part II (Leipzig, 1927), p. 19; cf. *SAK*, pp. 104 f.

[35] URU+A.

[36] Scheil, *Mém.*, IV, 8, and X, 12; cf. De Mecquenem, *Mém.*, XII, 71. For other bricks recently discovered in the "Villa royale" cf. De Mecquenem, *Mém.*, XXV, 211. The tombs of this period at Susa are particularly rich in funerary equipment; cf. *ibid.*, pp. 209–11 and 227–36.

in Kimash, where he quarried copper, while Madga to the south of Kimash furnished him gypsum.[37] His numerous references to the use of lapis lazuli arouse our interest, for this highly prized stone, in antiquity as today, must be sought in eastern Iran, and in Gudea's time commercial relationships with the plateau could not have been interrupted.

Perhaps because he was definitely afraid of the breakup of his empire, Gimil-Sin consolidated the rule over the more doubtful and troublesome regions in the hands of a single personage. This individual was Warad-Nannar, whose many titles make dry reading but are nevertheless highly significant. He was merely the *ishakku* or prince of some districts; these were Lagash (surely after Gudea's disappearance), Zabum, the land Gutebum, the "City of the Divine Gimil-Sin," Hamazi, and Ganhar. Over others he was *shakkanakku* or governor; these included Uzargarshana, Bashime, Timat-Enlil, Urbillum, Ishar, the Su(bartu) peoples, and the land Karda.[38]

One region neither Gimil-Sin nor his subordinate could conquer. Elam and Anshan might be made subject, but an independent state continued to flourish in Simash concurrently with the dynasty of Ur. In this land Girnamme and Tazitta I had been followed by the kings Ebarti and Tazitta II. Enbi-

[37] Statue B, vi 21 ff.; Cylinder A, xvi 7 ff.; cf. *SAK*, pp. 70 f. and 106 f.

[38] Thureau-Dangin, "Une inscription d'Arad-Nannar," *RA*, V (1898–1902), 99–102, and VI, 67 f.; cf. *SAK*, pp. 148 ff.

luhhan, the succeeding ruler, was a contemporary of Ur's next and last sovereign, Ibi-Sin.[39]

The accession (in 2207) of this unfortunate appears to have taken place under peaceful circumstances, though no one then alive can have believed that Ur was still all-powerful. For a time the pretext of its former might was maintained, and a "devastation" of Shimurrum gave its name to a year. Likewise a mention of the *ishakku* of Awak, Sharrum-bani, in the business documents of the second year and, moreover, the occurrence of business documents at Susa dated in his second and third years[40] indicate that Elam for a time remained loyal. But then came revolt and invasion; and it was the misfortune of Ur that its ruler weakened at the very moment when two young and vigorous states, Mari and Simash, were attacking, one from each side.

From Simash Enbiluhhan moved down into the Elamite lowlands and entered Susa. Like a true sovereign Ibi-Sin promptly met and worsted the invader; after his victory he boasted that like a storm he had overwhelmed in one day the land Awan and the cities Adamdun and Susa and had captured Enbiluhhan or, as he knew him, Enbilua.[41] But Simash was not to be denied. Her next ruler, Kindattu, again

[39] On the tablet listing the Simash kings, only *E- . . . -luhhan* is legible; the name is completed from the name Enbilua in an inscription of Ibi-Sin; see below.

[40] *Mém.*, Vol. X, No. 121, and Vol. XVIII, No. 79.

[41] Gadd and Legrain, *Royal Inscriptions*, Nos. 210 f. and 289.

occupied Susa; and his control was absolute. With tactful strategy his first move was the propitiation of the local deity, and later scribes tell us that he piously restored the temple of Inshushinak.[42] Meanwhile he had been winning to his side other lands formerly under the control of Ur. Thus Huhunuri rebelled from Ibi-Sin, who claims its subjection. He calls it "the key to the land Elam," but a variant text reads "the key to the land Anshan"; and doubtless Kindattu of Simash, who now ruled Anshan and Elam, made him pay dearly for his victory.[43]

The Third Dynasty of Ur was now clearly on the defensive; and Ishbi-Irra, the man of Mari, swept down from the northwest upon Nippur and advanced against Kazallu, whose *ishakku* fearfully implored aid from his suzerain. Indignantly Ibi-Sin replied that no one need be in terror; as sovereign he would be aided by Enlil and by the Elamites, who were now marching toward Ur; his victory over Ishbi-Irra was therefore assured.[44] This was a blind faith, and in

[42] Scheil, *Mém.*, III, 56 f. (Nos. 37 and 39). In the lists Kindat(t)u is called a son of Tan-Ruhuratir; this is evidently due to confusion with Idaddu II in the list of the Simash kings.

[43] The reading of this formula, which appears in Gadd and Legrain, *Royal Inscriptions*, Nos. 290 and 292, has been corrected by Professor Poebel. According to this inscription, Huhunuri or Huhnuri should be located east of Eshnunna and Der, on the border of Marhashi or Barahshi.

[44] Barton, *Miscellaneous Babylonian Inscriptions* (New Haven, 1918), No. 9, pp. 57–59; L. Legrain, *Historical Fragments* (*PBS*, Vol. XIII), Nos. 3, 6, and 9; cf. S. Langdon, "Ibi-Sin and the Fall of the Kingdom of Ur," *RA*, XX (1923), 49–51. A complete tablet of this correspondence between Puzur-Numushda and Ibi-Sin, now in the Oriental Institute Museum, will be published by Professor Poebel.

foreign captivity he had occasion to rue his words. The people of Elam, or rather of Anshan and Simash, came to Babylonia, not to help but to plunder; and to Anshan they carried off the last ruler of Ur, Ibi-Sin, together with his god Nannar (2183 B.C.).[45]

We do not know what spoil Kindattu reaped from his conquest. He can have won little save movable property, for he obtained no land in the alluvium; and his name was so quickly lost to posterity that the honor of the conquest was denied him and his destruction of Ur ascribed to another. His own dynasty continued in Elam and in Simash, but these were far removed both culturally and physically from Baby-

[45] Omen in Boissier, *Choix de textes relatifs à la divination*, II (Geneva, 1906), 64; see now Weidner in *MAOG*, IV (1928–29), 236, and cf. the fragment in King, *Catalogue of the Cuneiform Tablets . . . . of the British Museum, Supplement*, No. 2833. On Nannar cf. the inscription of Gimil-ilishu cited on p. 60. A Nippur lament ascribes the capture of Ibi-Sin to Elam; cf. Langdon, *Historical and Religious Texts* (*BE*, Ser. A, Vol. XXXI), pp. 6–8.

It has long been supposed that the capture of Ibi-Sin is referred to in an inscription of Ashurbanipal of Assyria, who declared that Nana of Uruk had been captured by an Elamite, Kudur-Nahhunte, and held captive in Susa for 1535 (*variant:* 1635) years. Kudur-Nahhunte would thus be the name of the Elamite who wrought the damage. For such an assumption cf. King, *History of Sumer and Akkad*, pp. 304 f.; Weidner in *MVAG*, XXVI, Heft 2 (1921), 49 f., and again in *MAOG*, IV (1928–29), 236; R. C. Thompson in *Cambridge Ancient History*, I, 471; *et al.*

The connection is highly improbable. The new list of Simash kings indicates that Kindattu ruled Elam at the time of Ur's fall; despite Scheil, "Kutir-Nahhunte I" *RA*, XXIX (1932), 67–76, a ruler of that name in Elam at so early a date is altogether improbable. The first individual of that name to appear in Elamite records was approximately contemporary with Hammurabi of Babylon. The reference of Ashurbanipal is far better explained in another way; cf. Olmstead, *History of Assyria*, p. 486, and see below, p. 111.

lonia; consequently it found little mention in the tangled web of affairs within the Land of the Two Rivers.

With Ibi-Sin's death the tiny city-states of Babylonia won back that local independence they had enjoyed before Ur gave unity to the land. A little kingdom again came into being at Hurshitum, the modern Tuz Khurmatli. There its king, Puhia, son of Asirum, erected his own palace with bricks inscribed in Akkadian.[46] In Ganhar Masiam-Ishtar dedicated a cylinder seal to his king, Kisari.[47] In Der, a ruler whose name is lost commemorated by a Sumerian inscription the building of a temple and the restoration of the city Der which he loved.[48] Far more important than these, however, were the two kingdoms of Isin and Larsa. The one was founded by Ishbi-Irra, the man of Mari, the other by Naplanum.

Gimil-ilishu, successor to the founder of the Isin dynasty, ruled in Ur also; he tells us that he brought back Nannar, the god of Ur, from Anshan.[49] Whether this was accomplished by force of arms or by diplomacy he does not say, but we surmise the latter. For

[46] Scheil, "Notes d'épigraphie," *RT* XVI (1894), 186, and XIX (1897), 64; Ungnad, "Vorderasiatische Schriftdenkmäler," Heft 1 (Leipzig, 1907), No. 115; cf. *SAK*, pp. 172 f.

[47] *Collection De Clercq, Catalogue*, Vol. I, No. 121 and pp. 82 f.; cf. *SAK*, pp. 174 f.

[48] From a stele carried to Susa as booty by an Elamite, published by Scheil, *Mém.*, IV, 3; cf. *SAK*, pp. 174 f.

[49] Gadd and Legrain, *Royal Inscriptions*, No. 100.

Kindattu, as king of Simash, had now yielded to Idaddu I, whom we know from his own inscriptions as Idadu-Inshushinak, a man of some moment. He himself claimed to be a son of Bebi, an individual otherwise unknown; but the twelfth century scribes of Shilhak-Inshushinak, who included an Idaddu in their lists of the earlier kings,[50] knew him as the "descendant" of Hutran-tepti,[51] and it is possibly one of his year formulas which reads "year when the bronze statue of Hutran-tepti was made."[52]

In Idaddu's case we have the first example of a practice frequently to be detected in the later Elamite changes of rule, a gradual advancement from a relatively insignificant position to one of great importance, often to royalty itself. The titles of the offices

[50] These lists, hereafter cited merely as the "lists," are parts of three texts: (1) *Mém.*, V, 20 f. (No. 71); (2) *Mém.*, XI, 63 (No. 95); (3) *Mém.*, XI, 64 ff. (No. 96); cf. Hüsing, *Quellen*, No. 48.

[51] The sense of the Elamite words *ruḫu šak*, here translated "descendant," is still vague; cf. Hüsing, *Quellen* p. 21. In the Achaemenian inscription of Darius these words are used to translate Old Persian *napa*, "grandson"; but Akkadian texts of the Hammurabi period translate the words by *mâr aḫatim*, "son of a sister," a phrase found again in the Babylonian Chronicle in the Assyrian period. Neither of these translations seems to be accurate or to agree with the native Elamite texts, which appear to justify only the vaguer meaning, "descendant." For speculations on the meaning of the phrase cf. F. W. König, "Mutterrecht und Thronfolge im alten Elam," *Festschrift der Nationalbibliothek in Wien* (1926), pp. 529–52; also P. Koschaker, "Fratriarchat, Hausgemeinschaft und Mutterrecht in Keilschriftrechten," *ZA*, XLI (1933), 55, n. 3.

[52] *Mém.*, Vol. XXIV, No. 385. Shilhak-Inshushinak also declared that Hutran-tepti restored the temple of Inshushinak in Susa; cf. his brick, *Mém.*, III, 54 (No. 33).

held during this period were those which had been borne by the most important figures in Elam during the period of the Third Ur Dynasty; although they originated in Babylonia, their use in Elam did not in the least imply subservience to the lowlands.

Idadu-Inshushinak very probably began his career as *ishakku* of Susa; he then became both *ishakku* of Susa and *shakkanakku* of the land Elam. In this office, by an Akkadian inscription, he tells of fortifying Susa and surrounding it with a rampart, of beautifying Kizra, Hubbu, and other parts of Susa, of erecting the walls of the temple on the Susian acropolis, and of depositing therein a limestone water basin to the honor of Inshushinak. The curse which he invokes on those who may dare to damage his monuments appeals to Inshushinak and Shamash, Inanna (or Ishtar) and Sin.[53] Doubtless this was inscribed while Kindattu was still the reigning monarch. Then Idadu-Inshushinak, as Idaddu I, became king of Simash or, as his son called him, king of Simash and Elam.[54] We may well hesitate to admit the defeat of a man of this caliber at the hands of Gimil-ilishu of Isin.

Idaddu's son, Tan-Ruhuratir, likewise began his career as *ishakku* of Susa. Promptly he entered into the life and intrigues of Babylonia by marrying Mekubi, daughter of Bilalama, *ishakku* of Eshnunna. For safety in her new home Mekubi erected a tem-

[53] Scheil, *Mém.*, VI, 16–19; cf *SAK*, pp. 180 f.

[54] Inscription of Tan-Ruhuratir in Scheil, *Mém.*, XIV, 26.

ple to Inanna, the goddess of the Susian acropolis.[55] Eventually Tan-Ruhuratir became the eighth king of Simash (*ca.* 2145–2125); but bricks of Shilhak-Inshushinak, a thousand years later, attest his continued interest in the temple of Inshushinak at Susa.[56]

The ninth king of Simash was a second Ebarti (*ca.* 2125–2115), who may likewise have advanced to the sovereignty through many intermediate offices. On the Susa tablets, however, we have only the year formula which he decreed at the time he reached the highest office in the land, "year after Ebarti became king"[57] Idaddu II (*ca.* 2115–2083), son of Tan-Ruhuratir, was more fortunate. He, too, began public life as *ishakku* of Susa, and while serving in this capacity he strove persistently to obtain the local deity's approval. His own bricks commemorate the construction of the wall of Uruanna, the Susian acropolis;[58] and other bricks inscribed with duplicate Akkadian and Sumerian texts tell how he renovated the old walls of the temple with new bricks to the honor of

---

[55] Scheil, *Mém.*, II, 80, and IV, 9; now complete in *Mém.*, XIV, 24 f.; cf. *SAK*, pp. 180 f.; Poebel in *AJSL*, XLIX (1932/33), 137; H. Frankfort, *Tell Asmar and Khafaje* (*OIC*, No. 13), pp. 25–32.

[56] Scheil, *Mém.*, III, 56, and V, 90 (No. 36). The element *ta-an* of names in *Mém.*, Vols. XXII–XXIV, shows that the ruler's name was Tan (*not* Kal or Rip)-Ruhuratir.

[57] Scheil, *Mém.*, Vol. XXIII, Nos. 291–305.

[58] Scheil, *Mém.*, X, 13; cf. Poebel in *AJSL*, XLIX 137.

Inshushinak.[59] His scribe Ishmenni and his servant Pududu dedicated to him, as *ishakku* of Susa, their personal seals; but like kings of the Third Ur Dynasty he intrusted to his judge, Kuk-Shimut, his own royal seal.[60] Eventually he, too, was recognized as the ruler of Simash, becoming the tenth king of that dynasty; and like his predecessor he also employed date formulas. One year is dated by the destruction of Zidanu; another tells of the devastation of Shindi-libbu; a third mentions the erection of a temple to Inanna of Uruanna.[61] Taken all in all, he was a monarch of much power and of many conquests.

Meanwhile a mighty ruler had come to the throne of one of the numerous kingdoms within Babylonia. For a hundred years after the fall of Ur the predominant state in this region was the kingdom of Isin. Throughout this period the kings of Larsa enjoyed at best a local independence, possibly at times admitting vassalage to Isin. The fifth ruler of Larsa, Gungunum, was too strong an individual to tolerate this condition of affairs; immediately after his accession (2087) he turned to the northeast for conquest. There Der was still independent under its own

[59] Sumerian texts: Scheil, *Mém.*, II, 69, and XIV, 27 f.; Akkadian: *Mém.*, II, 72.

[60] Scheil, *Mém.*, XIV, 28 f.; *RA*, XXII (1925), 148 f.

[61] Dossin, *Mém.*, Vol. XVIII, Nos. 123 f., 85, and 125; cf. also Nos. 120–22, "year after the tablet-house was built," and Nos. 84, 127, and 172, not all of which may, however, belong to Idaddu. I owe these readings to the kindness of Professor Poebel. Documents 67–68 and 80–197 in *Mém.*, Vol. XVIII, may all be assigned approximately to this period.

king, now Anumutabil, who had himself already begun to expand by sending an ambassador into Eshnunna and bringing to an end the dynasty of Kirikiri
and Bilalama.[62] Gungunum quickly reduced Anumutabil to the status of a *shakkanakku*, added the troops
of Der to those he had brought from Larsa, and penetrated the eastern mountains in his third year to de-
stroy the city Bashimu.[63] This was a direct thrust
at Idaddu II and the kingdom of Simash.

We are ignorant of the causes which led to this
war. Possibly Idaddu himself had once invaded
Babylonia, and Gungunum was merely undertaking
reprisal. Whatever the case, at the very time when
the kingdom of Simash was seemingly at the peak of
its power, this war brought disaster to Elam. Gungunum's fifth year is dated by a conquest of Anshan;
the Akkadian inscription of Anumutabil of Der, his
subordinate, tells how this *shakkanakku* smote the
heads of the peoples of Anshan, Elam, and Simash,
and how he destroyed Barahshi.[64] Idaddu himself,
the king of Simash, suddenly disappears.

[62] Frankfort, *Tell Asmar and Khafaje*, pp. 32 f., also *Tell Asmar,
Khafaje, and Khorsabad (OIC,* No. 16), pp. 23–29.

[63] Date formulas of the Larsa Dynasty gathered by E. M. Grice,
Chronology of the Larsa Dynasty ("Yale Oriental Series," *Researches,*
Vol. IV, Part 1). An alleged conquest of Zabshalu and the Su(bartu)
peoples by Ur-Ninurta, apparently documented by Poebel, *Historical
Texts,* p. 138, is now abandoned. Professor Poebel, in an unpublished
manuscript kindly placed at my disposal, "Zur Geschichte Elams zur
Zeit der Dynastien von Isin, Larsa und Babylon," has shown that the
formula is that of the seventh year of Gimil-Sin of Ur.

[64] Lenormant, *Choix de textes cunéiformes,* No. 5; cf. *SAK,* pp. 176 f.;
T. Jacobsen, "An Unrecognized Text of Ilu-Mutabil," *AJSL,* XLIV

All this happened so rapidly that in later times the very scribes of Elam were at a loss. Glibly they gave the names of two kings presumed to follow Idaddu II on the throne, namely, Idaddu-napir ("Idaddu is god") and Idaddu-temti ("Idaddu is lord"). On this point, however, historical method demands a more critical attitude. On their very face these names are spurious, coined according to the widespread theory, prevalent even in Elam, that the ruler himself was a deity.[65] Further, as though to disprove the same Elamite scribes in their patriotic but distorted attempt to continue the dynasty, a tablet found at Susa bears the year formula of Gungunum's sixteenth year.[66] Obviously, no other explanation is possible than that Gungunum of Larsa defeated and killed Idaddu in battle and incorporated within his own growing empire the plain in which lay the city Susa. Thus quickly the Elamite kingdom collapsed, the Simash dynasty ceased, and foreign control over a part of Elam resulted.

(1927/28), 261–63; note also the cylinder seal dedicated to Anumutabil, *shakkanakku* of Der, by Bazizzu, his chief priest of Anu, in W. H. Ward, *Cylinders .... in the Library of J. Pierpont Morgan* (New York, 1909), No. 68; cf. Scheil in *RA*, XIII (1916), 134 f.

[65] Cf. C. W. McEwan, *The Oriental Origin of Hellenistic Kingship* (*SAOC*, No. 13).

[66] Scheil, *Mém.*, Vol. X, No. 124; this fact appears to have been hitherto unrecognized.

CHAPTER IV

DIVINE MESSENGERS OF ELAM, SIMASH, AND SUSA

IN OUR attempt to reconstruct the historical data concerning early Iran and Elam we were introduced to the land by an event told about a remote king of a Babylonian city, and we have seen that in these early times a power mightier than any in Sumer seems to have ruled the Elamite highlands. We have followed the rise of a dynasty of Awan contemporary with the kings of Agade and have traced the collapse of both before the invading hordes of Gutium. We have observed that a dynasty at Ur in Babylonia, rising after the bleak years of Guti rule, was paralleled by a dynasty in Elamite Simash, by which it was eventually overthrown. Finally, we have discovered that the last ruler of Simash was himself the captive of a Babylonian sovereign and that Elam once more bowed to a warring invader. We are now to see a proud Elamite in possession of Babylonian territory, even while his own Elam was saturated through and through with Babylonian culture.

A mighty struggle began in Babylonia about the middle of the twenty-first millennium. New peoples, filtering in from Syrian Amurru, had already brought a disposition to quarrel with any and all comers; and when three new monarchs in one year rose to power, each determined to rule supreme, trouble might well be anticipated. In 2050 B.C. Gungunum's successor gave place to Sumu-ilum in Larsa, Bur-Sin II came to the throne in Isin, and the First Dynasty of Babylon began under Sumu-abum. Early in his fourth year Sumu-ilum combated the Amorite tribes settled in Akuz and Kazallu; in his eighth he attempted to subjugate Ka-ida, the "Mouth of the Rivers." Success was apparently denied him, or at least he failed to retain his conquests, for Sumu-abum was compelled to attack Kazallu only five years later.[1] From events such as these we may safely conclude that the land was in turmoil and confusion.

The exploits of one individual form a brief interlude in these years, for Ilu-shuma of Ashur may have invaded Babylonia in the time of Sumu-abum. His own inscription claims that he brought freedom to Ur and Nippur, which were nominally at least under the control of Larsa; if the granting of freedom be taken to mean freedom from taxes, the inscription must be understood definitely to imply invasion. He entered the lands east of the Tigris also, for he asserts that he freed Awal, Kismar, and Der of the god Sataran; the

---

[1] Date formulas of the First Dynasty of Babylon, in M. Schorr, *Urkunden des altbabylonischen Zivil- und Prozessrechts* ("Vorderasiatische Bibliothek," Vol. V), pp. 582–609. See also *Reallexikon der Assyriologie*, II, 164 ff.

warrior must almost have reached Elamite territory.[2] Nevertheless, the claim of this ruler stands as an isolated statement; there are no other historical data to deny or to confirm it. Whatever may have been Ilu-shuma's achievement, it had no enduring result.

The history of Babylonia during the next few years is marked by the attempts of two rulers to combat, regain, or control Kazallu east of the Tigris where Amorites had entered. Sumu-ilum of Larsa smote the district in his twenty-second year (2028 B.C.). A decade later the Babylonian Sumu-la-ilum began an eight-year contest with the Amorite Iahzer-ili, whom he drove from the city. We may suspect that the fugitive did not remain away permanently, for two years later the walls of Kazallu had to be destroyed, and Iahzer-ili was not declared officially dead until five years after this date.

Such disturbances within Babylonia once more gave complete freedom to Elam. There a new dynasty came into power, a dynasty which lasted as long as the far-famed First Dynasty of Babylon and which was almost equally important.

The first king of this line, Ebarti (*ca.* 2020–2001), is given no genealogy in the lists of Shilhak-Inshushinak. That he was not in a position of great importance before his accession is suggested by a seal of his

[2] Cf. Ebeling, Meissner, and Weidner, *Die Inschriften der altassyrischen Könige* (Leipzig, 1926), pp. 6–9; on the dating cf. King, *Chronicles Concerning Early Babylonian Kings*, II, 14.

servant Gimil-Bau which marks him as a private individual; then a seal of the servant of his son Kuktanra designates him as king,[3] and his full title, "King of Anzan and Susa,"[4] appears. He seems to be mentioned in a Babylonian omen text,[5] and the reason is not far to seek: he was the father of Shilhaha,[6] better known as Shimti-Shilhak, who is widely heralded as the father of Kudur-Mabuk.[7]

The exploits of Shilhaha (*ca.* 2000–1986), or rather of Shimti-Shilhak, are unknown to us, although they must have been noteworthy. Generation after generation traced back to him its ancestry, and his building activities on the temples of Nannar and Inshushinak in Susa were long remembered.[8] He it was who made the suzerain of greater Elam the lordly superior of the petty kings in local districts. Henceforth the highest title in the land—and Shilhaha himself received it

[3] Scheil in *RA*, XXII (1925), 158–60, taken in part from Documents 4, 7, and 40 of *Mém.*, Vol. X.

[4] From the Addahushu inscription; cf. Scheil, "Inscription d'Adda-Bakšu," *RA*, XXVI (1929), 1–7. Ebarti also built at the Inshushinak temple in Susa according to bricks of Shilhak-Inshushinak; cf. *Mém.*, III, 55 (No. 34) and 59 (No. 44; cf. *Mém.*, V, 91).

[5] Cf. Weidner in *MAOG*, IV (1928/29), 239 n.

[6] So according to the lists.

[7] Shimti-Shilhak would be the Babylonian pronunciation of the Elamite name Temti-Shilhak; the *t* is reproduced by *š* as it was in the name Hishep-ratep, which the Old Akkadian (Sargonid) scribes rendered by Hiship-rashir. That Shimti is also the Kassite *shimdi* (equated with *nadânu*, "to give") is improbable, for *temti* (*tepti*) means "lord."

[8] Nannar inscription of Addahushu, above, n. 4; Shilhak-Inshushinak bricks, *Mém.*, III, 53 (No. 32).

—was *sukkalmah*, "exalted messenger." Since this title was of more importance than "king," it must refer to the ruler's relationship to the gods, and we might therefore translate it by "divine messenger" or even "angel"! Shilhaha also instituted the use of another title, *adda*, "father"; doubtless this refers to the sovereign's relationship to his subjects. Its use has puzzled many a historian of Babylonia through its adoption by Shilhaha's own son, Kudur-Mabuk. A third title, "king," would have marked a man as mighty in Babylonia; this signified little in Elam, where Shilhaha was only incidentally "King of Anzan and Susa."[9]

Along with the additional epithets *adda* and "king" hereafter employed by the supreme ruler, the latter might equally treasure the titles "*sukkal* of Elam and Simash" and "*sukkal* of Susa," for he himself had once held these offices. As such they were, however, strictly subordinate to the title *sukkalmah*, as the word *sukkal*, "minister," "plenipotentiary," shows; and, since Susa was an Akkadianized city, its *sukkal* was the least important of the realm. Nevertheless, even he might expect greater power, for Shilhaha restored the step-by-step policy of throne succession already noted in earlier periods. Upon the death of the *sukkalmah* it appears that the *sukkal* of Elam and Simash himself became *sukkalmah*; the *sukkal* of Susa, who was often locally known as the king of Susa,

[9] The full titulary is given in the Addahushu inscription, on which see the preceding note.

advanced to the office of *sukkal* of Elam and Simash. A new *sukkal* of Susa was thereupon chosen, probably by the *sukkalmah*, for it would seem that the new subordinate was almost invariably a member of the supreme ruler's own family. At any rate, the fortunate individual may often have been a minor, for by such a choice the *sukkalmah* would retain the imperial power with less risk to his own life.

Our information about the period is secured largely from business documents of Susa. A few other texts, written perhaps during the early reigns, have been found in a place known today as Malamir, a hundred miles to the southeast.[9a] These, though important from the economic standpoint, add little to our knowledge of the political situation throughout the ensuing centuries. The tablets from both sites are written in dialectic Akkadian strongly impregnated with Elamite elements. During the early part of the period the personal names are for the most part Elamite. As time passes, the names tend more and more to become purely Akkadian, although the names of the months and titles of professions often remain in the native tongue.

Some of the Susian texts from the first part of the period are temple documents,[10] receipts for sheep and

[9a] The Malamir texts, first published in *Mém.*, IV, 169 ff., are re-translated in *Mém.*, Vol. XXII.

[10] *Mém.*, X, 14–80, Nos. 1–120 and 122 f. Personal names indicate that many of these documents are contemporary with Ebarti, the first ruler of the dynasty. Note the year formulas in Nos. 69, 75, and 98.

oxen destined for the palace of the *sukkal* and for sacrifices to the deities. The latter contributions usually go to Inshushinak or to Inanna, the lady of the acropolis, to whom sacrifices were sometimes offered in the palace of the *sukkal*. Other recipients of such gifts are Shimut, Nahhunte, Nergal, Enki or Ea, and Nin-egal, the lady of the palace. Place names in these documents include Zabzalu, better known as Zabshalu, from which a messenger came to Susa, and Simash, Ashgupe, Gurumutak, Lahrin (perhaps the later Lahiru), Zaban, and Dur Shulgi.

The majority of the later texts are simple memoranda of rents and mortgages, sales and exchanges, wills and documents of administration, and adoption records.[11] They are not unlike those of the same period which have been discovered in Babylonia; nevertheless, the language, as has already been remarked, is greatly influenced by the Elamite currently spoken, and some features show customs at variance with those practiced in the lowlands.[12]

More important from the standpoint of international and local history are the data these texts furnish us for a study of the chronology of the period. In Elam, as in all other ancient lands, the curse was an effective weapon. No less powerful was the invoca-

---

[11] *Mém.*, Vols. XXII–XXIV, Nos. 1–395, some of which were first published in *Mém.*, Vol. XVIII.

[12] Cf. E. Cuq, "Les actes juridiques susiens," *RA*, XXVIII (1931), 47–71, and "Le droit élamite," *RA*, XXIX (1932), 149–82.

tion of a mighty deity; and, since the ruler was the god's representative upon earth, the practice of swearing to the truth of a statement by the name of the local chief or the supreme sovereign was in high favor. Consequently the gods Inshushinak and Ishmekarab were often called upon by the contracting parties at Susa; at Malamir the goddess Shalla, the Hurrian Shala, alone or with her suzerain, Inshushinak, was frequently invoked. Fortunately for the historian, in place of the deity the name of a more earthly ruler is sometimes mentioned; thus in the Susian texts the *sukkal* of the city is often named, together with one of his more potent overlords, the *sukkal* of Elam and Simash or the *sukkalmah*. This type of invocation in the documents has shed so much light on the internal political situation of Elam throughout this period that the lists of the land's rulers compiled by Elam's own Shilhak-Inshushinak can often be proved inadequate and in one or two instances can actually be corrected.

Thus today we may discover a fact which was apparently unknown to the twelfth-century antiquarian, namely, that at the time Shilhaha or Shimti-Shilhak was the *sukkalmah* of Elam his subordinates were Shirukduh as the *sukkal* of Elam and Simash and Shimut-wartash as the *sukkal* of Susa.[13] The lists tell

---

[13] Cf. the table on p. 229. The seal of Documents 242 and 325 (*Mém.*, Vol. XXIII) apparently names the first four *sukkalmah*'s: Shilhaha, Shirukduh, Siwepalarhuppak, and Kuduzulush. *Mém.*, Vol. XXIV, No.

us that the former was a "descendant" of Shilhaha; we would expect as much, for Shilhaha seems to have revived this scheme of succession and would naturally place a relative upon the minor throne. Shimut-wartash, though ruler of Susa, left his own inscription on the island Liyan, where he dedicated to the goddess Kiririsha a votive cylinder.[14]

In Babylonia it was not Shilhaha but his son Kudur-Mabuk who became famous. This Elamite, entering the lowlands about 1995 B.C., made himself at home in Emutbal, the district around Larsa, and threatened the independence of this sovereign city. His own inscription actually proclaimed him the "father" of Emutbal. This was a title borrowed from Elam; it was of more honor than "king," yet of less prestige than *sukkalmah*. As we have seen, it had been employed by his own father, Shilhaha, but as used by the son it designated his subservience to the supreme ruler of all Elam, the *sukkalmah*.

Sin-iqisham was just beginning his reign at Larsa and could ill afford such a challenge to his power. He began the offensive the following year by an attack on Ka-ida and Nazarum.[15] In retaliation Kudur-Mabuk

---

346, however, shows Shirukduh supreme over Shimut-wartash (*sukkal* of Elam and Simash) and over Siwepalarhuppak (*sukkal* of Susa). Nos. 87, 221 f., and 246 invoke the name of Shimut-wartash alone, probably as *sukkal* of Susa.

[14] M. Pézard, *Mém.*, XV, 91 f.

[15] Gadd and Legrain, *Royal Inscriptions*, No. 266.

sought alliance with Isin, where Zambia came to the throne in Sin-iqisham's fifth year. In that year the latter claimed the defeat of Elam and Zambia;[16] we may doubt the veracity of the claimant, for before the year was out he was supplanted by Silli-Adad, and the new king at his accession appears humble indeed. He calls himself the nourisher of Nippur, the *ishakku* of Ur, Larsa, Lagash, and Kutalla;[17] but these are scarcely royal epithets, and it is quite possible that Silli-Adad was vassal to the Elamite. When he dared call himself "king" in the date formulas, he was at once deposed and Warad-Sin, Kudur-Mabuk's own son, was placed on the throne (1989 B.C.).

For a few years the son was nominal ruler, and the date formulas are in his name; the father was, however, in actual control. The second year is dated by an invasion of Kazallu and its neighboring district Mutiabal.[18] Zabum of Babylon reports a conquest of Kazallu in the same year. This is significant, for it may mean that Zabum was allied with the Elamite to meet a common danger, or that he was actually a vassal of the foreigner. The latter is probably the more accurate picture, for Kudur-Mabuk himself relates how he massacred the armies of Kazallu and Mutiabal in Larsa and Emutbal and how he guaranteed the existence of battle-scarred Kazallu, although

---

[16] *Ibid.*; also in Grice, *Records from Ur and Larsa* ("Yale Oriental Series," *Babylonian Texts*, Vol. V), p. 20.

[17] Gadd and Legrain, *op. cit.*, No. 121.   [18] *Ibid.*, No. 266.

he destroyed its walls.[19] Again in this inscription the Elamite declares himself the *adda* of his subjects; this time he is *adda* of Amurru, meaning doubtless the Amorite peoples whom he had just conquered in Kazallu and Mutiabal.

For five years of Warad-Sin's reign in Larsa the royal inscriptions are all from the hand of Kudur-Mabuk. Finally Warad-Sin is alone when he dedicates a sanctuary to Inanna of Hallab for his own life and for the life of his father.[20] Why Kudur-Mabuk should disappear so suddenly is a puzzle that needs unraveling. Possibly he was recalled to Elam by the death of his father, Shilhaha, although the automatic succession of Shirukduh to the office of *sukkalmah* and Shimut-wartash to the position of *sukkal* of Elam and Simash hardly required his presence. Perhaps he was needed in Elam to assist in the naming of the new *sukkal* of Susa, Siwepalarhuppak,[21] although the right to designate the Susa subordinate probably belonged solely to the new *sukkalmah*. At any rate, throughout the remainder of Warad-Sin's twelve-year reign in Larsa the son was left in full charge, and Kudur-Mabuk reappears only with the accession of his sec-

[19] Thureau-Dangin, "Une inscription de Kudur-Mabuk," *RA*, IX (1912), 121–24; cf. now Barton, *RISA*, pp. 324 f.

[20] *CT*, XXI, 31 f.; cf. *SAK*, pp. 214 ff.

[21] Shirukduh over Shimut-wartash and Siwepalarhuppak: *Mém.*, Vol. XXIV, No. 346; Shirukduh over Siwepalarhuppak: *Mém.*, Vol. XXII, Nos. 62 and 134 (=*Mém.*, Vol. XVIII, No. 201). The name of the new Susa official is probably to be divided thus: Siwe-palar-huppak.

ond son, Rim-Sin, in this city.[22] Again he is titled
adda of Emutbal; and he is even more closely associated with Rim-Sin than he had been with Warad-
Sin, for father and son now make joint dedications
for their own lives.[23] Then Kudur-Mabuk again disappears; and Rim-Sin, whose reign of sixty-one years
shows that he must have been a mere child at his accession, makes the dedications alone.

There is no information concerning the reign of
Shirukduh (*ca.* 1985–1966), although it would seem
that his subordinate ruler of Simash and Elam, Shimut-wartash, died in office and that Siwepalarhuppak
advanced to this position while Kuduzulush I became
the new *sukkal* of Susa. Then with the death of Shirukduh the accession appears to have moved forward
quite regularly; Siwepalarhuppak became *sukkalmah*
(*ca.* 1965–1946), with Kuduzulush as his *sukkal* of
Elam and Simash, and Kutir-Nahhunte[24] as the newly chosen *sukkal* of Susa.[25] The new *sukkalmah* him-

[22] The picture of the Babylonian situation here presented was made
possible only by the assistance of Professor Olmstead, who in an unpublished manuscript has examined the sources for the period and compared the date formulas with the relevant royal inscriptions. The number
of the Larsa date formulas has recently been increased by the publication
of text No. 266 in Gadd and Legrain, *Royal Inscriptions.*

[23] Lenormant, *Choix de textes cunéiformes,* No. 70; cf. *SAK,* pp. 218–21.

[24] Nahhunte is the proper spelling of this deity's name in the twelfth
century; for the sake of consistency, in this name as in others, minor
variations in spelling have been disregarded in this work.

[25] Siwepalarhuppak over Kuduzulush: *Mém.,* Vol. XXII, No. 63;
Vol. XXIII, No. 200; Vol. XXIV, No. 346, note; cf. also Vol. XXII, No.
64; Kuduzulush over Kutir-Nahhunte: *Mém.,* Vol. XXIII, No. 201.

self left no extant inscriptions, but centuries later he was named as the first of Susa's rulers to bring a certain precious wood to Ulpuhshi-igi-balap, where subsequent sovereigns could transport it to the capital;[26] and the scribes of Shilhak-Inshushinak knew that he had restored Inshushinak's temple on the acropolis.[27]

Meanwhile in Babylonia Elam's descendant Rim-Sin appeared to be making remarkable headway. In his fifteenth year he became embroiled with the peoples of Uruk, Isin, Babylon, Rapiqum, and Sutium and claims to have come out the victor. Fifteen years later (1947) his conquest of Isin was a genuine triumph, and he seemed to be well on the way to the control of the lowlands. He reckoned without Hammurabi, who came to Babylon's throne in that very year. This intrepid lawgiver began almost immediately a policy of expansion; he attacked Malgium in his fourth and tenth years, plundered Rim-Sin's recent conquest, Isin, in his seventh, and entered Emutbal or Larsa's own territory in his eighth. By 1918 Rim-Sin was hard-pressed; quite naturally he appealed to his ancestral Elam, where perhaps Kuduzulush I was now the *sukkalmah* (*ca.* 1945–1918). Most unwisely the Elamites answered the appeal. Using Marhashi or Barahshi as their base, they attacked Subartum, Gutium, Eshnunna, and Malgium.[28] Their

[26] Inscription of Shutruk-Nahhunte; see below, pp. 106 f.

[27] *Mém.*, III, 58, and V, 91 (No. 41).

[28] This formula, fragmentary in Poebel, *Babylonian Legal and Business Documents* (*BE*, Ser. A, Vol. VI, Part 2), p. 62, is now complete in Lang-

defeat by the army of Hammurabi meant not only Rim-Sin's loss of his kingdom in the following year, when the ruler of Babylon swept through Larsa; it meant not only Elam's loss of prestige in foreign countries; the attempted succor brought about the collapse of the empire in Elam and the overthrow of the régime. Although no foreigner invaded the land, the defeat in Babylonia was apparently so severe that Elam fell a prey to its own internal conflicts. At any rate, we know little of its history for almost seventy years.

One ruler only emerges with a certain degree of clarity. This is Addahushu, who declared himself a son of a sister of Shilhaha and whose reign, if reign it was, appears to have been recognized in Susa only. He was, in fact, denied an official title in most of his inscriptions, merely claiming to be the shepherd of the people of Susa or of Inshushinak. His deeds included the erection of a temple for the god Narute and a bridge for Inshushinak.[29] Further, a district

---

don, "Oxford Editions of Cuneiform Texts," II, 31; I owe the corrected reading of the formula to Professor Poebel.

In connection with the often assumed, but probably erroneous, identification of Hammurabi with Amraphel, it may here be stated that the name Chedorlaomer of Genesis, chapter 14, would obviously be Kudur-Lagamar in Elamite, but that no ruler named Kudur-Lagamar has yet come to light.

[29] Mém., VI, 26; IV, 10; cf. SAK, pp. 182 f. There is no way of evaluating the inscription of Tetep-mada, who also bore the curious title "shepherd of Susa, son of a sister of Shilhaha"; cf. Scheil, "Un prince susien nouveau," RA, XXIV (1927), 41.

was named for him, and a tablet with a seal impression of a servant of his points to the use of date formulas, for it bears the date "year of Shumu-abi."[30] He, too, finally attained the coveted position of *sukkal* of Susa, and in this office dedicated anew the temple of Nannar in commemoration of the first two rulers of the dynasty: Ebarti, the King of Anzan and Susa; and Shilhaha, the *sukkalmah*, the *adda*, the King of Anzan and Susa.[31]

We are ignorant of the events which permitted reorganization of a stable kingdom. Perhaps around 1850 the same Kutir-Nahhunte who as a mere child had been *sukkal* of Susa more than sixty years before revived the type of government which had been popular in the days of his fathers. As his subordinates he chose Tata, whose full name was Atta-merra-halki, to be *sukkal* of Elam and Simash, and Temti-agun to be *sukkal* of Susa.[32] The latter, calling himself a son of a sister of Shirukduh, wrote an inscription in Akkadian; that royal documents should be written in a foreign language shows how great had been the penetration of Semitic influences at Susa in the years im-

---

[30] Dimtu-Addahushu, *Mém.*, Vol. X, Nos. 72 and 75; date formula, *Mém.*, Vol. X, No. 2 (cf., however, No. 21).

[31] Scheil, "Inscription d'Adda-Bakšu," *RA*, XXVI (1929), 1–7. For Shilhak-Inshushinak bricks mentioning this ruler cf. *Mém.*, III, 55 (No. 35).

[32] Kutir-Nahhunte over Temti-agun: *Mém.*, Vol. XXII, Nos. 131 and 157; Vol. XXIII, Nos. 202 f.; Vol. XXIV, Nos. 347, 368, 374–78, 382 *bis*, and 392. Tata, *sukkal* over Temti-agun: *Mém.*, Vol. XXIV, No. 391; cf. also *Mém.*, Vol. XXIII, No. 321; Vol. XXIV, Nos. 379 and 383.

mediately preceding. The text dedicates a temple to Ishmekarab, the deity so frequently invoked in the business records, for the life of the *sukkalmah* Kutir-Nahhunte and for the lives of the members of his own family.[33] Also in Akkadian, and likewise for the life of Kutir-Nahhunte, Temti-agun dedicated a temple and several statues to Inshushinak by a text which has been fully preserved only in a copy made seven hundred years later by Shilhak-Inshushinak, who added in Elamite his own interpretation of its meaning.[34]

Temti-agun in time became *sukkal* of Elam and Simash, perhaps through the premature death of Tata, with Kutir-Shilhaha as the new appointee in Susa. Then Temti-agun became the supreme ruler (*ca.* 1840–1826), with Kutir-Shilhaha and Kuk-Nashur I in the lesser positions.[35] The latter was a son of a sister of Temti-agun, or so he claimed to be, when, as *sukkal* of Susa, he granted land to a favorite of his court.[36] When time raised Kutir-Shilhaha to the office

[33] Namely, Lila-ir-tash, Temti-hisha-hanesh, and Pilki, his *hashduk* mother; the phrase should perhaps be rendered "revered (or 'honored') mother." The inscription is published in *Mém.*, VI, 23; cf. *SAK*, pp. 184 f.; F. W. König in *Festschrift der Nationalbibliothek in Wien*, p. 542.

[34] *Mém.*, VI, 25; cf. Scheil in *RA*, XXIX (1932), 69–71. For a text of Shilhak-Inshushinak referring to Kutir-Nahhunte, Temti-agun, and Akkad see *ibid.*, pp. 71–75; Père Scheil's dating must be rejected.

[35] Temti-agun, *sukkalmah* over Kuk-Nashur: *Mém.*, Vol. XXIII, No. 167; cf. also Nos. 204 f. and 325. Kutir-Shilhaha over Kuk-Nashur: *Mém.*, Vol. XXIII, No. 210.

[36] *Mém.*, Vol. XXIII, No. 283.

of *sukkalmah* (*ca.* 1825–1811), Kuk-Nashur, himself
now *sukkal* of Elam and Simash, again conferred land
upon his favorite.[37] He was no longer under the necessity of honoring his dead relative, and in this document Kuk-Nashur traces his ancestry back beyond
Temti-agun and beyond Temti-agun's alleged "ancestor" Shirukduh to Shirukduh's "ancestor" Shilhaha or Shimti-Shilhak; thus he too became another
of the "sons of a sister of Shilhaha" so well known to
the compilers of later lists.

For a time the new *sukkal* of Susa under Kutir-
Shilhaha appears to have been Shirtuh.[38] He claimed
to have been a son of a sister of Kuk-Nashur, his immediate superior, when, like his alleged relative, he
granted land to one of his own courtiers.[39] Perhaps
he presumed too much upon his masters, for he soon
disappeared and Temti-raptash became the *sukkal* or
king of Susa.[40]

Finally Kuk-Nashur became *sukkalmah* (1810–
1800). Although Temti-raptash and a second Kuduzulush were his nominal underlings,[41] he himself

[37] *Mém.*, Vol. XXIII, No. 282.

[38] Kutir-Shilhaha over Shirtuh, king of Susa: *Mém.*, Vol. XXII,
No. 18; cf. also Vol. XXIII, No. 211. Kuk-Nashur over Shirtuh: *Mém.*,
Vol. XXII, No. 137.

[39] *Mém.*, Vol. XXIII, No. 284.

[40] Kutir-Shilhaha, *sukkalmah* over Temti-raptash, king of Susa:
Mém., Vol. XXII, Nos. 10 and 133; Vol. XXIII, No. 169; cf. also Vol.
XXII, No. 117, and Vol. XXIII, Nos. 212–14.

[41] Temti-raptash over Kuduzulush: *Mém.*, Vol. XXII, Nos. 8 and 116;
Vol. XXIII, No. 183; Vol. XXIV, Nos. 341, 345, and 393. Kuk-Nashur

proudly enumerated all the titles he had won in the course of his career. As the *sukkalmah*, *sukkal* of Elam, Simash, and Susa, he continued to bestow crown lands upon his favorites; to Shukshu and Mahisi of the city Humman he granted land extending from Hutekuk to Huteshekin,[42] from Asirsir to Hitpuli,[43] and from Manhashhur to Shumahani. This document is important not only for its text and accompanying map; perhaps because the land given was situated near Babylonia, the charter received the current Babylonian year date, the first year of Ammizaduga, which shows that the document was composed in 1801 b.c.[44] To the god of Susa Kuk-Nashur was no less kind. One inscription reports the dedication of his sanctuary;[45] another, which describes the erection of a temple inclosure, like the text of Temtiagun was recopied by scribes of the twelfth century and so was preserved for posterity.[46] Kuk-Nashur

---

over Kuduzulush: *Mém.*, Vol. XXII, Nos. 32, 36 f., 67, and 86; Vol. XXIII, Nos. 195 and 215; Vol. XXIV, No. 340. In Vol. XXII, No. 160, Kuk-Nashur is called *sukkal* of Elam when Kuduzulush is king of Susa; this is not in accord with the scheme as here presented, although I can see no better solution to the difficulty.

[42] In Elamite *hute* means merely "site," "place."

[43] "The river Puli."

[44] Text copied by Ungnad in "Vorderasiatische Schriftdenkmäler," Vol. VII, No. 67; cf. Ungnad in *BA*, VI, Heft 5 (1909), 1–5, and restore with the help of *Mém.*, Vol. XXIII, No. 282.

[45] Scheil, *Mém.*, V, xii, republished in *Mém.*, VI, 28; cf. *SAK*, pp. 184 f.

[46] Scheil in *RA*, XXIX (1932), 68.

was evidently a powerful monarch; it was the irony of
fate that the same scribes who so faithfully copied his
text after many centuries confused him with a second
Kuk-Nashur, a "descendant" of Tan-Uli.

The succeeding reign of Temti-raptash (*ca.* 1799–
1791), who may have controlled Kuduzulush II and
Tan-Uli[47] as subordinates, would seem to have been
uneventful, although the large number of economic
documents which belong to his time may indicate an
increased amount of business activity in Susa.[48] Likewise there is no additional information concerning the
years of Kuduzulush II (*ca.* 1790–1781), although it
is certain that he too became *sukkalmah*.[49] His subordinates would seem to have been Tan-Uli and Temti-halki.[50] As *sukkal* of Susa the latter individual, by

[47] Although Père Scheil has published a seal of Puzur-Mazat, son of
Tan-Uli, in *RA*, XXII (1925), 149 f., this individual need not be a son of
the king, for the name Tan-Uli is borne by private individuals in the business documents; see the indexes of *Mém.*, Vols. XXII–XXIV.

[48] In addition to those cited above, *Mém.*, Vol. XXII, No. 101, and
Vol. XXIII, Nos. 218–20 and 240, invoke the name of Temti-raptash
alone; Vol. XXIII, No. 315, connects Temti-raptash with a *shakkanakku*, but this does not indicate the ruler's relationship to a Babylonian
king.

[49] *Mém.*, Vol. XXIII, No. 179. The scribe of this document also
wrote Nos. 216 and 219 f., dated to Temti-raptash, and No. 222, dated to
Shimut-wartash. Unless the latter is the second of the name, mention of
him at this time is at present an unexplainable fact.

[50] Tan-Uli, *sukkal* over Temti-halki: *Mém.*, Vol. XXIII, No. 177
(and, doubtfully, No. 186). Tan-Uli over Temti-halki: *Mém.*, Vol.
XXII, Nos. 20 and 113; Vol. XXIII, Nos. 171 and 247; Vol. XXIV,
Nos. 335–37, 339, and 369; cf. also Vol. XXII, No. 11; Vol. XXIII,
Nos. 188 and 196; Vol. XXIV, No. 370.

an Akkadian inscription in which he employs merely the title "king," dedicated a temple to "Inshushinak, the king of the gods," an epithet wrongly interpreted in our own day to obtain the name of a sovereign, "Inshushinak-shar-ilani."[51] When Tan-Uli became *sukkalmah* (*ca.* 1780–1771), Temti-halki was elevated to the office of *sukkal* of Elam and Simash according to the usual scheme, and Kuk-Nashur II became the new ruler in Susa.[52] Owing to an error of the Elamite antiquarians, this Kuk-Nashur was confused with the first of the name, and in memory of his supposed deeds several bricks were inscribed in the twelfth century B.C. Today we may correct the mistake and distinguish the individuals without too great condemnation of the later scribes.

Unfortunately, we have no data on Tan-Uli; but when Temti-halki in turn became *sukkalmah*, he, like others before him, rejoiced in the full titulary when he dedicated a temple to the chief deity of Susa. Again writing in Akkadian, he tells us that, like Kuk-Nashur I, he was a "son of a sister of Shilhaha."[53] Though eventually his titulary was forgotten, his

[51] Scheil, *Mém.*, II, 120.

[52] Tan-Uli, *sukkalmah* over Temti-halki: *Mém.*, Vol. XXII, Nos. 7 and 9; Vol. XXIII, No. 173; Vol. XXIV, Nos. 338 and 353. Tan-Uli over Kuk-Nashur: *Mém.*, Vol. XXII, No. 102; Vol. XXIII, No. 178. In Vol. XXIII, No. 206, Tan-Uli is called the *sukkal* over Kuk-Nashur; this too is not explainable at present. Temti-halki, *sukkal* over Kuk-Nashur: *Mém.*, Vol. XXIII, Nos. 208 f.; cf. also Vol. XXII, No. 85.

[53] *Mém.*, II, 77 f.; cf. *SAK*, pp. 184 f. Temti-halki bears the curious title "*sukkalmah* of Elam and Simash" in the text of *Mém.*, VI, 27; cf. *SAK*, *loc. cit.* Doubtless this is an oversight of the scribe.

deed was commemorated six hundred years later by Shilhak-Inshushinak.[54]

Incomplete and confused sources deprive us of the names of Temti-halki's successors. Were our materials complete, we might still find many gaps, for Elam's involved scheme of succession surely invited assassination. One other "son of a sister of Shilhaha" came into prominence, possibly before, but more probably after, Temti-halki. This was Kuk-Kirwash. We first meet him as a minor official, perhaps *sukkal* of Susa, under Bala-ishshan,[55] of whom it was later said that he, like Siwepalarhuppak, brought precious woods to the Susa temple.[56] Kuk-Kirwash in turn, probably as *sukkal* of Elam and Simash, had as his subordinate Tem-Sanit, whose early death seems to have brought Kuk-Nahhunte to the Susian office.[57] Finally he reached the summit of his political ambitions and became *sukkalmah*, having Kuk-Nahhunte and a third Kuk-Nashur as subordinates.[58] In the now antiquated Sumerian he tells how he restored a temple in Susa and surrounded it with a new wall.[59]

[54] Scheil, *Mém.*, III, 57 (No. 38).

[55] Bala-ishshan over Kuk-Kirwash: *Mém.*, Vol. XXIV, Nos. 348 f.; cf. Scheil in *RA*, XXIX (1932), 76.

[56] Shutruk-Nahhunte inscription; see below, pp. 106 f. For the seal of a scribal servant of Bala-ishshan cf. Scheil, "Cylindre Pala iššan," *RA*, XXIII (1926), 36.

[57] Kuk-Kirwash over Tem-Sanit: *Mém.*, Vol. XXIV, No. 351; over Kuk-Nahhunte: *Mém.*, Vol. XXIV, No. 352.

[58] Kuk-Nahhunte over Kuk-Nashur (written "Nashir"): *Mém.*, Vol. XXIV, Nos. 329 f.

[59] Scheil, *Mém.*, II, 74–76; cf. *SAK*, pp. 182 f.

Had we other original texts of this "descendant" of Shilhaha, perhaps we could discover his correct ancestry; unfortunately, the twelfth-century scribes who copied his record and added their own Elamite comments[60] knew him only as a son of Lankuku, a name otherwise unfamiliar; hence his exact position in the line of succession remains doubtful.

History often shows that the rulers and peoples of a weakening kingdom make every effort to recapture the glorious days of the past. Deliberate archaization is one of the methods used in attempting to restore that past; perhaps, therefore, we may see both weakness and archaization in the numerous claims to descent from the great Shilhaha. At any rate, about 1750 B.C. Elam fades almost entirely from our view. Inasmuch as Babylonia about this time falls under the shadow of the Kassites, we must turn to these and to Babylonia's history for light. There we shall try to discover whether Elam's fate is not reflected in the catastrophe which befell its neighbor on the west, the Land of the Two Rivers.

[60] Scheil, *Mém.*, V, 56 f. (No. 78). Other bricks of Shilhak-Inshushinak mentioning this ruler: *Mém.*, III, 58, and V, 90 (No. 40).

In the spring of 1932 the writer was permitted to examine an unpublished manuscript of Professor Poebel, "Zur Geschichte Elams zur Zeit der Dynastien von Isin, Larsa und Babylon," which had been completed several years earlier, but in which the threefold division of power in Elam, somewhat as described in this chapter, was proposed. Inasmuch as the writer had already at that time reached the conclusion that some such scheme was necessary to bring order out of chaos, he is glad to have been anticipated by so great an authority, and consequently places all the more faith in the accuracy of the picture as here presented.

CHAPTER V

THE KASSITE INTERLUDE

IT HAS been rightly stated that few conquerors left so great an impress of their power upon Babylonian peoples as did the Kassites, though we know little of their earlier history.[1] Fortunately, some idea of their linguistic connections may be gained from a list of Kassite words compiled by Babylonian scribes, who gave also their corresponding Akkadian translations.[2] Most of the preserved words, as well as the majority of the personal names,[3] demonstrate that the common people among the Kassites spoke a Caucasian language which was perhaps a near neighbor of Elamite.[4] Another list, which turns the names of Kassite rulers into Akkadian, adds further light on the question of their deities em-

[1] A. T. Olmstead, "Kashshites, Assyrians, and the Balance of Power," *AJSL*, XXXVI (1919/20), 120.

[2] Friedrich Delitzsch, *Die Sprache der Kossäer* (Leipzig, 1884), pp. 25 f.; T. G. Pinches, "The Language of the Kassites," *JRAS*, 1917, pp. 102–5.

[3] A. T. Clay, *Personal Names from Cuneiform Inscriptions of the Cassite Period* ("Yale Oriental Series," Vol. I). Many Kassite names occur in the Nuzi documents now awaiting publication.

[4] The studies of Georg Hüsing on this subject, though of doubtful value, are often stimulating; cf. *Memnon*, IV (1910), 22–30; *OLZ*, 1917, cols. 106–9, 178–81, and 205–9; *OLZ*, 1918, cols. 43–48 and 264–72.

bodied in the names.[5] The fact that more than one
deity has been identified with a given Babylonian god
points to the syncretism of several groups of gods before the invaders entered Babylonia. We are, however, able to discern that some of the Kassite gods are
of Caucasian type. Such are Shipak, equated with
Marduk; Sah, identified with Shamash; Hudha,[6]
likened to Adad; and Harbe, corresponding to Enlil.[7]
Others of their gods are of uncertain origin. Among
these are Kashshu, their eponymous deity, who
doubtless took his name from their land and may also
be Caucasian; Kamulla or Ea; Dur and Shugab,
equated with Nergal; Shuqamuna, likened to Nergal
and Nusku; Hala or Gula; Shumalia or Shibarru, "the
Lady of the Bright Mountains, who dwells on the
summits"; Mirizir or Beltu; and Gidar or Ninurta.

We may detect among the invaders another element also. The horse was a divine symbol to the Kassites; and their constant use of this animal, which became common in Babylonia only after their entry,
connects the intruders with the Indo-European
hordes who were at this time attacking the whole
northern boundary of the Fertile Crescent, namely,
the Hittites, the rulers of Mitanni, and perhaps an

[5] H. W. Rawlinson, *Cuneiform Inscriptions of Western Asia*, Vol. V,
Pl. 44, i and iv.

[6] Possibly to be read Hulahha.

[7] Cf. the Elamite deity Hurbi in col. i, l. 15, of the Naram-Sin treaty
text cited above, p. 35.

element among the Hyksos. This connection is further substantiated by the names of other Kassite deities. Shuriash, equated with the sun-god Shamash, is indubitably the Hindu Surya[8] and the Greek Helios. Maruttash, likened to Ninurta, has been identified with the Indian Marut. Buriash, another storm-god like Adad, appears to be identical with the Greek Boreas.

All these factors show that the Kassites were a conglomerate people, and we live too long after them to disentangle completely the various elements of their composition. Nevertheless, it seems clear that an Indo-European, and so ultimately Nordic, ruling caste had once lived among them and dominated a group of alien and largely Caucasian peoples. Normally, such conquerors force their language upon the subject peoples, but we have one example of the reverse in Mitanni, and the same situation may have developed among the peoples who came into history as the Kassites; their Nordic aristocracy may in time have forgotten its own language save as it was preserved in a few proper names. The native races had their revenge.

Like their ancestry, the site of the Kassites' homeland is doubtful. Later remnants would indicate that they descended upon Babylonia from the central Zagros, north of Elam. The great-grandson of their

[8] Cf. the occurrences of the element Surya (generally written Shuwar) in the Amarna letters: J. A. Knudtzon, *Die El-Amarna-Tafeln* ("Vorder asiatische Bibliothek," Vol. II), Part 2, p. 1568.

third king[9] claimed suzerainty over the Guti and over Padan and Alman, which should be the Holwan region. Shalmaneser III of Assyria, almost a thousand years after their entry, found in Namri, a territory of the Lullubi, a ruler Ianzu, whose name is merely the Kassite word for "king."[10] In the hill country to the east and northeast of Babylonia the name of the Kassites lingered on into classical times among the Kissean and Kossean tribes.[11] However, it is necessary to point out that this evidence is largely negative, for there was a land Kashshen to the north of Elam already in the twenty-fourth century B.C., at a time when it is highly improbable that the true Kassites had yet arrived.[12] This implies that they took their name from a country long before occupied, and one which may have retained its original designation long after new and newer peoples became assimilated. Perhaps it witnessed the amalgamation of the various elements—Indo-European, Caucasian, and other—which composed the historical Kassites; perhaps that syncretism had already taken place in another and more distant land.

Too often we speak of invasion and attack, or the rapid entrance or intrusion of newcomers into a land already populated. This seldom happens. New peo-

[9] Agum-kakrime; see reference to his inscription below, p. 94.

[10] Cf. Delitzsch, *op. cit.*, pp. 29–38, and see below, p. 143.

[11] See the excellent article by Weissbach on the "Kossaioi" in Pauly-Wissowa, *Real-Encyclopädie.*

[12] See the Puzur-Inshushinak inscription above, p. 37.

ples do appear on the horizon, and these may make one attempt, however feeble, to descend *en masse* into a coveted land. If repulsed, they begin a policy of peaceful penetration, during which they are gradually assimilated into the old stock, though losing little of their virility. Step by step their members advance in power, until they themselves, once despised and feared, are in control and rule the land.

Thus occurred the "conquest" of the Kassites in Babylonia. As early as 1896 B.C. Samsu-iluna of Babylon repelled a wholesale invasion of the lowlands by their hungry hordes. Thereafter for almost one hundred and fifty years they appear in the Babylonian business documents as harvesters, laborers, and hostlers.[13] The intervening steps in their rise to full power are lost, but we must assume that their advance was gradual and constant. With minds untutored save in borrowed ways, they finally reached the pinnacle of power, and Babylonia fell under the sway of the Kassite dynasty in 1749 B.C.

The first of their kings[14] was Gandash (1749–1734), who ruled sixteen years and in a half-literate inscription called himself "king of the Four World-Regions, king of Sumer and Akkad, king of Babylon."[15] Ob-

[13] Cf. A. Ungnad, "Die Kassiten," *Beiträge zur Assyriologie*, VI, Heft 5 (1909), 21–26.

[14] See Weidner, "Die grosse Königsliste aus Assur," *AOF*, III (1926), 66–77.

[15] T. G. Pinches in *Babylonian and Oriental Record*, I (1886/87), 54 and 78; for other references cf. Olmstead in *AJSL*, XXXVI (1919/20), 120.

viously, he was attempting to declare himself the legitimate successor of the dynasty which had just ceased. The twenty-two-year reigns of his immediate successors, a son Agum and Kashtiliash I, who may not have been descended from Agum, point to a stable kingdom and to undisturbed power, although the almost total cessation of business documents indicates commercial inactivity and possibly stagnation. Ushshi, son of Kashtiliash, ruled eight years; then came Abirattash and his son Tazzigurumash. A surprising fact is related of a monarch contemporary with the last rulers. This sovereign, Gulkishar of the independent Sealands territory (1684–1630), gave land on the bank of the Tigris in the region of Der to one of his subjects.[16] If Der northeast of Babylonia proper was in his control, the Kassites may at this time have been cut off from the route to their last homeland in the mountains.

Harba-Shipak and Tiptakzi followed Tazzigurumash, whose line was restored with the accession of a son, Agum-kakrime. He it was who proclaimed himself king of Padan and Alman, king of Gutium, in addition to the more regular titles king of Kashshu, king of Akkad, and king of the broad land of Babylon.[17] This may indicate that he felt obligated to pro-

[16] Enlil-nadin-apli's *kudurru*, published by H. V. Hilprecht, *Old Babylonian Inscriptions* (*BE*, Ser. A, Vol. I), No. 83; cf. P. Jensen in *ZA*, VIII (1893), 220–24.

[17] Rawlinson, *op. cit.*, Vol. II, Pl. 38, No. 2; Vol. V, Pl. 33; cf. Jensen in *KB*, III, Heft 1, 134 ff.; for other references see Olmstead, *op. cit.*, p. 121, n. 6.

tect his ancestral home in the mountains as well as the newly occupied regions in the plains.

Agum-kakrime was followed by Burna-Buriash, and he by an unknown and then by Kashtiliash II (1530–1512). The latter gradually closed in on the Sealands; and his brother marched against Ea-gamil, the last king of the Sealands, who took refuge in Elam.[18] Then the brother himself, Ulam-Buriash, came to the Kassite throne, and with his accession (1511) the dynasty seems to have become thoroughly acclimated to its new home in Babylonia. The subsequent so-called "Amarna" period does not here interest us.

Inscriptions of the Kassite rulers so far mentioned, though nowhere numerous, are totally lacking at Susa, and the excavators at that site appear to have run into a barren stratum for the period. Kassite occupation of Elam contemporaneous with Kassite sovereignty of Babylonia thus seems out of the question. On the other hand, it is certain that the Elamite dynasty founded by Ebarti and Shilhaha disappeared shortly after the First Dynasty of Babylon faded from the scene. In the case of Elam, the land may have become the prey of peoples who were themselves originally fleeing from the Kassite hordes. At any rate, for the obscurity which covers both Babylonia and Elam at this time the Kassites should doubtless be held strictly responsible.

[18] Cf. L. W. King, *Chronicles Concerning Early Babylonian Kings*, II, 22–24.

CHAPTER VI

KINGS OF ANZAN AND SUSA

WITH startling suddenness we emerge from the obscurity which covers Iran and Elam for four hundred years after the advent of the Kassites in Babylonia. A highly entertaining tale in a later chronicle relates that Hurpatila, king of Elam, besought the Kassite Kurigalzu III (1344–1320 B.C.) to give battle with him at Dur Shulgi, a fortress founded east of the Sealands by the great king of the Third Ur Dynasty.[1] The outcome of the battle, said the Elamite, should decide the fortunes of Elam. The forces engaged, Hurpatila was abandoned by his soldiers, and Elam became a portion of the empire of Kurigalzu.[2]

Although this particular chronicle is very untrust-

[1] Cf. the Dur Shulgi in Susa documents above, p. 73.

[2] Chronicle P, iii 10 ff., first published in translation by Pinches in *Records of the Past*, new ser., V (1891), 106 ff. Text: Winckler, *Altorientalische Forschungen*, I (Leipzig, 1893–97), 297 ff. Transliteration only: Delitzsch in *Abhandlungen der K. Sächsischen Gesellschaft der Wissenschaften*, phil.-hist. Klasse, XXV, No. 1 (1906), 43 ff.

The name Hurpatila is generally assumed to be Kassite; cf. G. Hüsing, *Quellen*, p. 19. Note, however, the name of the Elamite god Hurbi in the Naram-Sin treaty cited above, as well as such names as *Hurbi*-shenni and Tehip-*tilla* in Nuzi texts; cf. E. Chiera, *Joint Expedition with the Iraq Museum at Nuzi* (American Schools of Oriental Research, "Publications of the Baghdad School," *Texts*), Vol. II, No. 212:30, and No. 213:3.

worthy, the story is not wholly fiction. Hurpatila, it
now appears, was the legitimate ruler of Babylon,
where he ruled at least four years.[3] Driven out by
the Assyrians, he may well have taken refuge in Elam,
there to continue the battle with the Assyrian nominee, Kurigalzu. It is certain, however, that his cause
was utterly lost; in Susa Kurigalzu dedicated an agate
scaraboid to the god Sataran and a scepter head to
Enlil;[4] on the acropolis he left his own statuette with
an inscription recording the defeat of Susa and Elam
and the devastation of Marhashi.[5] An agate tablet
which had once been presented to Inanna in Susa for
the life of Shulgi of Ur the Kassite brought back to
Nippur, where he dedicated it anew to Enlil and on
it recounted once more his conquest of Susa in Elam.[6]

Almost immediately the attention of the Kassites
was diverted from Elam and centered on the regions
northeast of Babylonia whence came the supply of
fresh recruits for their armies. Arik-den-ilu of Assyria
attacked a little kingdom called Nigimti in the ranges
east of Arbela and then marched down into the dis-

[3] Cf. E. Unger in *Forschungen und Fortschritte*, X, Nos. 20/21 (July
10–20, 1934), 256.

[4] Scaraboid: Scheil, *Mém.*, VI, 30; cf. De Mecquenem, *Mém.*, VII, 135;
knob or scepter head: Scheil, *Mém.*, XIV, 32.

[5] Scheil in *RA*, XXVI (1929), 7.

[6] Hilprecht, *Old Babylonian Inscriptions* (*BE*, Ser. A, Vol. I), Nos. 15
and 43 and p. 31. For an inscription of Kurigalzu from Der with a drawing
of an Egyptian see Sidney Smith, "An Egyptian in Babylonia," *Journal
of Egyptian Archaeology*, XVIII (1932), 28–32.

trict housing the Iashubagalla, a tribe later associated with remnants of the Kassites in the mountains.[7] Adad-nirari I also raided the central Zagros, striking at the Guti and Lullubi remnants; after his war with the Kassite Nazi-Maruttash, the boundary between Assyria and Babylonia was established at Arman of Akarsallu, which is the Holwan region, extending into the mountains as far as the land Lullubium.[8]

Under these circumstances Elam quickly slipped away from Kassite overlordship; and Pahir-ishshan, son of Igi-halki, probably as a contemporary of Nazi-Maruttash (1319–1294), founded a new Elamite dynasty. Unfortunately, his achievements are completely unknown to us, save that he transported to an unknown site those same precious woods upon which Siwepalarhuppak and Bala-ishshan before him had so carefully labored.[9] Even he left the work to be carried on by his brother and successor Attar-kittah (ca. 1295–1286), who witnessed the arrival of the objects at the Susa temple. In like manner we know nothing additional of Attar-kittah; but his son, Huban-numena (ca. 1285–1266), seems to have been a ruler of tremendous energy. As "king of Anzan and

[7] Clay, *Babylonian Records in the Library of J. Pierpont Morgan*, Vol. IV, No. 49:6 ff.; cf. Ebeling, Meissner, and Weidner, *Die Inschriften der altassyrischen Könige*, pp. 50 ff.; *LAR*, Vol. I, § 69.

[8] Budge and King, *Annals of the Kings of Assyria*, I (London, 1902), 4–6; cf. *LAR*, Vol. I, § 73. Cf. *Synchronistic History* i 28 ff.; I have made use of the translation made by the late Professor D. D. Luckenbill for the Assyrian Dictionary of the Oriental Institute.

[9] Shutruk-Nahhunte inscription; see below, pp. 106 f.

Susa" and prince of Elam, he was the first to claim the title "expander of the empire"; and bricks bearing his Elamite inscription, discovered on the island Liyan in the Persian Gulf, confirm his claim. The inscription, which invokes the deities Huban, Kiririsha, the mother goddess of the island, and the Baha, perhaps the local protecting deities, records that Huban loved him and heard his petitions and that Inshushinak granted him the kingdom. As reward, for the lives of the women Mishimruh and Rishapanla he is erecting a chapel to these gods and uttering the pious hope that they give him a prosperous life and a peaceful kingdom.[10] His more illustrious successors, Shutruk-Nahhunte, Kutir-Nahhunte, and Shilhak-Inshushinak, vied with each other in commemorating the name of Huban-numena, who had erected a temple to Kiririsha of Liyan and to Huban and Kiririsha.[11] Shilhak-Inshushinak, to whom Huban-numena was

[10] Text: F. W. König, *Corpus inscriptionum Elamicarum. I. Die altelamischen Texte* (Hannover, 1926), No. 4C. This is a synthesis of (1) Pézard, *Mém.*, XV, 42 f., with variants from the Dieulafoy collection in the Louvre; (2) Weissbach in *ZDMG*, XLIX (1895), 693 f.; (3) fragments now in the Berlin Museum, copied by Bork.

In Susa only a fragment with the name Humban-ummenna, a variant spelling of the name, has been found; cf. Scheil, *Mém.*, III, 1 (No. 1). On all these cf. Hüsing, *Quellen*, No. 4.

[11] Shutruk-Nahhunte: Pézard, *Mém.*, XV, 66; Weissbach, "Shutruk-Nahhunte *A*," in his *Anzanische Inschriften* ("Abhandlungen der K. Sächsischen Gesellschaft der Wissenschaften," phil.-hist. Klasse, XII [1891], 117–50); cf. Hüsing, *Quellen*, No. 19.

Kutir-Nahhunte: Pézard, *Mém.*, XV, 73; Weissbach, "Kutir-Nahhunte *A*," in *Anzanische Inschriften*; cf. Hüsing, *Quellen*, No. 31.

Shilhak-Inshushinak: (a) temple to Kiririsha: Pézard, *Mém.*, XV, 76 and 80; Weissbach, "Shilhak-Inshushinak *D*" and "*A*," in *Anzanische*

even a "descendant" of the great Shilhaha, also testified that Susa and Inshushinak were not neglected.[12]

Untash-Huban (*ca.* 1265–1245), son of Huban-numena, justly acquired a great reputation as a builder. During his reign temples, sanctuaries, and other religious edifices in abundance were erected on the Susa acropolis, each carefully described by an appropriate Elamite inscription. Semitic deities thus honored were Nabu, who was held in high esteem and received both a temple and a statue, Sin, Belala, Bêlit-âli ("the Lady of the City"), and Adad; but even Adad was paired with Shala, known as early as the period of the *sukkalmah*'s, and the great majority of the buildings erected were for Elamite gods. Perhaps less pretentious were those for Napratep, Shimut, Pinikir, Ea-Sunkik ("Ea is king"),[13] Hishmitik and Ruhuratir, Nazit, whose building was under the protection of Huban and Inshushinak, and a deity whose name is written A.IP(or E).A.SUNKIK.[14] But Upurkupak's temple, according to the inscription, surpassed all others which had ever been erected to this deity; and

---

Inschriften; cf. Hüsing, *Quellen,* Nos. 57 and 59; (*b*) temple to Huban and Kiririsha: Pézard, *Mém.,* XV, 86; Weissbach, "Shilhak-Inshushinak B," in *Anzanische Inschriften;* cf. Hüsing, *Quellen,* No. 58.

[12] Scheil, *Mém.,* III, 59, and V, 91 (No. 43).

[13] Written ᵈNUN.SUNKIK; the translation of NUN by *Ea* in this name is uncertain, but cf. the deity *Ea-šarru* in Akkadian texts.

[14] Whether this is to be read phonetically is not certain.

Nahhunte received his dwelling because he had answered the prayer of Untash-Huban and performed what he requested. Still more magnificent were surely those for Huban and Inshushinak. Each separately received a new domicile, while jointly as the *melki ilâni*, "princes of the gods," they enjoyed a temple, as well as a sanctuary known as the *nûr kiprât*, "Light of the World-Quarters." Nor was Susa itself forgotten; Untash-Huban dedicated a temple and a chapel "for my city" to Inshushinak.[15] So numerous were these

[15] References to Untash-Huban texts:

A.IP.A.SUNKIK: *Mém.*, III, 3 (No. 2); cf. Hüsing, *Quellen*, No. 5.

Adad: *Mém.*, III, 14 (No. 6); cf. Hüsing, *Quellen*, No. 5.

Adad and Shala: *Mém.*, III, 11 (No. 5); cf. Hüsing, *Quellen*, No. 7.

Belala: *Mém.*, III, 28 (No. 14); cf. Hüsing, *Quellen*, No. 10.

Bêlit-âli: *Mém.*, III, 16 (No. 8); cf. Hüsing, *Quellen*, No. 7.

Hishmitik and Ruhuratir: *Mém.*, III, 19 (No. 10); cf. Hüsing, *Quellen*, No. 7.

Huban: *Mém.*, III, 31 (No. 17); cf. Hüsing, *Quellen*, No. 9.

Huban: *Mém.*, III, 29 (No. 15); cf. Hüsing, *Quellen*, No. 8.

Huban and Inshushinak (*nûr kiprât*): *Mém.*, III, 32 (No. 18); cf. Hüsing, *Quellen*, No. 11.

Huban and Inshushinak (*melki ilâni*): *Mém.*, III, 31 (No. 16); cf. Hüsing, *Quellen*, No. 9.

Inshushinak (temple): *Mém.*, III, 38 (No. 21); cf. Hüsing, *Quellen*, No. 5.

Inshushinak (*giguna*): *Mém.*, III, 34 (No. 19); Weissbach in ZDMG, XLIX (1895), 692 f.; cf. Hüsing, *Quellen*, No. 13.

Nabu: *Mém.*, III, 9 (No. 4); cf. *Mém.*, III, 15, and Hüsing, *Quellen*, No. 6.

Nabu: *Mém.*, III, 15 (No. 7); cf. Hüsing, *Quellen*, No. 7.

Nabu: *Mém.*, V, 7 (No. 66); cf. Hüsing, *Quellen*, No. 6.

Nabu: *Mém.*, III, 36 (No. 20); cf. *Mém.*, III, 15, and Hüsing, *Quellen*, No. 12.

Nahhunte: *Mém.*, III, 27 (No. 14); cf. Hüsing, *Quellen*, No. 10.

Napratep: *Mém.*, III, 17 (No. 9); cf. Hüsing, *Quellen*, No. 7.

Nazit: *Mém.*, III, 21 (No. 11); cf. Hüsing, *Quellen*, No. 9.

constructions that they argue for him abundant re-
sources and extensive conquests; but these were recorded on steles, of which Shutruk-Nahhunte preserved one, while of the rest all save fragments of
another have since disappeared.[16] Untash-Huban
dedicated to Huban and Inshushinak a limestone
statue of himself by a bilingual inscription in which,
it is interesting to note, the Elamite characters already show the beginnings of the later forms.[17] His
almost exclusive use of the Elamite language for the
other records is a sign of nationalistic feeling which
resulted in increasing opposition to Akkadian culture.

In his reign Elamite metallurgy attained its climax
in a life-size bronze statue of Napir-asu, wife of Untash-Huban, which was cast hollow in a single piece,

NUN.SUNKIK: *Mém.*, III, 24 (No. 12); cf. Hüsing, *Quellen*, No. 9.
    Pinikir: *Mém.*, III, 7 (No. 3); cf. Hüsing, *Quellen*, No. 5.
    Pinikir (temple): *Mém.*, III, 9 (No. 4); cf. *Mém.*, III, 15, and Hüsing,
Quellen, No. 6.
    Shimut: same as Bêlit-âli.
    Sin: *Mém.*, III, 25 (No. 13); cf. Hüsing, *Quellen*, No. 10.
    Upurkupak: *Mém.*, III, 39, and XI, 88 (No. 23); cf. Hüsing, *Quellen*,
No. 14.
    "For my city" (written *al-lum-mi-ma*, to be analyzed *alu-u-mi-ma*):
Mém., III, 38, and V, 88 (No. 22); cf. Hüsing, *Quellen*, No. 5.
    "For my city" (*giguna*): *Mém.*, III, 36, and V, 87 f. (No. 20); cf.
Hüsing, *Quellen*, No. 12.

[16] Shutruk-Nahhunte text: Scheil, *Mém.*, III, 43 (No. 25); cf. Hüsing,
Quellen, No. 21. Stele fragments: M. Pézard, "Reconstitution d'une
stèle d'Untaš-[nap] GAL," *RA*, XIII (1916), 119–24; cf. also M. Rostovtzeff,
"La stèle d'Untaš-[nap]GAL," *RA*, XVII (1920), 113–16.

[17] Scheil, *Mém.*, XI, 12 ff. (No. 89); cf. Hüsing, *Quellen*, No. 15.

its interior filled with fused metal. The queen wears a thin cloth over shoulders and breasts and a long, sweeping "bell skirt" descending to the ground. Details of the dress ornamentation are carefully reproduced, as are bracelet and ring on her folded hands. An Elamite inscription warns him who discovers and destroys the statue, or who obliterates or erases the name of Napir-asu in the inscription, that the anger of Huban, Kiririsha, and Inshushinak will descend upon him, that Belti, the great goddess, will deny to him fame and family.[18]

The accession of Kashtiliash III in Babylon (1249) found Untash-Huban ready to embark upon foreign conquest. His pretext for undertaking a war with the lowlands may be discovered in the story of Agabtaha, a leather-worker who fled from Hanigalbat to Kashtiliash and made for him a leather shield. In payment he received an estate near the city Padan on the northeast border of Babylonia.[19] The Elamite may well have felt that this was territory which belonged to Elam, not Babylonia. The ensuing conflict appears to have been altogether one-sided; the sole purely Akkadian inscription of Untash-Huban commemorates this, perhaps his greatest achievement. He captured Immiria, the protecting god of Kashtiliash, and carried him to the Susa acropolis, where Huban, In-

[18] G. Lampre, *Mém.*, VIII, 245 ff., Pls. 15 f.; Scheil, *Mém.*, V, 1 ff. (No. 65); cf. Hüsing, *Quellen*, No. 16.

[19] Scheil, *Mém.*, II, 95.

shushinak, and Kiririsha could guard him forever.[20]
The stone bearing the grant of Kashtiliash which
caused the strife was likewise brought to the capital.

Elam may have suffered from internal troubles in
the next few years, for Untash-Huban was followed
not by a son but by his uncle, Unpatar-Huban, son
of the dynasty's founder, Pahir-ishshan.[21] This may
explain why Tukulti-Ninurta I of Assyria, without
resistance from the Elamites, could penetrate the
Zagros from Tarsina, an inaccessible mountain between the cities Sha-sila and Barpanish on the southern bank of the Lower Zab, into the region of the
widespreading Guti between the lands of Suqush and
Lalar.[22] The Assyrian was again unopposed, after his
victory over Kashtiliash, when he added to his conquests a long list of border towns which were sometimes Elamite and sometimes Babylonian.[23]

Unpatar-Huban ruled only a few years when he
was succeeded by his brother, Kidin-Hutran (*ca.*
1242–1222); the latter retaliated on Tukulti-Ninurta

[20] Scheil, *Mém.*, X, 85.

[21] So in the Shilhak-Inshushinak lists. *Unpatar* is consistently read
Unpahash by Scheil, but cf. König in *MVAG*, XXX, Heft 1 (1925), 36,
n. 54.

[22] Annals: Messerschmidt, *Keilschrifttexte aus Assur historischen Inhalts*, Heft 1 (Leipzig, 1911), No. 16 obv. 17 ff.; cf. *LAR*, Vol. I, § 149.

[23] Schroeder, *Keilschrifttexte aus Assur historischen Inhalts*, Heft 2
(Leipzig, 1922), No. 60 iii 58—iv 83; cf. *LAR*, Vol. I, § 166. The town
Turnasuma should lie in the region of the Mê Ṭurnat (in Elamite, Durun),
while Ulaiash, if it is near the Ulai, must be near the source of the Karkhah
east of modern Mandali.

by invading Babylonia. The one and one-half years' reign of Enlil-nadin-shumi, Tukulti-Ninurta's puppet on the throne of Babylon, was brought to a sudden close by this unexpected raid of Kidin-Hutran, who captured Der, sacked its temple of Anu, and penetrated even to Nippur before returning to Elam. Tukulti-Ninurta promptly repaired the damage in Babylon by enthroning Kadashman-Harbe for a year and a half, and then Adad-shum-iddina (1238–1233). The Elamite was not, however, to be denied. Again he raided the lowlands; crossing the Tigris he advanced as far west as Isin and as far north as Maradda, just west of Nippur, before retreating in safety to his homeland.[24] The energy which enabled him to make these telling raids is obvious; it is therefore a striking commentary on the accidental manner in which our Elamite sources have been recovered that the record of his exploits is found only in Babylonian literature, and that, aside from the lists of Shilhak-Inshushinak, the name of Kidin-Hutran does not appear in Elamite records.

Kidin-Hutran was followed by Halludush-Inshushinak, of whose relation to his predecessors we are ignorant and of whose reign we know nothing.[25] He in turn was succeeded by a son, Shutruk-Nahhunte (*ca.* 1207–1171). This sovereign inaugurated the

[24] Chronicle P, iv 14 ff.; cf. Winckler, *op. cit.*, I, 124. On the site of Maradda cf. Clay in *OLZ*, XVII (1914), 110–12.

[25] Cf. Hüsing, *Quellen*, p. 18.

really great period of Elamite history, a period we might with some justification designate as the "classical" period.

One inscription of Shutruk-Nahhunte, could we but translate it accurately, would give us some idea of his numerous activities. Unfortunately, the text is extremely difficult and in many places the meaning is obscure. An introduction describes the transportation of a stele from Aia to Susa and its dedication to Inshushinak. The record then states that many earlier kings had not known the place where certain choice woods[26] were to be found, but that he importuned Inshushinak, his god, who heard his prayers. The route lay by way of Tahirman, Teda, and Kel, then by way of Hashmar[27] and Shahnam. Further, many former kings had never heard of the places called Shali, Mimurashi, and Luppuni. With Inshushinak's aid he discovered the place where the choice woods grew; and there he forested, just as did a few kings whose names he did not know, and just as did Siwe-palarhuppak, Bala-ishshan, Pahir-ishshan, and At-

---

[26] The Elamite words here are *husa hitek*. That the former means some sort of timber should long ago have been clear from the Persian texts in *Mém.*, Vol. IX, where it is often preceded by the determinative for wood; cf., for example, *Mém.*, Vol. IX, No. 139:16 and 18; No. 174:4. This must also be the correct meaning of the Elamite *husame*, e.g., *Mém.*, V, 20 ff. (No. 71), iii 15 ff.: "In Ekallat a temple of Inshushinak with . . . . wood had been built."

[27] The Hashmar pass mentioned in Assyrian records is to be located where the Diyala breaks through the Jebel Hamrin; cf. Weidner in *AOF*, IX (1933/1934), 97.

tar-kittah. Thus with his god's aid he achieved that which many had sought to do and few had accomplished; he, too, brought choice woods to Susa, where by the grace of Huban and Inshushinak he worked them and then in the temple on the acropolis dedicated them to Inshushinak, his god.[28] With just pride he boasted that things which former kings had not done he had been enabled to accomplish, and all these achievements he had brought about for the glory of Huban and Inshushinak.[29] When he discovered a stele far up in Anzan, he was forced to admit that he did not know the name of the king who had erected it. The inscription which makes this frank confession continues with an obscure passage referring to Dur Untash, later known as Dur Undasi, on the Hithite or Idide River, and to a place Tikni; it concludes with a dedication of the stele as the ruler's offering to his beloved god.[30]

Other inscriptions of Shutruk-Nahhunte are more easily understood. With baked bricks he beautified a chapel of Inshushinak in Susa and uttered the prayer that the deity look with favor upon his good

[28] Weissbach, "Shutruk-Nahhunte C," in *Anzanische Inschriften*, after Loftus. Copy, also after Loftus, in König, *Corpus inscriptionum Elamicarum*, Part I, No. 28*A*; fragmentary duplicate: Scheil, *Mém.*, XI, 15 (No. 90). Transliteration: Hüsing, *Quellen*, No. 28; attempted translation: Scheil, *Mém.*, V, 15 ff. (No. 70).

[29] Scheil, *Mém.*, III, 46 (No. 27); cf. Hüsing, *Quellen*, No. 17.

[30] Scheil, *Mém.*, V, 12 f. (No. 69); cf. Hüsing, *Quellen*, No. 20. On the location of Dur-Untash and the Idide River see M. Streck, *Assurbanipal*, II, 48, n. 1.

deed.[31] When a temple of the goddess Manzat built by former kings fell into ruin, he removed the débris and searched diligently for the inscribed bricks which those rulers had placed in its walls; with his own new bricks he restored the temple to its former glory.[32] Stone basins for the cult of the Elamite gods, but especially for Inshushinak and Suhsipa, suggest that the sacrificial offerings were regularly performed.[33] The island Liyan belonged to Shutruk-Nahhunte's empire, and there he re-erected and rededicated to Kiririsha the temple which Huban-numena had once devoted to this goddess.[34] Practically every inscription proclaims opposition to Akkadian culture; Shutruk-Nahhunte's only text written in Akkadian is a dedication to Ishmekarab, an Akkadian deity well known in Elam since the days of the *sukkalmah*'s.[35]

Meanwhile Ashur-dan I (1189–1154) had begun his long reign in Assyria. Soon he turned upon the weak Zamama-shum-iddina of Babylon and wrested from

[31] Scheil, *Mém.*, III, 44 (No. 26); Weissbach, "Shutruk-Nahhunte B," in *Anzanische Inschriften;* cf. Hüsing, *Quellen*, No. 18.

[32] From brick fragments in the Berlin Museum. These were ascribed to Huteludush-Inshushinak by Hüsing, *Quellen*, No. 63, but see now F. W. König, "Die Berliner elamischen Texte VA 3397–3402," *WZKM*, XXXII (1925), 212–20; the text appears in König, *Corpus inscriptionum Elamicarum*, Part I, No. 42A-C.

[33] Scheil, "Légendes de Šutruk Nahhunte sur cuves de pierre," *RA*, XVI (1919), 195–200.

[34] Weissbach, "Shutruk-Nahhunte *A*," in *Anzanische Inschriften;* Pézard, *Mém.*, XV, 66; cf. Hüsing, *Quellen*, No. 19.

[35] Scheil, *Mém.*, II, 118; Scheil doubts its historicity.

him Zaban on the Lower Zab, Irria, and Akarsallu.[36]
Shutruk-Nahhunte at once realized the impotence of
Babylon, and with his son Kutir-Nahhunte marshaled Elam's forces. His own inscription speaks of a
camp in Eli, of capturing seven hundred cities as far
as Mara and then a hundred more.[37] He entered Babylonia. In Eshnunna he found a statue of a former
ruler and one of Manishtusu.[38] From Sippar he took
Naram-Sin's famous "Stele of Victory"[39] and the great
stone bearing Hammurabi's law code; a portion of
the latter was erased for his own inscription, but the
blank space was never filled.[40] In the vicinity of Kish
he seized as booty an obelisk of Manishtusu and two
more statues of the same sovereign, which his inscription declares he found "in Akkad."[41] He was now
in the land Karintash, and a stele of Meli-Shipak fell
into his hands.[42] Advancing to Babylon, he overthrew
the unfortunate Zamama-shum-iddina, who had

[36] *Synchronistic History* iii 9 ff.

[37] Scheil, *Mém.*, XI, 17 ff. (No. 91); cf. Hüsing, *Quellen*, No. 28a.

[38] *Mém.*, VI, 12 f., and X, 2; cf. Hüsing, *Quellen*, Nos. 26 f.

[39] *Mém.*, III, 40 (No. 24), and II, Pl. XI; cf. Hüsing, *Quellen*, No. 22.

[40] *Mém.*, IV, 11 f.

[41] Kish obelisk: Scheil, *Mém.*, II, 6 ff.; statues: *Mém.*, X, 2 f., and
III, 42; cf. Hüsing, *Quellen*, No. 25.

[42] Scheil, *Mém.*, IV, 163 ff.; cf. Hüsing, *Quellen*, No. 23. Restore
Karintash with the help of a Shilhak-Inshushinak text, *Mém.*, V, 31 f.
(No. 72), ii 10, and the neo-Elamite text of Shutruk-Nahhunte, *Mém.*,
V, 62 f. (No. 84), l. 11, variant. According to Hüsing, *Quellen*, p. 53,
Karintash would be modern Karind on the Baghdad-Kirmanshah road.

reigned but a single year (1174), and established his own son Kutir-Nahhunte on the throne.[43] Adding further insult, he laid tribute and tax upon the subjected districts, a stated number of talents and minas upon Dur Kurigalzu, Sippar, Dur Sharrukin,[44] and Opis. This tribute was doubtless intended for the erection and maintenance of temples to Babylonian deities, for there is mention of bricks which should restore the walls of their dwellings.[45] Then, loaded with monumental spoil, Shutruk-Nahhunte withdrew to Susa, where his trophies were dedicated to Inshushinak with new inscriptions and set up near the Inshushinak temple.[46]

Official Babylonian historians refused the title "king of Babylon" to Kutir-Nahhunte and gave it to Enlil-nadin-ahhe, who kept up the Kassite resistance three more years. Finally, in 1171 B.C., Kutir-Nahhunte put an end to the Kassite Dynasty once and for all. Late Babylonian odes then attempted to gloss over the unpleasant fact of the Elamite's rule by insisting that the gods of Babylon had themselves sum-

[43] So probably we are to restore the text of Nebuchadnezzar I in Winckler, *Altorientalische Forschungen*, I, 535 ff. Cf. p. 132, n. 55.

[44] Restored from Dur-shar- . . . . .

[45] Hüsing, *Quellen*, No. 67, drawn from Loftus; a recent copy, also after Loftus, in König's *Corpus inscriptionum Elamicarum*, Part I, No. 28C:I.

[46] For other objects brought to Susa at one time or another by members of this dynasty cf. Jéquier, *Mém.*, VII, 32 ff. For lists of the *kudurrêti* see De Morgan, *Mém.*, VII, 137 ff.; Scheil, *Mém.*, X, 87 ff., and XIV, 35; for maceheads see *Mém.*, XIV, 32 f.; for weights, *Mém.*, VI, 48, and XIV, 34; for other Kassite texts, *Mém.*, IV, 166, and VI, 49.

moned him to the throne.[47] The Elamite felt altogether differently, and Babylon ceased to be the capital. Its gods had shown themselves powerless, and the
image of Marduk himself was carried off to Susa,[48]
where Kutir-Nahhunte now succeeded his father on
the throne. On his way thither he wrested from her
temple one other famed Babylonian deity, Nana, the
Lady of Uruk. To the actual number of years she remained captive in Susa Ashurbanipal of Assyria added a round thousand when he declared that fifteen
hundred and thirty-five years before his time Kudur-
Nanhundi, an Elamite, had not feared the oath of the
great gods but had laid his hands upon the temples of
Akkad and carried away Nana to Susa.[49]

The reign of Kutir-Nahhunte in Elam (*ca.* 1170–
1166) appears to have been short. He had time to
rebuild the temple of Kiririsha on the island Liyan
and to dedicate it for his own life, for the life of
Nahhunte-Utu, his wife, and for the lives of her progeny.[50] He refounded the ruined sanctuary of the deity
Lagamal in Susa and placed it under the protection
of Inshushinak.[51] Before his accession to the throne
he had already surrounded the Inshushinak sanctuary

[47] A. Jeremias, "Die sogenannten Kedorlaomer-Texte," *MVAG*, XXI
(1916), 69–97, esp. pp. 80 ff. and 92 ff.

[48] Nebuchadnezzar inscription; see above, p. 110, n. 43.

[49] See below, p. 206.

[50] Pézard, *Mém.*, XV, 73; Weissbach, "Kutir-Nahhunte *A*," in *Anzanische Inschriften*; cf. Hüsing, *Quellen*, No. 31.

[51] Scheil, *Mém.*, III, 49, and V, 89 (No. 29); Weissbach, "Kutir-
Nahhunte *B*," in *Anzanische Inschriften*; cf. Hüsing, *Quellen*, No. 30.

on the northwestern part of the Susa mound with a
wall of baked brick panels or bas-reliefs portraying a
man-bull worshiping the date palm;[52] after his accession he placed his own statue within this sanctuary,
which he began to beautify on a large scale.[53] Death
brought a sudden end to his activities and placed a
greater conqueror than he on the throne. His decease
marked the beginning of a new era and the dawn of a
brief but better day.

[52] Scheil, *Mém.*, III, 47 (No. 28); Weissbach, "Kutir-Nahhunte *C*,"
in *Anzanische Inschriften;* cf. Hüsing, *Quellen*, No. 29. On the reliefs
themselves see J. M. Unvala, "Three Panels from Susa," *RA*, XXV
(1928), 179–85.

[53] Shilhak-Inshushinak inscription, *Mém.*, III, 50, plus V, 89 (No. 30);
complete, *Mém.*, Vol. XI, Pl. 11, Fig. 2; cf. Hüsing, *Quellen*, No. 43, and
Unvala, *loc. cit.*

CHAPTER VII

THE GLORY OF AN ELAMITE EMPIRE

SHILHAK-INSHUSHINAK (*ca.* 1165–1151 B.C.), brother of Kutir-Nahhunte, was without question the greatest of the Elamite rulers. His reign marks the summit of Elam's political attainments, and perhaps also the height of her commercial and economic importance; but the very effort to extend his borders was a contributing cause to the collapse of the empire after his death. Of these things we know little; we can only trace his achievements on the field of battle and attempt to picture the Susa of his time. All else lies hidden in unexcavated and unknown mounds of Elam.

An inscription written late in the reign gives some account of his early exploits.[1] It begins with a long invocation to gods worshiped in Elam: Huban, Inshushinak, Kiririsha, Nannar, Nahhunte, Temti, Sili, Shimut, Hutran, Tiru, the Nap-bahappi-hutip-nappip, perhaps deities guarding the dwellings of the gods, as well as the god of the heavens, the gods of Elam, and the gods of Susa. The king declares himself the son of Shutruk-Nahhunte, beloved "descendant" of the woman Beyak, beloved brother of Kutir-

[1] Scheil, *Mém.*, XI, 21 ff. (No. 92); cf. Hüsing, *Quellen*, No. 54.

Nahhunte, the chosen one of Nahhunte the mighty
prince² of the Elamite gods. He has inscribed this
stele for his own life, for the life of Nahhunte-Utu,
once the wife of Kutir-Nahhunte and now his own
mate, and for the lives of their children, namely, his
sons Huteludush-Inshushinak, Shilhina-hamru-Lagamar, Kutir-Huban, Temti-turka-tash, and Lili-ir-
tash and his daughters Ishnikarabbat, Urutuk-El-
halahu, Utu-e-hihhi-Pinikir, and Bar-Uli. He recites
his own and his wife's pious deeds toward Inshushinak, repeatedly asking the god's mercy and begging
that his prayers be heard and his requests granted.

All this is but introduction; the political historian
rejoices at what follows. In eight groups, corresponding perhaps to eight separate campaigns, Shilhak-Inshushinak lists the cities which he conquered. Each
group is preceded by a prayer and followed by the
name of the district in which the cities were located;
once the names of over two hundred and fifty such
places were to be read on this stele. Unfortunately,
today less than a hundred are clearly legible, and
only too often the names of the districts have been ob-
literated. Nevertheless, an analysis of the names is
well worth the time. The names most clearly recognizable are those beginning with *bît*, "house," or *sha*,
"of," for these indicate their Semitic origin. Others
bespeak their Kassite, or at least Caucasian, sources,
while others again are completely unknown.

² *Melku*, the Akkadian term!

The first group once contained forty-two place names. Today there are legible only Sha Shilitu, perhaps Sha Beltia, Bit Buli, Shenkuru, Bit Nappahe ("house of blacksmiths"), Sha Imire ("of asses"), Bit Nakiru (which may be the Nakri tribe subsequently defeated by Tiglathpileser III of Assyria),[3] and Bit Pilantu. In a second group only Sha Barbari ("of wolves") and Sha . . . . Nankari ("of . . . . carpenters") can be read. The third group once comprised thirty-one cities in the district Ukarsillam Ebeh. Since this includes the Akarsallu which had just been captured by Ashur-dan and the Ebih Mountain which Shamshi-Adad V of Assyria was to cross on his way from Zaban (modern Altun Köprü) to the city Mê Ṭurnat on the Diyala River,[4] it is not difficult to understand where Shilhak-Inshushinak had campaigned when he gives the names of the conquered cities. Here we find Sellam, Tunni, Matku (which must be Madga at modern Tuz Khurmatli, from which Gudea had once obtained gypsum), Bit Siniriba, Bit Katashman ("house of Kadashman"), Bit Lassi, Bit Sin-shemi (known also to Nebuchadnezzar I of Babylon, who granted land of its district on the Tigris to his priest of Enlil),[5] Bit Etelle, Appi-

[3] Cf. LAR, Vol. I, § 764.

[4] LAR, Vol. I, § 723; for the location of the Ebih Mountain see now Weidner in AOF, IX (1933/34), 96.

[5] Text in W. J. Hinke, Selected Babylonian Kudurru Inscriptions (Leiden, 1911), No. 5. A translation made for the Assyrian Dictionary of the Oriental Institute was at my disposal.

sini-beti, Sha Warad Egalli ("of the palace servant"), and Kiprat.

The fourth group lay in the district . . . . tilla and comprised eleven cities. The names Arrapha, Nuza, and perhaps Titurru ("the bridge") tell us at once that we are in the modern Kirkuk region, even though the remaining legible names, Hanbate and Sha Nishe ("of peoples") are unknown. With forty-one sites located in the Durun, Ebeh, Shatrak, and Ialman regions, we are back to the Turnat or Diyala, Ebih, and modern Holwan districts. The city names of this fifth group which may still be read are Tunnati, Sha Hanta, Bit Rie Rappi ("house of the chief shepherd"), Bit Bahe, Sha Purna Mashhum (a Kassite name meaning "of the protection of god"), perhaps Bit Ishtar, Huratu, Ishirtu sha Adad ("sanctuary of Adad"), Sha Anpima, the Great and the Small Bit Rituti, Bit Ittatu, Reshu, Bit Rikim Adad ("house of the thunder of Adad"), and Bit Mugia.[6] Bit Ishtar later found Tiglathpileser III in its midst, while Reshu is probably the Rashi tribe of Arameans, well known to the Assyrians from Sargon onward and located in the mountains east of Der, where was its capital, Bit Imbi.[7]

The sixth group once named forty-nine sites in the district Balahuta, Ialman, and A. . . .zahaya; even the names betray the modern Holwan region.

[6] Perhaps to be read Bit Ulgia.

[7] E.g., *LAR*, Vol. I, §§ 773 f., and Vol. II, §§ 34 and 82.

Here are Nahish Barare, Sha Hilik, Sha Balihu, Murattash (which Tiglathpileser I found south of the Lower Zab in the midst of the mountains Asaniu and Atuma),[8] Dunnu, Bit Uzali. . , Bit Hanipi, Sha Kupia, three Bitati ("houses"), Bit Nagia, Sha Kattarzah, Duhupuna (which Shamshi-Adad V was to discover south of the Ṭurnat River and Mount Ialman),[9] Annahhutash, Bit Sin-ishmanni, Bit Silia (Assyrian Bit Sa'alli or Sha'ali), with its capital Bit sha Ilti (known to the Assyrians as Dur Illatai, where Arameans took refuge[10]), Bit Zahmi, Bit Hubbani ("house of cisterns"), Sha Marazza, Sha Iklai, Sha Shangibari, Tintu Ili-erish, Bit Matimu, Bit Laqipu, Tintu, Bit Rikim Adad (already named in the preceding group), Bit Tamtea, and Harbatu. The last names of this group, proving that we have reached the Kassite homeland, are Bit Nap Shumalia ("house of the god Shumalia"), Bit Tasak Sunkik (or Bit Tarish Sharru), Bit Milshipak ("house of Meli-Shipak"), and Sha Burra Hutte. The group is closed with Bit Barbari ("house of wolves") and "the city Kaplu."

The seventh group names Bit Kilalla, Bit Nankari ("house of the carpenters"), Tan Silam, Bit Kunzubati, Puhutu, Nakapu, Zallat, Kishu, and Bit Rapiqu; the district name is . . . .kattar. The eighth group once named twenty-six sites; of these only Kitan (or

[8] *LAR*, Vol. I, § 232.

[9] *LAR*, Vol. I, § 724; restore to Duhupuna with Hüsing, *Quellen*, p. 80.

[10] *LAR*, Vol. I, § 790; cf. also § 806.

Natan), Nar Sillam ("the river of Sillam"), Harap, and Bit Kimil Adad are today wholly legible, while the name of the district cannot be read.

So much for this great stele, which continues with another dedication formula to the gods of Elam, the gods of Anshan, and the gods of Susa. Other stele fragments add other names. One cites the district Halman Niripuni and formerly named fourteen places in a district of which . . . .akmish Lanhu. . . . alone can be deciphered. Another names Niripuni Shuru-tuha as a district, and in an unknown region places the sites Makshia, Sha Kutu, Asse, Sha Kilka. . . . , Kishshimu, Harpa. . . . , and Talzana.[11]

The campaigns of Shilhak-Inshushinak stand out in bold relief after a study of these lists. First Akarsallu and then the Ebih Mountain region between modern Altun Köprü and the Diyala River fell into his hands. Thence he turned westward and reduced a number of Aramean tribes which, even at this early date, were settled well up the east bank of the Tigris. With the capture of Madga or Tuz Khurmatli he was in territory which in ordinary times was indisputably Assyrian and from which it was an easy step northward to Nuzi and Arrapha or Kirkuk. At this point he was less than seventy miles due east of Ashur; it is therefore not farfetched to assume that Shilhak-Inshushinak himself brought to an end the long reign of

[11] Scheil, *Mém.*, V, 33 (No. 73) and 35 (No. 74); cf. Hüsing, *Quellen*, Nos. 54*a* and *b*.

Ashur-dan (1154 B.C.). With Durun and Ialman he was back at the exit from the mountains of the Turnat or Diyala River in modern Holwan, from which he penetrated eastward into lands which had once housed the Kassites.

The Elamite's control was far from absolute. Although his brother had brought to an end the rule of Kassite kings in Babylon, he had been unable to retain the region, and at Isin in the northern part of the alluvium a new power had sprung into being. Under Marduk-shapik-zeri this power now began to interfere in the affairs of Assyria,[12] where, we may suspect, Elamite overlordship was the real cause of revolt and unrest following the death of Ashur-dan. Shilhak-Inshushinak could ill afford such intervention and at once left Elam to chastise the sovereign of Isin. Marching to the Tigris, where he defeated an army sent against him, he advanced to the city Hussi and proceeded up the Euphrates as far as Nimettu-Marduk, by which he may mean Nimitti-Enlil, the wall of Babylon.[13] There he may have met defeat, for it is clear that henceforth he held little control over any part of Babylonia or Assyria.

The great king still possessed, however, a mighty

[12] Weidner, "Aus den Tagen eines assyrischen Schattenkönigs," *AOF*, X (1935), 1–9.

[13] Text: Weissbach, "Incertum 1" (after Loftus), in *Neue Beiträge zur Kunde der susischen Inschriften,* "Abhandlungen der K. Sächsischen Gesellschaft der Wissenschaften," phil.-hist. Klasse, XIV (1894), 729–77; cf. Hüsing, *Quellen,* No. 54c.

empire. He ruled Liyan in the Persian Gulf, for there he restored Huban-numena's temple to Kiririsha and a joint temple to Huban and Kiririsha.[14] His territory reached inland almost to Persepolis, for bricks inscribed with his name and dedicated for his own life, for the life of his wife, and for the lives of their progeny have been found in territory of the Mamassani tribe halfway between Ramuz and Shiraz.[15] When the Balahute, located in the central Zagros, carried away vessels of Inshushinak, he brought them back by force, making his camp in Eli, Anzan, Ulan, and Sha Purna Mashhum.[16] Like Huban-numena and Shutruk-Nahhunte, he employed the title "expander of the empire," and no one had a better claim.

During his reign Inshushinak, once merely the local god of Susa, became the supreme deity of the realm; and temples to him arose in all parts of the kingdom. A single inscription mentions the erection of temples in Tettu, Sha Atta Mitik, Ekallat (whose deities were ordinarily Adad and Shala[17]), Berraberra, Sha Attata

[14] Pézard, *Mém.*, XV, 76, 80, and 86; Weissbach, "Shilhak-Inshushinak *A*," "*D*," and "*B*," in *Anzanische Inschriften*; cf. Hüsing, *Quellen*, Nos. 57–59. A stele found in Susa was doubtless originally from Liyan; cf. Scheil, *Mém.*, V, 38 (No. 76); Hüsing, *Quellen*, No. 49.

[15] E. Herzfeld, "Drei Inschriften aus persischem Gebiet," *MAOG*, IV (1928–29), 82–85; *AMI*, I (1929–30), 114, where there is a transliteration and translation by F. W. König; cf. *ZDMG*, LXXX (1926), 244, for old Elamite rock-reliefs at Naqsh-i-Rustam near Persepolis.

[16] Scheil, *Mém.*, III, 78 ff. (No. 54), iii 7 ff.; cf. F. W. König, "Drei altelamische Stelen," *MVAG*, XXX, Heft 1 (1925), 21.

[17] Cf. the Bavian inscription of Sennacherib, ll. 48 ff., conveniently translated in *LAR*, Vol. II, § 341. This text gives also the location, northeast of Babylonia proper in the debatable land.

Ekal Likrub, Marrut (probably the Nar Marrati or Sealands), and Sha Hantallak.[18] But the Lord of Susa was not honored to the total exclusion of other Elamite gods. Lakamar or Lagamar received a temple in Bit Hulmi and Huban one in Beptar Siyan Sit,[19] while the edifices erected to Kiririsha alone and to Huban and Kiririsha on the island Liyan have already been noted. From the enumeration of these temples we obtain further corroboration of the far-extending empire of Shilhak-Inshushinak. He had conquered the whole east Tigris country clear to the Lower Zab, while at least a part of the Sealands to the southwest of Susa was also in his possession. Doubtless some of the sites named are to be located within Iran at no great distance from the later capital of the Achaemenids, Persepolis.

A tremendous income from all parts of this empire now flowed in to Susa, and with wealth such as no Elamite ruler had before possessed he made this metropolis equal to the other great cities of his time. Many as were the industrial and commercial enterprises carried on by private individuals in the business and residential section, that part of the city which housed the palaces and temples was the scene of even greater activity. Shilhak-Inshushinak brought to completion the sanctuary of Inshushinak which his

---

[18] Scheil, *Mém.*, V, 20 ff. (No. 71); cf. König in *MVAG*, XXX, Heft 1 (1925), 29 ff. A temple to Inshushinak in . . . .en-ili is mentioned in the text of Scheil, *Mém.*, III, 82 ff. (No. 55), rev. 4 ff.

[19] Scheil, *Mém.*, V, 20 ff. (No. 71), on which see preceding note.

brother had begun; at the side of his brother's statue he placed his own image of baked brick and surrounded the temple with bas-reliefs on which was his prayer that Inshushinak look with favor on his good deed.[20] South of this he restored the sanctuary which Untash-Huban had erected to Pinikir[21] and the temple for Suhsipa, already worshiped by Shutruk-Nahhunte.[22] For the safety of himself and family he constructed a sacred inclosure in the sanctuary of Tab-migirshu;[23] in the inclosure of Beltia ("my lady") he incased the altar with new ornamentation and surrounded it with copper objects, while that for "Huban the exalted" had an alabaster stele.[24] He restored a temple for Manzat and Shimut, the latter of whom received particular attention as "the Elamite god."[25] For Inshushinak and Lagamar he rebuilt another, with the confession that he did not know the names of the kings who had first erected it,[26] and still another for Ishni-

---

[20] Scheil, *Mém.*, III, 50, and V, 89 (No. 30); complete, *Mém.*, Vol. XI, Pl. 11; see also *Mém.*, III, 52 (No. 31); cf. Hüsing, *Quellen*, Nos. 43 and 32, and J. M. Unvala in *RA*, XXV (1928), 180 f.

[21] *Mém.*, Vol. V, No. 71 iv 22 ff.; see reference above, p. 121, n. 18. On Pinikir cf. F. W. König, "Pinikir," *AOF*, V (1928/29), 101–3.

[22] *Mém.*, Vol. V, No. 71 iii 28 ff.; cf. also the stele inscription which is "Incertum 2" in Weissbach, *Neue Beiträge* (after Dieulafoy; cf. Hüsing, *Quellen*, No. 52); this mentions the deity Suhsipa and the place Karintash. A king Karintash (Kara-indash) appears to be named in *Mém.*, V, 31 (No. 72); cf. Hüsing, *Quellen*, No. 51.

[23] Scheil, *Mém.*, V, 59 (No. 79); cf. Hüsing, *Quellen*, No. 33.

[24] Scheil, *Mém.*, III, 82 ff. (No. 55), upper edge 1 ff. and right edge ii 1 ff.

[25] Stele: Scheil, *Mém.*, XI, 60 f. (No. 94); cf. Hüsing, *Quellen*, No. 53.

[26] Brick: Scheil, *Mém.*, V, 61 (No. 82); cf. Hüsing, *Quellen*, No. 34.

karab, known in the earlier period as Ishmekarab, who also protected a doorway in his own new dwelling and in whose honor he named a daughter Ishnikarab-bat.[27]

Doubtless it was to one of these deities that Shil-hak-Inshushinak erected the 14-foot-square sanctuary which was uncovered by excavations in the southern part of Susa and which housed a superb limestone statue of ·Puzur-Inshushinak. Perhaps the winding stairway of 120 steps descending over 85 feet to a lower level of the mound led to a temple dedicated to another of these gods.[28]

Such constructions as these paled into insignificance before two massive temples which arose on the southwestern corner of the citadel mound. Architects' drawings on fragmentary clay tablets prove that they were not erected at haphazard,[29] and chance has preserved for us an actual model of this portion of the mound. It is a low bronze table surmounted by reproductions of these temples, the smaller two-staged, the larger three-staged. At sight of them we involuntarily recall the "temple towers of glazed brick with horns of shining bronze" which Ashurbanipal destroyed at Susa some five hundred years later. Two standing-stones flank the larger temple, before which is the model of a stone platform with cups for the

[27] Stele: Scheil, *Mém.*, III, 82 ff. (No. 55), rev. 1 ff.; bricks: *Mém.*, III, 88, and V, 92 (No. 56); cf. Hüsing, *Quellen*, No. 37.

[28] De Mecquenem, "Constructions secondaires," *Mém.*, XII, 72 ff.

[29] *Mém.*, XII, 77.

sacrificial blood. A vase, another platform, and a stele are represented, as is also a sacred grove of trees; the latter in turn brings to mind Ashurbanipal's description of "sacred groves into which no stranger penetrates, whose borders he never oversteps." One of two nude shaved and crouching figures holds a vase to be used in the sacrifice. At one corner of the table an incription tells how Shilhak-Inshushinak made this bronze object and proclaimed its name "the Rising Sun."[30]

The first and smaller temple was erected over the site of Shulgi's temple to Ninhursag and was doubtless dedicated to the same goddess, though possibly she now bore a native name, such as Kiririsha or Pinikir. Four foundation deposits marked the temple proper, which measured about 50×25 feet, with additional rooms on all sides. Four other deposits marked the corners of the inner sanctuary, which was slightly less than 20 feet square. Statues of Puzur-Inshushinak and a stele of Manishtusu were to be observed within the temple, while the bronze statue of Napirasu, queen of Untash-Huban, adorned the interior of the holy of holies. On all sides of the temple extended a pavement of baked bricks laid in bitumen, the monotony of which was frequently broken by upright Elamite steles.[31]

---

[30] Gautier, *Mém.*, XII, 143–52; Scheil, *Mém.*, XI, 58 (No. 93); cf. Hüsing, *Quellen*, No. 56. For the Ashurbanipal references cf. the Rassam Cylinder vi 27 ff., conveniently translated in *LAR*, Vol. II, § 810.

[31] De Mecquenem, "Temple de Nin-har-šag," *Mém.*, XII, 70–72.

This temple likewise yielded in magnificence to the new edifice for the Lord of Susa, Inshushinak.[32] His temple stood on a platform over 130 feet long and half as wide, its corners oriented almost due north and south. Beneath its foundations of burned brick set in bitumen there were again eight foundation deposits, four under the corners of the temple proper, which measured over 67×33 feet, and four under the angles of the inner sanctuary, which was over 26×16 feet in size. These deposits consisted of statues of Puzur-Inshushinak inscribed with proto-Elamite characters; electrum pendants, bracelets, leaves, and rings; bronze basins and rolled bronze leaves; silver and stone vases; and tablets of Shulgi, the mightiest king of Ur's Third Dynasty. On either side of the temple gateway stood a life-sized lion of glazed clay; these were the "colossi, the guardians of the temple," described by Ashurbanipal, who added that fierce wild oxen adorned the gates.[33] The latter swung on huge inscribed stone sockets, whose inscriptions list the former kings who constructed Inshushinak's temple.[34] At the doorway decorative clay cones or glazed knobs told how Shilhak-Inshushinak dedicated the entrance

[32] De Mecquenem, "Temple de In-Šušinak," *Mém.*, XII, 67–69. Cf. also Jéquier, "Troisième royaume susien," *Mém.*, VII, 36 f.; De Morgan, "Trouvaille de la colonne de briques," *Mém.*, VII, 49–59; De Mecquenem, "Offrandes de fondation du temple de Chouchinak," *Mém.*, VII, 61–130. The latter references must, however, be used with caution, for many of the objects described are demonstrably of neo-Elamite manufacture.

[33] Cf. G. Lampre, *Mém.*, VIII, 164 ff., Figs. 324 f.

[34] Scheil, *Mém.*, XI, 63 ff. (Nos. 95 and 96); cf. Hüsing, *Quellen*, Nos. 48a and b.

to his god for his own life, for the life of Nahhunte-Utu, and for the lives of their children;[35] one knob was dedicated to Zana-Tentar, who would seem to be "the Lady of Babylon."[36] Also at the doorway inscribed bricks, a few of which were stamped, bore Shilhak-Inshushinak's boast that he restored what former kings had built and that he placed each of their names on bricks that their deed might be commemorated in his own day.[37]

The temple walls, unsupported by buttresses, were made of unburned brick veneered with well baked brick. Here and there an inscribed brick, sometimes glazed, recorded the name of a famous king who had erected the temple to Inshushinak. Thanks to the royal antiquary, many of the *sukkalmah*'s were so commemorated.[38] Kuk-Nashur and Kuk-Kirwash, each of whom by a Sumerian inscription had dedicated a temple within the temple area to the god, were especially honored; their Sumerian texts were reproduced, and for the edification of his readers Shilhak-

[35] Scheil, *Mém.*, III, 72 f., 75 f., and 77 (Nos. 50, 52, and 53); photograph of the latter: *Mém.*, Vol. I, Pl. 4, opp. p. 104; cf. Hüsing, *Quellen*, No. 44. Other knobs are described by Jéquier in *Mém.*, I, 123.

[36] Scheil, *Mém.*, III, 74 (No. 51); cf. Hüsing, *Quellen*, No. 44. If *Tentar* is the Akkadian TIN.TIR, this would indicate that the latter ideogram was actually so pronounced in Babylonia.

[37] Scheil, *Mém.*, III, 66 f., also Pl. 10, No. 4 (No. 48); V, 61 (No. 83); III, 69 f. (No. 49); cf. Hüsing, *Quellen*, Nos. 35 f. and 40. On the general subject of inscribed bricks at Susa cf. De Morgan, *Mém.*, I, 93–95 and 197 f.

[38] Scheil, *Mém.*, III, 53 ff., and V, 90 ff. (Nos. 32–45); cf. Hüsing, *Quellen*, No. 39.

Inshushinak confides that he has translated their inscriptions, found their names, and therefore commemorated their deeds.[39] But since an Akkadian text of Temti-agun, recording the dedication of a statue to Inshushinak for the life of his superior, Kutir-Nahhunte, received practically identical comments,[40] it is obvious that Shilhak-Inshushinak could neither read nor interpret the Sumerian! Still another type of brick set into the walls manifests the ruler's interest in the more immediate present; it names all his children and dedicates the temple as his offering for the city of Susa![41]

Within the building, columns of inscribed triangular bricks supported its wooden roof. Beautifully glazed bricks, singly and in reliefs, added the necessary color to the interior walls. But the most curious relief is of bronze. It portrays a number of warriors marching in single file, all identically clad in helmet with pointed visor, sleeveless jacket, short skirt, and upturned boots. Their beards are cut square and hang on the breasts, and tassels from the helmet cover the nape of the neck and ears. A short curved sword is held aloft in the right hand, a bow is suspended from the left, a mace is thrust through the skirt, while a strap over the right shoulder supports a quiver on the back. An inscription, today all but illegible, may

[39] Bricks: Scheil, *Mém.*, V, 56 f. (No. 78), and III, 60 (No. 46); *RA*, XXIX (1932), 68; cf. Hüsing, *Quellen*, No. 38.

[40] Brick: Scheil in *RA*, XXIX, 69 f.

[41] Scheil, *Mém.*, III, 61 f. (No. 47); cf. Hüsing, *Quellen*, No. 41.

treat of conquests and the presentation of booty to the deities Manzat, Nahhunte, Lagamar, Pinikir, and Kiririsha.[42]

The temple altar was guarded by an inscribed bronze rod, a hollow cylinder over 14 feet long cast in a single piece. The inscription describes its manufacture and its dedication to Inshushinak for the lives of the ruler and his family, but it also contains a lengthy curse on those who would damage his handicraft. The curse invokes Hutran, the beloved "descendant" of Kiririsha and Huban, as well as Huban and Kiririsha themselves, Inshushinak and Nahhunte.[43] Stele inscriptions tell us that Shilhak-Inshushinak erected a splendid new altar with ornamentation of copper, around which he set copper cult vessels and other objects, which may have included replicas of horned animals, for its protection. The same inscriptions add that he placed upon the altar objects which we may translate "magnificent likenesses" of Shutruk-Nahhunte, Kutir-Nahhunte, himself, Nahhunte-Utu, Shimut-nika-tash, his brother, and all his children; if these were indeed images, we need no longer question the deification of Elamite monarchs or of the entire ruling family.[44]

A paved court extending on all sides of the temple

[42] De Morgan, *Mém.*, I, 163 f., Pl. 13; Jéquier, *Mém.*, I, 123; Scheil, *Mém.*, XI, 86, Fig. 18; cf. Hüsing, *Quellen*, No. 42.

[43] Jéquier, *Mém.*, VII, 37; Scheil, *Mém.*, V, 39 ff. (No. 77); cf. Hüsing, *Quellen*, No. 45.

[44] Scheil, *Mém.*, III, 82 ff. (No. 55), obv. 18 ff.; *Mém.*, III, 78 ff. (No. 54), ii 1 ff.; cf. König, *MVAG*, XXX, Heft 1 (1925), 19 and 23.

was surrounded by a wall, doubtless bearing reliefs, and by numerous Elamite steles. Three of these we have already studied minutely, for they outlined Shil-hak-Inshushinak's far-flung conquests.[45] Two others described the erection of the temple and its sanctuary; of these, one was dedicated to Huban, Kiririsha, and Inshushinak, the other to Inshushinak alone.[46] A sixth listed the former kings who had erected a temple to Inshushinak and enumerated various sites throughout the kingdom where other temples to Elamite gods might be found.[47] A seventh described the building of a temple to Manzat and Shimut; an eighth has come down to us in fragments only.[48] These steles doubtless made an impressive appearance, but to the worshiping Elamites a sight more astounding must have been the southern entrance to the temple, reserved for trophies from foreign lands. Here were on display the great law code of Hammurabi, the splendid obelisk of Manishtusu, the famous "Stele of Victory" of Naram-Sin, and boundary stones without number bearing grants of land. These were the embodied proofs of the ruler's prowess in arms, of his distinction abroad and at home. They and the temple inclosure suggested the glory of the

[45] See above, pp. 113 ff. and 118.

[46] Scheil, *Mém.*, III, 78 ff. (No. 54) and 82 ff. (No. 55); cf. König, *op. cit.*, pp. 18 ff. and 22 ff. (Nos. 46 f.).

[47] Scheil, *Mém.*, V, 20 ff. (No. 71); cf. König, *op. cit.*, pp. 29 ff. (No. 48).

[48] Scheil, *Mém.*, XI, 60 f. (No. 94), and V, 10 (No. 68); cf. Hüsing, *Quellen*, Nos. 53 and 50.

Elamite empire; but after that empire had decayed, they remained but an echo of power gone forever.

History affords frequent examples of empires which reach their prime only to pass into immediate decline, and Elam was no exception. A process of disintegration began shortly after 1150 B.C., when Shilhak-Inshushinak gave place to Huteludush-Inshushinak, whom he had named first in the lists of his sons. Huteludush-Inshushinak himself many times claims descent from both Kutir-Nahhunte and Shilhak-Inshushinak, and once from the father of both, Shutruk-Nahhunte, as well. In reality it would seem that he was a son of Nahhunte-Utu, who was perhaps a daughter of Shutruk-Nahhunte married first to Kutir-Nahhunte and then to Shilhak-Inshushinak. Without daring to assume the title borne by his predecessors, "king of Anzan and Susa," Huteludush-Inshushinak persisted in calling himself the "expander of the empire," though without just cause. A tendency to archaize is noticeable both in the sign forms and in the content of his inscriptions, and this in itself suggests that the great days of Elam were in the past. The fact that no inscription of his has been found on the island Liyan in the Persian Gulf may indicate that Liyan was now lost to his kingdom, although his erection of a temple for Upurkupak in Shalulikki, later Shallukea, proves that at least a part of the Sealands was yet subservient.[49]

[49] Brick: Scheil, *Mém.*, XI, 75 (No. 99); cf. Hüsing, *Quellen*, No. 62; Harper, *ABL*, Nos. 789 and 1311; Waterman, *RCAE*, II, 52 and 414 ff.

The constructions of Huteludush-Inshushinak in Susa were neither pretentious nor numerous. In Kipu, perhaps a part of the temple area, he erected a temple to Ishnikarab for his own life, for the lives of his legitimate brothers, and for the lives of his sons, daughters, and relatives.[50] For the goddess Manzat he made a stone door socket for his own life, for the life of Nahhunte-Utu, his revered mother, and for the lives of his legitimate brothers. This he placed in the temple of Manzat and Shimut which had been erected by Shilhak-Inshushinak, and again he calls the latter deity the "Elamite god."[51] With small flat green-glazed bricks he constructed a diminutive rectangular chapel for Inshushinak and declared that the anger of Huteludush-Inshushinak and of the ancient Shilhaha should descend upon him who disturbed it.[52] A stele which may be attributed to him calls upon the gods of Anshan and the gods of Susa as well as Inshushinak, Kiririsha, Nahhunte, Upurkupak, Tiru, and Manzat.[53] Although remembered by the neo-Elamite Shutruk-Nahhunte,[54] it is clear that Huteludush-Inshu-

[50] Brick: Scheil, *Mém.*, XI, 71 (No. 98); cf. Hüsing, *Quellen*, No. 60; F. W. König in *Festschrift der Nationalbibliothek in Wien* (1926), p. 530.

[51] Scheil, *Mém.*, XI, 69 (No. 97); cf. Hüsing, *Quellen*, No. 65.

[52] Jéquier, *Mém.*, VII, 38. Texts: Scheil, *Mém.*, XI, 72 f. (No. 99), and V, 60 (No. 80); Weissbach, "Incertum 3," in *Neue Beiträge*; cf. Hüsing, *Quellen*, Nos. 61 f.

[53] Scheil, *Mém.*, V, 37 (No. 75). There attributed to Shilhak-Inshushinak; but cf. Hüsing, *Quellen*, No. 64.

[54] Brick: Scheil, *Mém.*, V, 62 f. (No. 84).

shinak was a ruler of little importance and that during his reign the power of Elam rapidly declined.

The appearance of a great king in Babylonia, Nebuchadnezzar I, coincided with the disintegration of the Elamite power. The Babylonian made the most of his opportunity. In his own inscription he recounts the victories of the Elamite Shutruk-Nahhunte and his son over the Babylonians and tells of his resolve to avenge these victories or to die in the attempt. With the remnant of his people he penetrated the country of the Elamites and reached the sources of the Uknu or Karkhah River, probably at a point east of Mandali, where he awaited their attack. Backed by the army of his predecessor on the throne, Huteludush-Inshushinak was not loath to give battle. The warriors of Babylonia, as Nebuchadnezzar himself admits, were badly smitten, his cavalry forced to flee in disorder. He dared not risk a second engagement but retreated to Dur Apil Sin. As he puts it: "The Elamite followed, and I fled before him; I sat down on the bed of weeping and sighing."[55] He then appealed to Marduk, who had been held captive in Elam since the days of Kutir-Nahhunte. Marduk heard his laments and commanded Nebuchadnezzar to bring him from hostile Elam.[56]

[55] Rawlinson, *Cuneiform Inscriptions of Western Asia*, Vol. III, Pl. 38, No. 2; cf. Winckler, *Altorientalische Forschungen*, I, 535 f.; Olmstead in *AJSL*, XXXVI (1919/20), 147 ff.

[56] *CT*, Vol. XIII, Pl. 48; cf. Winckler, *op. cit.*, I, 542 f.; Olmstead, *loc. cit.*

Thus far the Babylonian had been totally unsuccessful; and if Huteludush-Inshushinak had been able to hold loyal his Elamite subjects, he might have claimed a complete victory. But Ritti-Marduk, lord of the "house" of Karziabku, a land not far from modern Holwan, transferred his support to the Babylonian monarch;[57] and two priests of the god Ria, Shamua and his son Shamaia, in the city Din Sharri not far from Susa, fled from the face of the Elamite king and were received by Nebuchadnezzar.[58] With such unexpected help, Nebuchadnezzar could renew his attack. Since Der no longer admitted Elamite suzerainty, it was made the base for a forced march of thirty hours into Elam. Heat, dust, and lack of water impeded his progress; but Huteludush-Inshushinak, for what reason we know not, offered no opposition, and Nebuchadnezzar reached the Ulai River not far from Susa. There the Elamites finally gathered and, as the Babylonian told it, gave such battle that the sun was darkened as when dust storms sweep by. Ritti-Marduk valiantly distinguished himself against his former master, and at the command of Ishtar and Adad "the king of Elam turned back and stood on his mountain," that is, died. Nebuchadnezzar triumphed; he

[57] Ritti-Marduk *kudurru* in L. W. King, *Babylonian Boundary Stones and Memorial Tablets in the British Museum* (London, 1912), No. 6, pp. 29–36; location by Billerbeck, *Das Sandschak Suleimania*, pp. 13 f.

[58] Shamua *kudurru* in King, *op. cit.*, No. 24, pp. 96–98; cf. Olmstead, *loc. cit.* Din Sharri occurs in Ashurbanipal's inscriptions; cf. translation in *LAR*, Vol. II, § 806.

captured the land of Elam; he plundered its possessions.[59] Lowland and highland he filled with destruction and made like a desert; when at last Nebuchadnezzar returned to Babylonia he was not alone, for
with him Marduk took the highroad, the path of joy,
the desired way to Babylon from hostile Elam.[60]

Likewise the god Ria was taken from Din Sharri
and carried to the alluvium to rejoice the hearts of
Shamua and Shamaia. In the city Hussi, not long since
ravaged by Shilhak-Inshushinak, a permanent home
for the deity was established and was deeded for his
maintenance. Included in this grant were lands of
Opis and Dur Sharrukin, once tributary to Shutruk-
Nahhunte, as well as the region of Hussi of Bit Sin-
asharidu on the bank of the Takkiru Canal, Bit Bazi
on the Royal Canal, and Bit Akarnakkandi, which
was specifically designated as the city of the god Ria.[61]
Ritti-Marduk also prayed his new lord to grant freedom to his own ancestral lands. He declared that
under a former king they had been free, but that
under an enemy rule and contrary to their custom—
he is obviously referring to the Elamites—they had
been brought under the dues of Namar. Nebuchadnezzar promptly released from these dues the lands

[59] Ritti-Marduk *kudurru* in King, *loc. cit.*, corrected by Thureau-
Dangin, "Un synchronisme entre la Babylone et l'Elam," *RA*, X (1913),
97 f.

[60] Rawlinson, *Cuneiform Inscriptions of Western Asia*, Vol. IV, Pl. 20,
No. 1; cf. Olmstead, *op. cit.*, pp. 148 f.

[61] Shamua *kudurru*; see above, n. 58.

of Bit Karziabku, together with their horses, cattle, flocks, and woods, and proclaimed the independence of the citizens. A curse, which threatens any governor of Namar who shall infringe this royal charter, invokes Ninurta and Adad; Shumalia, "the lady of the shining mountains, who dwells on the summits"; Nergal and Nana; Shahan, the shining god, son of the temple of Der; Sin and the Lady of Akkad; and the gods of Bit Habban.[62]

Nebuchadnezzar also claims that he overthrew the mighty Lullubi and despoiled the Kassites.[63] We know nothing of an expedition into Lullubi territory save when he attacked Elam, and he may only be referring to Lullubi troops in the Elamite army; his defeat of the Kassites may in turn refer only to his supplanting their dynasty. His claim of conquest over Elam was doubtless exaggerated, and his unlimited control of the country is denied by the fact that a younger brother of Huteludush-Inshushinak named Shilhina-hamru-Lagamar succeeded to the Elamite throne and was remembered into New Elamite times.[64] Nevertheless, it is certain that with the death of Huteludush-Inshushinak the dynasty begun by Pahir-ishshan withdrew from active participation in international affairs.

[62] Ritti-Marduk *kudurru;* see above, n. 59.   [63] *Ibid.*

[64] Brick of Shutruk-Nahhunte: Scheil, *Mém.*, V, 62 f. (No. 84). On the relationship of this king to his predecessor cf. Koschaker in *ZA*, XLI (1933), 53, n. 8.

For a time the scene of attempted conquest by westerners shifted to the north of Elam, where Ashur-resh-ishi followed Nebuchadnezzar in claiming a defeat of the Lullubi and all the Guti in their mountain regions.[65] A few years later Marduk-nadin-ahhe of Babylon defeated Tiglathpileser I of Assyria and captured, together with its gods Adad and Shala, the city Ekallate, which had once been taken by Shilhak-Inshushinak.[66] Tiglathpileser responded by crossing the Lower Zab well up in the mountains and attacking the lands Murattash and Saradaush.[67] Some time after his tenth year Tiglathpileser fought another skirmish with the Babylonians above the city Zaban opposite Arzuhina or modern Altun Köprü; he then secured the city Arman and the plain of the city Salum and plundered from Akarsallu as far as Lubdu; by crossing the Radanu River he made the cities at the foot of Mounts Kamulla and Kashtilla a part of his kingdom.[68]

Despite these raids there was no material advance of any Babylonian power into the eastern mountains,

[65] Annals: Budge and King, *Annals of the Kings of Assyria*, I, 20; cf. *LAR*, Vol. I, § 209.

[66] Bavian inscription of Sennacherib, ll. 48 ff., in Rawlinson, *Cuneiform Inscriptions of Western Asia*, Vol. III, Pl. 14; cf. *LAR*, Vol. II, § 341.

[67] Annals: Budge and King, *Annals of the Kings of Assyria*, I, 58; cf. *LAR*, Vol. I, § 232; cf. Olmstead, "Tiglath-Pileser I and His Wars," *JAOS*, XXXVII (1917), 174, and *History of Assyria*, p. 66.

[68] *Synchronistic History* ii 14 ff.; annals: Schroeder, *Keilschrifttexte aus Assur historischen Inhalts*, Heft 2, No. 66:10 ff., and No. 69:15 ff.; cf. *LAR*, Vol. I, §§ 293 and 331; cf. Olmstead in *JAOS*, XXXVII, 183.

while Elam itself seems to have disappeared completely as a political entity. Two of the three kings of the Second Dynasty of the Sealands, Simmash-Shipak and Kashshu-nadin-ahi, bear names which bespeak their Kassite origin, and Mar-biti-apal-usur (*ca.* 996–991 B.C.), who followed the Bazi Dynasty, was called a "descendant of Elam";[69] but these facts tell us absolutely nothing about the land itself. In the northwestern part of Susa, where Kutir-Nahhunte and Shilhak-Inshushinak had erected a sanctuary to Inshushinak, tombs covered the site of the earlier buildings; and even the tombs were hopelessly poverty-stricken.[70] For a period of over three hundred years after the death of Huteludush-Inshushinak our Elamite sources are completely silent. Thus it is no exaggeration to say that with his death, so far as Elam is concerned, come dark centuries.

[69] L. W. King, *Chronicles Concerning Early Babylonian Kings*, II, 51 ff. and 62.

[70] De Mecquenem, "Fouilles de Suse," *RA*, XIX (1922), 131 ff. and 139 f.

CHAPTER VIII

INDO-IRANIANS IN THE
ZAGROS MOUNTAINS

THROUGHOUT the early historical periods
thus far described, the inhabitants of the Zagros Mountains seem to have belonged to
that group of people which has been called, for want
of a better name, the Caucasian. To this group we
have ascribed the Elamites, the Kassites, the peoples
of Gutium, and other autonomous populations of the
highlands. A remote connection of their language
with the Tamil dialects in India has further suggested
that the entire plateau of Iran was inhabited by members of this group.

The coming of the Kassites into Babylonia, with
their inclusion in the historical perspective, in itself
argues, however, for the entry of another race of
people, the Indo-Iranians, into the land. Although
the Kassites were not themselves of this race, they
appear to have experienced some contact with Indo-
Iranian peoples, whence came several non-Caucasian
deities into their pantheon. The region in which this
contact took place must have been Iran, and the manner of its accomplishment is not difficult to imagine.

Across the steppes of Turkestan from the plains

north of the Caucasus and the Caspian Sea, Indo-Iranian chieftains and their horse-borne warriors swept into Iran about the beginning of the second millennium B.C. Once within the plateau, their forces divided. One branch descended southeastward into India, there to impose its language upon the subjugated peoples and to develop it into what is known as Sanskrit. The other, a smaller branch, advanced into western Iran. From it the Kassites learned of the sun-god, Surya, the pest-god, Marut, and the storm-god, Burya, and discovered that the horse, the warrior's animal par excellence, also far excelled the slow ox and ass as a draft animal.

The western wing of the Indo-Iranian invaders did not, however, pause at the Zagros ranges. Its leaders drove on westward to the great bend of the Euphrates, where, in Mitanni, they settled down after their long trek to enjoy the doubtful blessings of aristocratic rule. Their names are basically Indo-Iranian, not far removed from those of their one-time compatriots, the future Hindus; their gods bore Indo-Iranian names—Indra, Varuna, Mitra, and the Nasatya; their warriors were known by a word familiar in Sanskrit as *marya*, "heroes"; and their documents dealing with the typically Indo-Iranian pursuit of horse-training reveal early Indo-Iranian, almost Sanskrit, numerals.

This outpouring of Indo-Iranian dynasts was not without its contemporary parallel in the western

Orient. We can only conjecture the origin of the Hyksos who subdued Egypt in the eighteenth century B.C., but few today can doubt that among them were Aryans speaking a dialect of the *centum* group of Indo-European. Contemporaneously, a stratum of the same branch of Aryans swept over the Caucasian basic stock of Anatolia; its final achievement was the centralization of power in the city now known as Boghazköy, the capital of a great Hittite empire. The origin of these peoples should probably be looked for in the west rather than in the east.

The Hyksos lost control of Egypt about 1580 B.C., but the Indo-European Hittite kings remained in power to the thirteenth century, when the "Sea Peoples" brought ruin to their kingdom and threatened the safety of Egypt. The Indo-Iranian dynasts of Mitanni fell prey a century earlier to their distant cousins in Anatolia and to a revived Assyrian empire. Their small aristocracies had succumbed earlier still to the Caucasian substratum as had their fellows among the Kassites; their written language was Caucasian, and when they were conquered scarcely a vestige of Indo-Iranian culture remained behind. Their penetration into the bend of the Euphrates is, however, of great historical importance. It would appear that they were but an advance guard of the great mass of the same stock which entered Iran; while they were reaching the northwestern frontier of Mesopotamia as early as 1500 B.C., their relatives in the eastern branch were descending into India. One may well

suppose that the intervening highlands of Iran were
occupied during the subsequent centuries by the peoples who a half millennium later enter the stage of
history as Iranian Medes and Persians. The Caucasian peoples retained their autonomy only in the Zagros regions, a fact which accounts for the absence of
Indo-Iranian names in the historical records of Assyrian kings who penetrated these mountains down to
the ninth century B.C.

We have already become familiar with the names
of some of these independent districts, but others are
entirely new. On the northern border of Elam, quies-
cent by 900 B.C., was the land of the Ellipi. This included the mountain valleys to the northeast of Der,
extending perhaps to modern Nihavend and reaching
as far north as the Baghdad-Kirmanshah–Hamadan
trail. Slightly north of this were remnants of the Guti
and the Kassites; and, as in earlier periods, the people
known as the Lullubi still occupied the fertile Shehrizor plain and guarded the northern approaches to the
chief commercial road leading to and from the plateau. Sometimes there is mention of a land Namri,
long since associated with Bit Hamban and hence
with the exit of the Diyala River from the mountains;
but Namri is more often merely an indefinite Assyrian
expression for the southeastern lands, while the common designation for the ancient territories of the
Lullubi was Zamua, or Mazamua when it became an
Assyrian province. North of this region again, but
still south and southeast of Lake Urmia, was the land

of the Mannai, while west of the lake extended the land Parsua or Parsuash, the first stopping-place of the Persians on their way to Parsumash and then to Parsa.

These territories—Ellipi, Zamua (including Namri and the land of the Lullubi), Mannai, and Parsuash—were the foremost obstacles to Assyrian extension of power in the Zagros throughout the subsequent years. They were likewise the scene of the first contact between Assyrians and Iranians.

The Assyrian Adad-nirari II (911–890) claims to have marched from beyond the Lower Zab River by the borders of Lullubium and Zamua as far as the passes of Namri,[1] but it was not until the revival of power under Ashurnasirpal (885–860) that any real advance into the Zagros was attempted. In his reign Assyrian warriors attained the Awroman mountain range east of the Shehrizor. After three campaigns the region was partially subdued, and a provincial capital, Dur Ashur, was erected on the site of an older city, Atlila, to serve as the grain center of the rich area.[2] One of the opponents encountered bore

[1] Annals: *Keilschrifttexte aus Assur historischen Inhalts*, Heft 2, No. 84 obv. 23 ff.; cf. *LAR*, Vol. I, § 360.

[2] Annals: Budge and King, *Annals of the Kings of Assyria*, I, 254 ff.; cf. *LAR*, Vol. I, §§ 448–58. On the topography cf. Billerbeck, *Das Sandschak Suleimania*, pp. 21–38; A. T. Olmstead, "The Calculated Frightfulness of Ashur nasir apal," *JAOS*, XXXVIII (1918), 209 ff.; E. A. Speiser, "Southern Kurdistan in the Annals of Ashurnasirpal and Today," *Annual of the American Schools of Oriental Research*, VIII (1926/27), 1–41.

the Semitic name Nur-Adad; the rest—Musasina, Kirtiara, Ameka, Arashtua, Sabini, and Ata—all have names we can safely assign to the Caucasian group of languages. We are therefore forced to conclude that, if once there had been an Indo-Iranian intermixture with the natives in this part of the Zagros, none of its traces remained by 900 B.C.

The pressure of the Indo-Iranians, or, as we may now truly call them, the Iranians of the plateau, soon made itself felt in the mountains. As they advanced westward into the Zagros they took over from the native chieftains the control of the walled cities and proved themselves no less formidable opponents to Assyrian warriors than had been their predecessors. This we first witness in the reign of Shalmaneser III. In 856 this sovereign found in Zamua two Caucasian chiefs, Nikdime and Nikdiara.[3] In 844 a ruler Ianzu, whose name is but the ancient Kassite word for "king," was recognized as an Assyrian vassal in Namri.[4] His revolt in 835 was the signal for further Assyrian conquest in the east. Namri and Parsua were entered; the land of the Madai or Medes was

---

[3] For references to the texts and for source criticism see A. T. Olmstead, *Assyrian Historiography* ("University of Missouri Studies, Social Science Series," Vol. III, No. 1 [May, 1916]), pp. 21–28; for convenient translations see for the first campaign *LAR*, Vol. I, §§ 561, 609, and 644. On the topography of the reign cf. Billerbeck, *Das Sandschak Suleimania*, pp. 42–66; Olmstead, "Shalmaneser III and the Establishment of the Assyrian Power," *JAOS*, XLI (1921), 345–82.

[4] Cf. *LAR*, Vol. I, §§ 573 and 637.

encountered near modern Sakiz, some hundred and thirty miles east of Arbela; and south of the Zeribor Lake, in Harhar, hereafter the Assyrian border fortress, the royal image was installed for worship.[5] Again in 829 the generalissimo of the Assyrian army advanced against Ualki of the Mannean land; between this and Parsua, west of Lake Urmia, he encountered Artasari, whose name, compounded with a very common Iranian element, shows how the new race was pouring into the region.[6] In the next year Parsua and Namri were re-entered.[7] We may be certain that Zamua all this time was securely under Assyrian domination, for in 830 B.C. the high office of eponym was held by the governor of Mazamua, Hubaia.[8]

When revolt within Assyria ended the reign of Shalmaneser,[9] the eastern regions once more became autonomous. Not so Parsua west of Lake Urmia, which was entered by a new power in the Armenian highlands, Haldia, whose king left a stele in the Keleshin Pass southwest of the lake.[10] This state of affairs was intolerable from the Assyrian standpoint. Forces of

---

[5] Cf. *LAR*, Vol. I, § 581; for the location of Harhar see Billerbeck, *Das Sandschak Suleimania*, p. 63.

[6] Cf. *LAR*, Vol. I, § 587.   [7] Cf. *LAR*, Vol. I, § 588.

[8] Olmstead, "The Assyrian Chronicle," *JAOS*, XXXIV (1915), 361; cf. *JAOS*, XLI (1921), 374, n. 61.

[9] Cf. Olmstead, *History of Assyria*, pp. 153 f.

[10] Sayce in *JRAS*, 1894, pp. 691–705; C. F. Lehmann-Haupt, *Corpus inscriptionum Chaldicarum*, Textband, 1. Lfg. (Berlin und Leipzig, 1928), pp. 24–34; 2. Lfg. (Berlin und Leipzig, 1935), pp. 132–60.

the new ruler, Shamshi-Adad V (825–812),[11] advanced into Mannai and Parsua as well as into Mesu and Gizilbundu, lands which may be located in the valley of the Jaghati River flowing into Lake Urmia. Here was met an Iranian, Piri-shate; if it is true, as the annals state, that this individual was king of the region, we are witnessing the transference of power from Caucasian to Iranian overlords. This conclusion is corroborated by the names Irtisati, Satirai, Artasiraru, and possibly Mamanish, belonging to kings of the land Nairi on the Armenian border. However, when Assyrian forces advanced southward from Parsua into the land of the Madai or Medes, possibly in the region of the snow-capped Takht-i-Balkis, they encountered a chieftain Hanasiruka whose name sounds peculiarly Caucasian. Iranian domination of the northern Zagros had not, therefore, been achieved by 822 B.C., and the movement of Iranians from the plateau cannot yet have been completed.

In his fourth year Shamshi-Adad initiated a campaign against Babylonia by traversing Ebih, the southern part of the mountain range known as the Jebel Hamrin, and capturing the cities of Mê Turnat and Di᾽bina in regions long since known to Shilhak-Inshushinak of Elam. In his fifth year the Assyrian

[11] Annals: *KB*, I (Berlin, 1889), 174–87; Weidner, "Die Feldzüge Šamši-Adads V. gegen Babylonien," *AOF*, IX (1933/34), 89–104; cf. *LAR*, Vol. I, §§ 718–22. On the topography and Iranian names cf. Billerbeck, *Das Sandschak Suleimania*, pp. 66–69; G. Hüsing, "Vorgeschichte und Wanderungen der Parsawa," *Mitteilungen der Anthropologischen Gesellschaft in Wien*, LX (1930), 258 f.

crossed the Lower Zab River, the Ebih Mountain, and the Ṭurnat or Diyala, pressed through Mount Hashmar, and descended upon Der (modern Badrah), which was robbed of its treasures. The inhabitants of Der, we are told, forsook their city for Elam; from Parsamash, soon to be familiar as Parsumash and to house the Iranian Achaemenes, as far as Bit Bunakki on the headwaters of the Karkhah, there was plundering, devastation, and conflagration.[12]

Toward the last of Shamshi-Adad's reign, Namri joined forces with his enemies, and the succeeding sixty-five years witnessed a temporary decline of Assyria. Eight expeditions, nevertheless, were directed against the Madai or Medes, two against the Mannai, and four against Namri. These amounted to little, for the star of Haldia was again in the ascendancy. King Menuash occupied Parsua, then left his inscription on the Tash Tepe south of Lake Urmia in Mannean land.[13] The Assyrian Adad-nirari III (812–782) is merely repeating an old formula, therefore, when he claims conquest of Ellipi, Harhar, Araziash, Mesu, Madai, Gizilbundu, Munna or Mannai, Parsua, and other lands.[14] His successors were even more impotent than he.

We enter upon the last period of Assyrian history

[12] O. Schroeder, *Keilschrifttexte aus Assur historischen Inhalts*, Heft 2, No. 142; cf. Weidner in *AOF*, IX, 101–4.

[13] C. F. Lehmann-Haupt, *Corpus inscriptionum Chaldicarum*, Textband, 1. Lfg., pp. 45–47.

[14] *KB*, I, 190 f.; cf. *LAR*, Vol. I, § 739. For the whole period cf. Olmstead, *History of Assyria*, pp. 158–61.

with the accession of Tiglathpileser III (746–728). As we examine his records we notice that his opponents in the east bear names which show inextricable mingling of Kassite or Caucasian, Aramean, and Iranian races; the increasing predominance of the latter is of great importance, for it forbodes the establishment of Iranian empire.

One line of Assyrian advance[15] in the second year of the reign brought about the return of the fertile Shehrizor to the status of a province whose governor could, in later years, assist in the deportation of little groups of Zagros inhabitants to faraway Syria. In this region were engaged the forces of Tuni of Sumurzu, Miki of Halpi, and the land of Bit Hamban.

A second line of attack was pursued in the mountains somewhat more distant, but we find it difficult to locate exactly the "lands" and cities mentioned. Most of their names are of Caucasian origin, as are nearly all place-names in this region down to the latest period. The names of the individuals encountered are often more suggestive. Some of these were Kaki, king of Bit Zatti; Tunaku in Bit Abdadani; Mitaki; Battanu in Bit Kapsi; Bisi-hadir of the city Kishisa (later familiar as Kishesim); and Ramateia of Araziash, who furnished products typical of mountain ranges and fertile valleys—horses, cattle, sheep,

---

[15] Annals: I have been permitted the use of Professor Olmstead's unpublished reconstruction of the annals of Tiglathpileser III. For the published annals see P. Rost, *Die Keilschrifttexte Tiglat-Pilesers III* (Leipzig, 1893), pp. 6 ff.; cf. *LAR*, Vol. I, §§ 766–68 and 773 f. On the topography cf. Billerbeck, *Das Sandschak Suleimania*, pp. 72–94.

and lapis lazuli. Careful study of the topography of this expedition makes it probable that Assyrian forces advanced to the region around Bane and Bistan, roughly about one hundred and twenty-five miles east of Arbela over difficult terrain. From Bit Abda-dani, for many years an Assyrian dependency, the Semitic Mannu-kima-sabe was required to furnish three hundred talents of lapis lazuli (almost ten tons, if we are to believe the record!) and five hundred tal-ents of copper.

The year 737 found a still greater campaign under way. Upash of Bit Kapsi, whose territory was again entered, fled to Mount Abirus, possibly a peak of the Penja-Ali-Dagh northwest of modern Hamadan. Other chieftains, Bur-Dada, Ushuru, and Tanus, like-wise found safety only in flight. Iautarshi, whose Iranian name bespeaks his origin, betook himself to the vicinity of the Rua range, which extended, so we are told, into the salt desert and so is perhaps the Penja-Ali-Dagh itself. Encouraged by these suc-cesses, the eponym canon could well declare that the campaign was actually directed against the land Mada, the land of the Medes, for it was in this very region that Iranian Medes coalesced into a kingdom.

Inscriptions intended for display likewise picture the advance, though less accurately than the annals. In these we discover the land Parsua, the city Zakruti of the mighty Medes, and the land Nishai; and here we read the claim of tribute from the lands of the

Medes and the Ellipi and from the chieftains of all their mountains as far as Mount Bikni. The mention of Parsua is curiously out of place unless we can see behind the name groups of peoples from Parsua traveling from the shores of Lake Urmia southeastward toward Hamadan. The city Zakruti is still puzzling, although some have equated it with the Sagartioi tribe of the Persians, mentioned by Herodotus.[16] Nishai, however, is too familiar from the famous Nisaean breed of horses for its mention here to be only accidental. The Ellipi we have long known, while Mount Bikni years ago was identified with the Demavend;[17] and the comparison of "Bikni, the mountain of lapis lazuli," with the famous blue stone so desired throughout antiquity is sufficient to prove its identity with the bluish snow-clad peak towering over the modern capital of Iran, Teheran.[18] There is no need to declare Tiglathpileser's claim an overstatement, though that is, of course, possible. It is rather an understatement, for "tribute" may just as well have included commercial purchases and voluntary gifts as compulsory payments.[19]

When Sargon (722–705) inherited the throne of As-

[16] iii. 93; cf. the references in Prášek, *Geschichte*, I, 85, n. 1.

[17] Winckler, *Die Keilschrifttexte Sargons*, I (Leipzig, 1889), xxvii, n. 3.

[18] Cf. Olmstead, *History of Assyria*, p. 362.

[19] Herzfeld, *AMI*, VII (1934), 24–26, follows the doubtful lead of Prášek, *Geschichte*, I, 18–20, in distinguishing between "Medes" or "mighty Medes" and "Medes on the border of Mount Bikni."

syria he was faced with the immediate problem of preserving and expanding the provincial organization in the Zagros and of combating the influence of the Haldian empire to the north and east. Danger first threatened in the kingdom of the Mannai south of Lake Urmia, where an Iranian chief, Mitatti of the land Zikirtu, had persuaded the natives to revolt from their lord Iranzu. The latter appealed to Sargon, who drove the rebels out in 719;[20] but three years later the new sovereign Aza was slain by Mitatti and another Iranian, Bagdatti. Sargon restored the line-of Aza with a brother, Ullusunu,[21] but the pressure of Haldia proved too strong and he too defected. Another expedition from Assyria quickly brought him to his senses, expanded the province Parsuash by the addition of six districts, and made Harhar, temporarily known as Kar Sharrukin, once more the capital of a province, which also included six new districts. If, as seems likely, we are to locate this city in the southeastern reaches of the Shehrizor, we are not surprised to find that the kingdom of Ellipi with its sovereign Talta is mentioned in this connection, and that twenty-eight Median village lords here paid their respects to the Assyrian commander.

Again in 715 Haldian forces entered Mannean land.

[20] Annals: A. G. Lie, *The Inscriptions of Sargon II*, Part I (Paris, 1929), corrected by Olmstead, "The Text of Sargon's Annals," *AJSL*, XLVII (1930/31), 259–80. For the year 719 see Lie, *op. cit.*, pp. 8 ff.; cf. *LAR*, Vol. II, § 6.

[21] Lie, *op. cit.*, pp. 12 ff.; cf. *LAR*, Vol. II, §§ 10 f.

With a native governor, Daiaukku, whose son was a
Haldian hostage, they conspired to overthrow Ullusunu and seized twenty-two fortresses in the land.
This time likewise Sargon acted quickly.[22] Daiaukku,
whose name was rendered in Greek as Deioces, together with his family was captured and deported to
Hamath in Syria, and peace was brought to the dis-
rupted land. A revolt in the lower Shehrizor was also
subdued in this year, two new regions added to the
province, and Kar Sharrukin strengthened to prevent
a recurrence of the event. The matter-of-fact account
in the Assyrian annals is unexpectedly enlivened by a
letter which relates the actual events of the strength-
ening of this city and describes a foray into the land
of the Medes; it must therefore be seen as the real
source of the annals themselves,[23] which declare that
twenty-two city prefects of the Medes again delivered
their gifts in this capital. Details of other engage-
ments also may be discovered in the reliefs which
once adorned the palace of Sargon. There we see the
capture of the city Kishesim in the province of Parsuash, a triple-walled fortress equipped with magnificent flanking towers; Sikris in the Kar Sharrukin
province, a simple high-walled inclosure also provided
with flanking turrets; Kindau, to whose chief gate a
causeway leads over a swamp; and other cities sur-

---

[22] Annals: Lie, *op. cit.*, pp. 16 ff.; cf. *LAR*, Vol. II, §§ 12–15.

[23] Harper, *ABL*, No. 126; cf. Waterman, *RCAE*, I, 86 f. In this letter
it is stated that the Medes are quiet.

rounded by moats or protected by lofty walls and battlements.[24]

These reliefs also depict for us the inhabitants of the Zagros at this period, native and Iranian alike. The hair is cut short, usually curled, and held in place by a red fillet, though often low caps with broad forehead bands are worn; the short beard also is curled. Over a short-sleeved girdled tunic reaching to the knee is worn a curious sheepskin coat which on peaceful occasions hangs over both shoulders, open in front, but in battle serves for protection, replacing the Assyrian leather collar and mail breeches. Like their opponents, some of these Zagros chieftains go barefoot; but a conspicuous part of the costume consists of high laced boots, a few of which have the upturned point we have often considered Hittite, but which are indispensable in mountainous regions. For weapons they carry neither bow nor sword; the regular weapon of offense is a long spear, of defense, a rectangular wicker shield.[25]

An elaborate report of Sargon's expedition of 714[26] tells us more of these individuals. Crossing Mount

---

[24] Harhar: Botta and Flandin, *Monument de Ninive*, Vol. I (Paris, 1849), Pl. 55; Kishesim: *ibid.*, Pls. 68 and 68 *bis;* Sikris: *ibid.*, Pl. 64; Kindau: *ibid.*, Pl. 61; Bit Bagaia: *ibid.*, Pl. 76; Kisheshlu: *ibid.*, Vol. II, Pl. 147. Cf. Billerbeck, *op. cit.*, pp. 98–101 nn.

[25] Cf. Billerbeck, *Das Sandschak Suleimania*, pp. 163–67; Olmstead, *History of Assyria*, p. 244.

[26] Thureau-Dangin, *Une relation de la huitième campagne de Sargon* (Paris, 1912); other fragments in Schroeder, *Keilschrifttexte aus Assur historischen Inhalts*, Heft 2, No. 141. Cf. *LAR*, Vol. II, §§ 140 ff.

Kullar in the valley of the Lower Zab north of the Shehrizor, Sargon and his warriors soon reached Mannean land, where they were greeted by Ullusunu. In Parsuash the governors of Namri, of the land of the Medes, and of many other lands hastened to present their gifts—"prancing horses, swift mules, [Bactrian] camels." To the casual reader the names of these chieftains are uninspiring, but the specialist examines with care the elements which indicate Iranian origin. Here came Talta of Ellipi, a member of the old racial stock, but with him three Iranian chieftains from the bottom lands south and east of the Shehrizor: Uksatar, the first Cyaxares; Durisi; and Satareshu. Nor were they alone. Other chieftains from the Zagros and the Iranian plateau joined in presenting their gifts to the great power of the Orient, Assyria. Their names are preserved for us in two lists, one of which is at times a mere epitome of the second but often adds still other names.[27] At this late date we are amazed at the large number of Caucasian rulers, such as Paiaukku and Mashdaiaukku, whose names, like that of Daiaukku or Deioces, contain elements occurring abundantly in the texts from Nuzi. Yet the number of individuals whose names we may with little hesitation call Iranian is not small. Auarparnu em-

[27] One list is in the account of Sargon's eighth campaign, ll. 42–49; cf. *LAR*, Vol. II, § 147. The other is in Prism A, ll. 14–37, published by Winckler, *Die Keilschrifttexte Sargons*, II, Pl. 44; I have been able to use a revised copy of the prism text, prepared by Luckenbill for the Assyrian Dictionary; for translation cf. *LAR*, Vol. II, § 192. Cf. the good notes on Iranian names in König, *Älteste Geschichte*, pp. 55–58.

bodies the element *aura,* "lord," which in Achaemenian times is found in the name of the great god of all beings, the "Wise Lord," Auramazda. Bagbararna, like the land name Bit Bagaia, which may have been translated into Semitic to become Bait Ili ("house of the god"), contains the element *baga,* already familiar from the Iranian words of Kassite times. Satarpanu, like Satareshu, contains the Assyrian transcription of the word *khshathra,* known from Old Persian as "kingdom." Ashpabarra, compounded of the word for "horse" and the verb "to bear," evidently means "the cavalryman." Doubtless the inability of the Assyrian scribe to reproduce on his clay tablet the wealth of Iranian sounds as he heard them in other names, such as Ushrai, Hardukku, and Arbaku,[28] hides from us still other Iranian elements in proper names. No member of that expedition, however, can have failed to recognize the distinctions between Caucasian and Iranian in feature, dress, and language; we may even conjecture that when the Madai, inhabitants of Media, henceforth are mentioned in Assyrian annals the scribe meant peoples of the Iranian group.

Sargon's ninth year witnessed a brief excursion into Ellipi and Media in the east.[29] A Median province on

[28] Obviously the source whence came the name Arbaces in the Ctesias list; see below, p. 176, n. 15.

[29] Lie, *op. cit.,* pp. 28 ff.; cf. *LAR,* Vol. II, §§ 23 f. The fact that *Bit Daiaukki,* formerly seen as one of the objectives of this year, was a misreading (cf. Lie, *loc. cit.,* and see Thureau-Dangin in *RA,* XXIV [1927], 75, n. 3) has been totally ignored by later authors.

the frontier of Ellipi, Bait Ili, together with other districts within the mountains, was subdued as far as
the land of the Manda. Tribute is claimed from forty-
five city lords of the Medes and from Talta of Ellipi.
The Assyrian forces may indeed have advanced beyond modern Hamadan, for cylinder inscriptions declare that they conquered from Hashmar as far as
Simash on the border of the distant eastern Medes,[30]
and Simash like Ellipi was on the Elamite frontier.

[30] Winckler, *Die Keilschrifttexte Sargons*, II, Pl. 43, l. 14; cf. *LAR*,
Vol. II, § 118; the phrase hitherto read as *adi (mâtu)ṣimaš̌patti (mâtu)ma-
dai* . . . . must be interpreted thus: *adi (mâtu)ṣimaš patti (mâtu)madai*
. . . . , "as far as the land of Simash on the border of the land of the
Medes. . . . ."

CHAPTER IX

A NEW ELAMITE KINGDOM

ALTHOUGH Elam disappeared as a great power in the twelfth century B.C., it is inconceivable that government in this land as well as in all southwestern Iran can have disintegrated completely. Some day perhaps we shall discover the names of local chieftains who maintained a semblance of power in their own districts and who appeared great to their subjects. The future may disclose to us rulers whose sovereignty centered around modern Shiraz and who extended their domain to the southeast, thus being unknown to our sources. We may even learn that when Elam again appeared as a political power it was as the result of pressure of new immigrants, possibly kinsmen of those very Iranians who were so hardily pressing into the northern Zagros, or mayhap Arameans entering the plateau from southern Babylonia. At present we are hopelessly at sea; the very name of the land is unmentioned in connected sources from about 1150 to 821 B.C. We know nothing of its internal condition even at the latter date, when Shamshi-Adad V declares that it participated against him in a battle at Daban.[1]

[1] Annals: *KB*, I, 174 ff.; cf. *LAR*, Vol. I, § 726, and discussion in Olmstead, *History of Assyria*, pp. 156 f.

Escape from this uncertainty comes only in 742 B.C. At this time, a Babylonian chronicle informs us, Huban-nugash, son of Huban-tahrah, became king of Elam.[2] Not too literally may we accept this dictum. It now appears that throughout the first part of the subsequent period there was no single kingdom of Elam, only a kingdom of Anzan and Susa. The sovereign of this empire, like the rulers of the twentieth and nineteenth centuries B.C., could attain to supreme power only step by step. Beginning perhaps as king of Susa, an individual could, through family prestige or political intrigue, eventually reach the highest office. In Babylonia the ruler of the comparatively subordinate city Susa was known as the king of Elam. This title was therefore a complete misnomer which for years puzzled historians of the lowland.

Huban-nugash was the first ruler of Susa of whom we have record; our Babylonian sources, when dealing with Elamite affairs of this time, speak only of him. His sister was wife to Huban-immena, in whom we must see the first king of this new Anzan and Susa empire. Neither ruler is mentioned in the contemporary records of Tiglathpileser III, who, besides overcoming the mountain clans north and east of

---

[2] Babylonian Chronicle B, i 9 f.; I have been able to use the translation made for the Assyrian Dictionary by the late Professor D. D. Luckenbill from the text last published in *CT*, Vol. XXXIV, Pls. 43 ff.

The name is given as "Ummanigash, son of Umbadara," in Ashurbanipal's Cylinder A, vi 52, in Streck, *Assurbanipal*, pp. 54 f.; cf. *LAR*, Vol. II, § 810.

Ashur, was likewise engaged in reducing the Aramean tribes along the east bank of the Tigris.[3] When the Assyrian Sargon became more ambitious, Huban-nugash of Susa tried his own hand at conquest.[4] Endeavoring to assist Merodach-Baladan, Sargon's enemy in Babylonia, the Elamite won a skirmish near Der, although he failed to capture the city (720 B.C.). His own death three years later brought to a temporary halt Elamite attacks on the lowland.

Successor to Huban-nugash in Susa was his nephew, Shutruk-Nahhunte II (717–699);[5] the real claim to future power of this individual lay in the fact that he was son of the great king of Anzan and Susa, Huban-immena. How long he remained in the Susa office we do not know; his own inscription advises us that when he had attained to the kingship of the realm of Anzan and Susa through the aid of his deity Inshushinak, he erected for this god a chapel.[6]

[3] Rost, *Die Keilschrifttexte Tiglat-Pilesers III*, pp. 4 ff.; cf. *LAR*, Vol. I, § 764; see Olmstead, *History of Assyria*, pp. 176 f. Nakri and Pahhaz, attacked at this time, had already been mentioned by Shilhak-Inshushinak; see above, p. 115.

[4] Lie, *The Inscriptions of Sargon II*, Part I, pp. 6 f., restored with Olmstead, *AJSL*, XLVII (1930/31), 262 f., but compared with Babylonian Chronicle B, i 33 ff. On the event cf. Olmstead, *Western Asia in the Days of Sargon of Assyria* (New York, 1908), pp. 44 f., and *History of Assyria*, p. 251.

[5] Babylonian Chronicle B, i 39 f.; in the Susa temple Ashurbanipal found a statue of Ishtar-Nanhundi, who is, of course, our king.

[6] Scheil, *Mém.*, V, 62 f. (No. 84); it is this inscription which gives to Shilhina-hamru-Lagamar and Huban-immena the title of king (see above, p. 135). Other texts of this ruler: Scheil, *Mém.*, III, 90, and V, 93 (No. 57); V, 67 f. (No. 85).

This the modern archeologist has discovered in a building over twenty-five feet square on the southeastern part of the Susa acropolis.[7]

To the reign of Shutruk-Nahhunte II must also be attributed several other inscriptions from Elamite territory. One, written on a stele found at Susa and long since ascribed to the anointing priest Shutruru, relates the erection of more than thirty statues in as many cities of the kingdom.[8] Others are found on rock reliefs far to the east of Susa near the plain now called Malamir south of the river Karun. Long before Shutruk-Nahhunte this plain had possessed an important Elamite settlement; early business documents, as well as numerous tells and ruin heaps, bespeak its onetime commercial prosperity.[9] Script, language, and representations prove that the reliefs and inscriptions of Hanni, son of Tahhihi, prince of Aiapir, also belong to the period of the neo-Elamite kingdom.[10]

One of these reliefs portrays the bearded Hanni with head swathed in a cloth similar to that worn in the same region today. A plaited tress of hair hanging to his waist is actually a pigtail; a robe descending to his knees is decorated with a band of rosettes and then with long tassels; a skirt extends to his feet. Be-

[7] De Morgan, *Mém.*, VIII, 34 f.

[8] Scheil, *Mém.*, V, 69 ff. (No. 86).   [9] See above, pp. 72 ff.

[10] König, *Geschichte Elams*, p. 34, equates "son of Tahhihi" with *ben Tahhai*, meaning a man of the nomad Tahha tribe; however, Harper, *ABL*, No. 282 (Waterman, *RCAE*, I, 194 f.), shows that the Aramean Tahha tribe did not dwell in Elam.

hind him stands his priest, Shutruru, while a warrior with his bow and musicians with their instruments show that his court was maintained in the best oriental style. The inscription, dedicated to the deities Tepti, Tirutir, Tirutur,[11] Napirshipak, Man(?), Huban, and Nahhunte, speaks of achievements of the king Shutur-Nahhunte, son of Indada, and of buildings or steles erected in Aiapir and Shilhite. This king may not be our Shutruk-Nahhunte, but his name suggests that he was a member of the same family and dynasty.[12]

The relief in another ravine represents Hanni, his wife, perhaps their children, and a second man who is probably the king. The latter wears a helmet projecting in front and covering the nape of the neck behind; his beard is long and straight. A robe reaching to his knees is belted tightly at the waist, while his feet are bare.[13]

The deeds of Shutruk-Nahhunte were not limited

[11] Or should we read Tirushak? See T. J. Meek, *Old Akkadian, Sumerian, and Cappadocian Texts from Nuzi* ("Harvard Semitic Series," Vol. X [Cambridge, Mass., 1935]), p. xiii; cf., however, the Elamite deity Tiru in *Mém.*, V, 37 (No. 75), l. 15, and in *Mém.*, XI, 21 ff. (No. 92), obv. i 9, where I do not believe that we should read *Ti-shup* (i.e., Teshup).

[12] Relief: Jéquier, *Mém.*, III, 133 ff. Text: Scheil, *Mém.*, Vol. III, Pl. 23 and pp. 102 ff. (No. 63); also published by Weissbach in his *Neue Beiträge zur Kunde der susischen Inschriften*, "Abhandlungen der K. Sächsischen Gesellschaft der Wissenschaften," phil.-hist. Klasse, XIV (1894), 742 ff. Other reliefs in this ravine show processions of men and animals; cf. Jéquier, *Mém.*, Vol. III, Pls. 27–29.

[13] Jéquier, *Mém.*, Vol. III, Pls. 26 and 32*b*. Text: Scheil, *Mém.*, III, 108 ff. (No. 64).

to architectural monuments or self-extolling inscriptions. Like his predecessor he, too, supported Merodach-Baladan in Babylon, a policy that appeared none too wise when Sargon captured Dur Athara, scarcely sixty miles from Susa, and made it the capital of a new province.[14] Consequently the Elamite proceeded to the hill country east of Der; his subsequent loss of a few border fortresses east of the Tigris in the vicinity of Der was more than compensated by the repulse of an Assyrian attack on Bit Imbi in the land Rashi eastward in the mountains.[15] Campaigning in this region was, even for Sargon, too difficult, and success came only when his cohorts were able to advance over well-kept trails. Such a road—the one leading from Baghdad to Hamadan—favored his troops in 708 B.C., when the well subsidized ruler of Ellipi, Talta, departed this life. In the fratricidal war which followed, one son, Nibe, sought the aid of Shutruk-Nahhunte, who provided forty-five hundred bowmen; the other, a son by an Iranian wife, if we may trust his name, Ishpabara, appealed more successfully to Assyria, which established him on the throne.[16]

[14] Lie, *op. cit.*, pp. 42 ff. On the location of the city cf. Streck in *MVAG*, XI, Heft 3 (1906), 18 f., where the name is read *Dûr-Abiḥara;* Olmstead, *Western Asia in the Days of Sargon of Assyria*, p. 130, n. 4.

[15] Lie, *op. cit.*, pp. 50 ff. A location of Bit Imbi in the Dasht-i-Gawr with Billerbeck, *Das Sandschak Suleimania*, pp. 123 f., seems too far north to meet the geographical requirements.

[16] Lie, *op. cit.*, pp. 72–75. Cf. Olmstead, *History of Assyria*, p. 249; Harper, *ABL*, Nos. 159–61 and 174 (Waterman, *RCAE*, I, 108–11 and 116–19); and *LAR*, II, § 65.

Shutruk-Nahhunte was far from oppressed by these setbacks, although his next move likewise resulted in failure. He brought Merodach-Baladan back from an enforced retreat in the swamplands, added to his forces a large number of Elamite bowmen and cavalry under the leadership of Imbappa, Tannanu, and ten division commanders, and obtained for the Babylonian a brief reign. Unfortunately, a number of the Elamite troops were put to rout when Sennacherib attacked Kutha in 702, while the main body, deserted by its allies when the Assyrians stormed Kish, was severely crippled and lost its baggage.[17]

Following up his success, Sennacherib advanced along the Kirmanshah road against the Iasubigallai and the remnants of the Kassites, who, he declares, had not been submissive to the kings his fathers.[18] He could not have progressed deeply into the mountains, however, for shortly afterward Ellipi became restless. The governor in Harhar declared that matters were quiet enough in his own immediate region, but that Ishpabara on the south was definitely on the warpath. Further, he reported, Uaksatar or Cyaxares in the bottom lands of the Shehrizor, who had offered gifts to Assyria in Sargon's eighth year, was heading a conspiracy against the prefect of a city within the

[17] Text in Sidney Smith, *The First Campaign of Sennacherib* (London, 1921), ll. 5–27; see now Luckenbill, *Annals of Sennacherib* (OIP, Vol. II), pp. 48 ff., and cf. *LAR*, Vol. II, §§ 257–59.

[18] Bellino Cylinder, ll. 20–26; see now Luckenbill, *Annals of Sennacherib*, pp. 58 f., and cf. *LAR*, Vol. II, §§ 277 f.

Harhar province.[19] In righteous anger against the unfaithful Ellipi, Sennacherib raided their royal residences Marubishti and Akkuddu and annexed a part of the land to Harhar. The fate of Uaksatar remains unknown, although tribute from the Medes is claimed as a result of this expedition and he may have recognized Assyrian suzerainty.[20]

In a monarchy, defeat in battle is often the signal for revolution at home. Shutruk-Nahhunte's throne may already have been insecure as a result of his reverses abroad. When, in 700, his ally Merodach-Baladan was forced to flee Babylon for the Elamite city Nagitu on the Persian Gulf, his overthrow was certain. Our Babylonian sources tell us that the new "king of Elam" was Hallushu, whom we know as Hallushu-Inshushinak (699–693), brother of the first sovereign of Susa, Huban-nugash, and son of Huban-tahrah.[21]

This sovereign bided his time five years. Then, when the Assyrian troops were searching for Merodach-Baladan at the mouth of the Ulai River among the Elamite districts of Nagitu, Hilmu, Pillatu, and

[19] Harper, *ABL*, No. 645; Waterman, *RCAE*, I, 448 f.

[20] Bellino Cylinder, ll. 27–33; cf. Luckenbill, *Annals of Sennacherib*, pp. 59 f., and *LAR*, Vol. II, §§ 279–82.

[21] See his inscription published by Scheil, *Mém.*, III, 100 f., and V, 93 f. (No. 62). Cf. also Babylonian Chronicle B, ii 32–34. The name cannot be read *Hallutush;* the last sign is usually *šu*, but once it is *su* (Streck, *Assurbanipal*, pp. 214 ff., iii 6), while Ashurbanipal, who discovered his statue in the Susa temple, writes his name *Hallusi* (Cyl. A, vi 54; cf. Streck, *op. cit.*, pp. 54 f.; *LAR*, Vol. II, § 810).

Hupapanu (694 B.C.), he determined on a bold course. Moving straight against Sippar in the central part of the lowland, he massacred its inhabitants and sent Sennacherib's own son, Babylon's sovereign, to Elam for a sure execution. On the throne he placed Nergal-ushezib, who added to the conquests the territory from Nippur to Uruk—practically all of Babylonia.[22]

These were impressive achievements; and Hallu-shu-Inshushinak could well claim to be the empire's expander, as he does when, as the beloved servant of Huban and Inshushinak, he constructs for the Lord of Susa a sacred room lined inside and out with glazed brick.[23] Unfortunately, his conquests could not be sustained. In retaliation for the loss of his son, Sennacherib put to death the son of the Elamite, and his army in the south took Uruk from Nergal-ushezib. The Elamites withdrew, and Nergal-ushezib followed suit, but in a renewed attack was himself captured by the Assyrians at Nippur. Hallushu-Inshushinak had not, however, returned to his homeland soon enough. His disappointed subjects revolted and dethroned him late in 693 B.C.[24]

Kudur-Nahhunte (693–692) is called the new king of Elam in the Babylonian sources; his actual relationship to the kingdom of Anzan and Susa as to his

[22] Babylonian Chronicle B, ii 35–46.

[23] Cf. Jéquier, *Mém.*, I, 128; for the text see n. 21.

[24] Babylonian Chronicle B, ii 47—iii 9. Annals: for convenience see Luckenbill, *Annals of Sennacherib*, pp. 38 f., 73 ff., and 89 f.; cf. *LAR*, Vol. II, §§ 246 f., 318–21, and 354. Cf. Olmstead, *History of Assyria*, pp. 290–92.

predecessors is completely unknown. It is likely that his capital was neither Anzan nor Susa but Madaktu, a city in the upper Karkhah River valley.[25]

Sennacherib at once realized the opportunity offered by the change in Elamite rulers. If with Ninevite troops he struck from the north into Rashi and the Elamite possessions east of Der, their army would be prevented from re-entering the plains of Babylonia; Mushezib-Marduk, whom the Elamites had substituted for the decapitated Nergal-ushezib, would be left without an ally; and the beleaguered Assyrian troops in the south could return to Assyria in all safety. The plan was wisely conceived and boldly executed. Rashi was ravaged, Bit Imbi captured, and the passes which led to Bit Bunakki and Tell Humbi on the headwaters of the Karkhah were carried. Madaktu was endangered, and Kudur-Nahhunte withdrew deep into the mountains to Hidalu, probably to be located on the modern Karun River.[26] The Elamite need not thus have retreated, since the

[25] A location of Madaktu at the ruins near Derre-i-Shahr in the Saimarreh plain on the Karkhah River fits the geographical requirements better than does Oppert's location on the Ab-i-Diz north of Dizful, or Billerbeck's at Kalat-i-Raza just northwest of Susa. For the latter views see Billerbeck, *Susa* (Leipzig, 1893), pp. 70–72; Streck, *Assurbanipal*, p. 44, n. 2.

[26] For location cf. Streck, *op. cit.*, p. 324, n. 3; Billerbeck, *Susa*, p. 72. The city is named in the Achaemenian documents from Susa in *Mém.*, Vol. IX, Nos. 65 and 238. Billerbeck's location at Diz-Malkan on the middle Karun is on the direct road between Dizful and Isfahan, only seventy miles in a straight line from Susa and forty miles from Malamir. This site would be a natural retreat for Elamite kings fleeing Madaktu or Susa.

January torrents made it impossible for Assyrian troops to reach Madaktu and Sennacherib was compelled to order a retreat. His tactics had nevertheless proved highly successful. The Assyrians in southern Babylonia returned home safely, and a palace revolution cost Kudur-Nahhunte his throne and life after but ten months of rule.[27]

No trifler was his brother and successor, a second Huban-immena (692–688), known to Assyrians as Umman-menanu. To the support of Mushezib-Marduk in Babylon he mustered a mighty army. It comprised forces of Anzan, of which he must have been sovereign; of Parsu(m)ash, not the Assyrian province west of Lake Urmia but the district known to Shamshi-Adad V as Parsamash and probably already in the hands of the Persian Achaemenes; of Ellipi, now largely beyond Assyrian influence; and of a score of Aramean tribes east of the Tigris or bordering on the Persian Gulf. Against this formidable army Sennacherib dared offer resistance only when it had advanced to Halule on the Tigris in northern Babylonia. The Assyrian annals recite a magnificent paean of victory; the sober Babylonian chronicle indicates that the affair ended in a drawn battle.[28]

Again calamity fell upon the Elamites, for in April of 689 the leading spirit of the confederacy, Huban-

[27] Babylonian Chronicle B, iii 9–15. Annals: for convenience see Luckenbill, *Annals of Sennacherib*, pp. 39 ff., 88 f., and 90 f.; cf. *LAR*, Vol. II, §§ 248–51, 351, and 355.

[28] Luckenbill, *Annals of Sennacherib*, pp. 41 ff.; cf. *LAR*, Vol. II, §§ 252–54; Babylonian Chronicle B, iii 16–18.

immena, suffered a stroke of paralysis. Deprived of his aid, Babylonian offense degenerated to a weak defense, and in November Sennacherib recaptured Babylon. By the following March Huban-immena was dead,[29] and with him died also the Elamite hopes of additional conquest in Babylonia. Our sources for the eight-year reign of his successor, Huban-haltash[30] I (688–681), are completely silent.

According to Babylonian sources, a second Huban-haltash (681–675) ascended the throne "in Elam" upon the death of the first. In the eyes of Esarhaddon the new sovereign was pro-Assyrian, for he put to death a fugitive son of Merodach-Baladan. Thereupon the refugee's brother, Naid-Marduk, found it expedient to desert Elam and become an Assyrian ally; in reward he was intrusted with the administration of the Sealands.[31]

According to Elamite or at least Susian sources, however, the successor to Huban-haltash I was Shilhak-Inshushinak II, son of Ummanunu, that is, a son of that Huban-immena who had halted Sennacherib at Halule. In Susa this ruler erected a temple to Dilbat, the "lady of the city," on the bronze door sockets of which he wrote his Elamite inscription.[32] It is cer-

[29] Babylonian Chronicle B, iii 19–27.

[30] In Akkadian, Humba-haldashu and later Umman-aldash.

[31] Babylonian Chronicle B, iii 39 ff.; R. C. Thompson, *The Prisms of Esarhaddon and Ashurbanipal* (London, 1931), p. 15.

[32] Scheil, *Mém.*, XI, 78 (No. 101); cf. Jéquier, *Mém.*, VII, 38. In *Mém.*, I, 127, Jéquier describes a fragmentary unpublished stele of this ruler, and in *Mém.*, I, 131, some unpublished bricks with inscriptions.

tain that hereafter Assyria befriended the successors of Huban-haltash II and opposed the family of Shil-hak-Inshushinak, whom we may consider the legitimate Elamite sovereign. In the light of these and subsequent facts, it is clear that henceforth there was no single ruler of great importance in Elam. On the contrary, there were many kings, rulers in Susa, in Madaktu, in Hidalu, and probably in other cities as well. The great days of Elam as an international power were gone. Internecine warfare was rampant, and Assyria wisely played one sovereign off against another.[33]

The failure of Esarhaddon's first Egyptian campaign may have led Huban-haltash II to throw in his lot with the ruler of Susa. Doubtless from the vicinity of Bit Imbi and Der, Elamite troops fell upon Sippar, scarcely twenty-five miles from Babylon.[34] In retaliation Esarhaddon instigated a plot which replaced Huban-haltash by his brother Urtaki (675–663),[35] of whose loyalty he was nevertheless suspicious.[36] Eventually his fears were allayed, and the official archives at Nineveh received a copy of his letter to Urtaki, which is as full of innocuous phrases as is the formal conversation of one diplomat with another in our own

[33] Cf. König, *Geschichte Elams*, pp. 19 ff.

[34] Babylonian Chronicle B, iv 9 ff.

[35] Esarhaddon Chronicle, obv. 16–18, in Sidney Smith, *Babylonian Historical Texts* (London, 1924), pp. 12 ff.

[36] Omen query in Knudtzon, *Gebete*, No. 76.

day.[37] It was a striking tribute to the friendly relations between the two sovereigns that the statues of Ishtar and other gods, long since captive in Elam, were returned, we presume voluntarily, to their homes in Babylonia in 672 B.C.[38] To and from Elam went dispatches of private individuals and public officials. A certain Pahuri, possibly an ambassador of Urtaki at the Assyrian court, received many letters written in his native Elamite, and some of these also made their way into the royal archives.[39] Even Susa, though not controlled by Urtaki, felt the influence of this free intercourse. A prism of Esarhaddon, shortly after it was composed in 673 B.C., found its way into the city,[40] and Assyrian omen texts were there copied in Akkadian and translated into the native tongue.[41] After 672, although the Elamite was often encouraged to violate his oaths of friendship,[42] peace between Urtaki and the Assyrian continued unbroken throughout the remaining lifetime of Esarhaddon.

[37] Harper, *ABL*, No. 918; cf. Waterman, *RCAE*, II, 138 f.

[38] Babylonian Chronicle B, iv 17 ff.; Esarhaddon Chronicle, obv. 21–23.

[39] Weissbach, "Susische Thontäfelchen," *BA*, IV (1902), 168–201; additional notes by Bork in *BA*, V (1906), 401–4. None of the letters is dated, and their translation is exceedingly difficult.

[40] Scheil, *Mém.*, XIV, 36 ff.

[41] Scheil, *Mém.*, XIV, 49 ff.; "Déchiffrement d'un document anzanite relatif aux présages," *RA*, XIV (1917), 29 ff.

[42] Harper, *ABL*, No. 328; cf. Waterman, *RCAE*, I, 226 ff.

CHAPTER X

MEDIAN AND PERSIAN CHIEFTAINS

B Y THE beginning of the seventh century B.C. strange faces began to appear in Iran. Striking out from their "Cimmerian darkness" north of the Caucasus, the Gimirrai, as the Assyrians knew them, poured through the passes to the south. Some turned definitely westward, after striking obliquely the Haldian kingdom, and entered the Anatolian plateau. Others, together with or followed by Scythians or Ishguzai, passed to the east of Haldia and descended into the valleys of Iran. These were not harmless nomads seeking pasturage for their peaceful flocks. They were hard-riding, horse-borne robbers bent on plunder, unlettered, uncouth, but fearfully capable.

The land of the Manneans, south and southeast of Lake Urmia, was the first halting-place for those who entered Iran. Esarhaddon of Assyria (681–668) knew that they had wrested from his control the city of Dur Enlil in this land and that Sharru Iqbi was in grave danger of falling into their hands.[1] He knew also that his own troops, sent to punish the Mannean Ahsheri for hostile acts, were threatened by these

[1] Knudtzon, *Gebete*, Nos. 19 f. and 16.

same Cimmerians, from whom no quarter could be expected.[2] Publicly he maintained that he scattered the Manneans and killed their ally, Ishpakaia the Scythian;[3] but years later his own son, in whose reign Ahsheri was still a rebel, informs us that the Mannean had seized Sharru Iqbi in the days of his father. Assyrian administration of the land was therefore at an end.

It was a serious loss. From this region of northwest Iran south to the Nisaean plain below Bisitun, the Zagros had long been noted for its horses; the plain in front of modern Hamadan was no less famous. Far to the east within the territory of the distant Medes lay the land known in later times as the Choara, also famed for its riding horses, cattle, flocks, and camels. Hitherto the country of the Manneans with its fertile, well-watered valleys had furnished a large number of the horses and draft animals used by the Assyrian army. That army, to maintain its mobility and to oppose with success the horse-riding Scythians and Cimmerians, required these animals. If the Mannean territory could no longer supply them, another region must be raided. This could be accomplished only by fast-riding cavalrymen penetrating ever more deeply into unknown terrain, hastily rounding up whatever animals could be found, and driving them with all

[2] *Ibid.*, No. 24.

[3] R. C. Thompson, *The Prisms of Esarhaddon and Ashurbanipal*, p. 19.

dispatch to Assyrian soil. There could be no attempt at conquest, and no provincial organization need therefore be set up. Speed alone was the essential item, horses and draft animals the sole object.

We learn of such undertakings through the liver omen queries which Esarhaddon directed to the sun-god. Behind these texts, inscribed at the very moment when success or failure was imminent, lies the stark reality of fear and danger. Medes, Scythians, and Cimmerians must all be considered.

One series of raids set out from Bit Kari for Media.[4] Although we are ignorant concerning the exact destinations, it is possible that only the Nisaean and Hamadan plains were first entered. Farther and farther afield the attempt to procure mounts led the daring Assyrians. Finally it was determined to enter that fabulous region, the Choara, flanked by the Salt Desert and the snow-capped Demavend. We hear that cavalrymen have gone to gather horses from the land Kuk Kuma and the city Ramadani and are planning to advance as far as Arri, the Choara, although Cimmerians and Manneans are expected to interfere.[5] We discover that raiders who have advanced through a city Antarpati, known as Andirpattianu to Sargon, hope to arrive at Patush Arri ("toward the Choara") on the edge of the Salt Desert, although the chieftain

---

[4] Knudtzon, *Gebete*, Nos. 30 f.; Klauber, *Texte*, Nos. 19 f.

[5] Klauber, *Texte*, No. 22.

Eparna or the people of Saparda may prove trouble-some.[6]

Such an undertaking could not be left unnoticed in the royal inscriptions which were written by 673 B.C. The words which describe it, pardonably boastful, may be thus paraphrased:

As to the land Patush Arri[7] on the edge of the Salt Desert within the land of distant Medes, bordered by Mount Bikni (the Demavend), the mountain of lapis lazuli, whose soil none of the kings my fathers had trod, from it I carried off the powerful city lords Shidir-parna (Chithrafarna or Tissaphernes) and Eparna together with their riding horses, cattle, flocks, and camels.[8]

We do not know how literally this may be interpreted. The raid whose outcome the king viewed so dubiously in the liver omen was doubtless the actual reason for the preparation of this part of the prism inscription, but even such a raid was noteworthy. No Assyrian had ever advanced farther into Iran, or indeed as far.

In the same connection the royal texts declare that three Median city chieftains voluntarily presented themselves at Nineveh and begged to be reinstalled in their own rebellious cities. These were Uppis of Partakka,[9] Zanasana of Partukka, and Ramateia of

[6] *Ibid.*, No. 21.

[7] The Pateischoreis of Strabo *Geogr.* XV. iii. 1. Cf. Spiegel in *ZDMG*, XXXII (1878), 717; P. Haupt in *JAOS*, XLIV (1924), 158; Herzfeld in *AMI*, VII (1934), 26–28.

[8] R. C. Thompson, *op. cit.*, p. 21.

[9] Against the usual equation of this name with Greek Paraetacene cf. Herzfeld in *AMI*, VII (1934), 16 and 28.

Uraka Zabarna. Again we are unable to judge the accuracy of the claim that these were restored to their cities with Assyrian help and subjected to taxes imposed by Assyrian governors.[10] If it is true, as one scholar has suggested, that the cities may be connected with the lands Parthia and Hyrcania,[11] a fairly accurate knowledge of geography must be presumed on the part of the Assyrian writer, though this, too, could have been obtained on such an ambitious raid as has already been described.

Toward the last years of his reign Esarhaddon determined to recapture the onetime province of the Manneans. As we have already learned, the Cimmerians had occupied this territory in the days of his father; and although they now declared that the land belonged to Assyria, another informant of the king proclaimed this an utter misstatement of fact. His letter to Esarhaddon is our only source, and even it gives expression to fear that the undertaking may prove unsuccessful. To judge from the next Assyrian ruler's difficulties with the land of the Manneans, his fear was altogether justified.[12]

The fact, however, that Assyrian raids into territories as far distant as the Choara could even be contemplated by the year 673 B.C. automatically precludes the existence of a powerful Median kingdom,

[10] R. C. Thompson, *op. cit.*, p. 21.

[11] Herzfeld in *AMI*, VII (1934), 28 f.

[12] Harper, *ABL*, No. 1237; cf. Waterman, *RCAE*, II, 358 ff.

such as is described by Herodotus, at that date. Since the "Father of History" only too often has been proved correct where his critics thought him wrong, we might well examine what this fifth-century Greek has to relate, remembering that he obtained much of his information about Median origins from the descendants of a Mede, Harpagus.

Once upon a time, says Herodotus,[13] when the Medes were living scattered in villages, there was among them an upright chieftain, Deioces, son of Phraortes. Having become an arbitrator in his own locality, widely recognized for his upright judgments, his services were in great demand throughout other parts of the land. Eventually he found that his duties were too onerous and troublesome, whereupon he refused to serve any longer in this capacity. The Medes then summoned an assembly and offered him the kingship. Once in power, Deioces forced his subjects to build Ecbatana, the modern Hamadan, with seven walls circumscribed about one another. Strict in the features which characterize the "Great King," Deioces was also severe but equitable in administration, so that the six great Median tribes[14] willingly accepted his domination. His reign of fifty-three years was followed by the twenty-two-year rule of his son, Phraortes, who first made the Persians subject to the

[13] i. 95 ff.

[14] The names of these tribes are successfully disposed of by König, *Älteste Geschichte*, p. 6.

Medes and who ended his life in a premature attack on the Assyrians. Phraortes' son, Cyaxares, had barely ascended the throne when Scythians overthrew his kingdom; for twenty-eight years these rode around the country, plundering and committing violence. Finally Cyaxares regained control of Iran, brought to an end the kingdom of Assyria, and boasted a reign of forty years before he yielded to his son Astyages. The son ruled thirty-five years and then was overcome by Cyrus the Persian in 550 B.C.[15]

We have already recognized Deioces in the Mannean Daiaukku deported by Sargon of Assyria in 715 B.C. The kingdom ascribed to him by Herodotus, whose chronology would assign Deioces to the years 728–675 B.C., did not, therefore, exist. The accuracy with which the Greek renders the names of Deioces and his successors should, however, warn us not to

[15] The *terminus ad quem* of Median history is established by the Nabunaid–Cyrus Chronicle.

The king list of Ctesias (ed. Müller, pp. 41 ff., from Diodorus Siculus *History* ii. 32 ff.), is but a curious amplification of that in the account of Herodotus. This physician-historian at the court of Artaxerxes II, where the "royal parchments" were at his disposal, merely doubled the number of kings given by Herodotus. Though his names are genuinely Iranian, his history is practically without any foundation; for a critical discussion see Prášek, *Geschichte*, I, 105 ff. The following table (see Rawlinson, *The Seven Great Monarchies* [New York, 1885], II, 85 and 571) indicates the Cnidian's procedure:

HERODOTUS			CTESIAS				
1. Anarchy	35 years		1. Arbaces	28 years		3. Sosarmus	30 years
2. Deioces	53		2. Maudaces	50		4. Artycas	50
3. Phraortes	22		5. Arbianes	22		7. Artynes	22
4. Scythians	28						
5. Cyaxares	40		6. Artaeus	40		8. Astibaras	40
6. Astyages	35		9. Aspandas	38			

dispose of his other data too lightly. The unfortunate Daiaukku may actually have been pictured to successive generations of Medes as the founder of their dynasty. Nevertheless, we enter actual history only with the alleged accession of his son, Phraortes, whose dates were known to Herodotus as 675–653 B.C.

Over a century and a half later, when Darius the Great was striving so diligently to win the Persian throne, a certain Phraortes declared that his real name was Khshathrita and that he was of the family of Cyaxares.[16] Here, then, is the key to the riddle of the Herodotean Phraortes: his name likewise was Khshathrita. Whether the latter was merely his throne name[17] or whether Herodotus knew that he too, like the contemporary of Darius, was actually named Phraortes,[18] need not concern us. We have, however, no occasion to doubt that his active years began about 675 B.C., especially when we meet him in the liver omen queries dating from the last years of Esarhaddon under an Assyrianized name form, Kashtariti.[19]

When we first meet Kashtariti, whom we shall henceforth designate as Khshathrita, he is not king of Media. Instead, he is the chieftain of the city Kar

---

[16] Bisitun inscription of Darius, ii 14 ff.; cf. Weissbach, *Die Keilinschriften der Achämeniden* (Leipzig, 1911), pp. 28 f.

[17] So Prášek, *Geschichte*, I, 140.

[18] So König, *Älteste Geschichte*, pp. 29 f.

[19] So a keen deduction of König, *ibid.*

Kashshi, the name of which betrays its location in the old Kassite homeland in the central Zagros. The Herodotean story of the founding of the Median capital at Ecbatana[20] is still in the future.

The liver omen queries describe his activities rather fully. We find him and his Median troops attacking the cities Karibti and Ushishi,[21] or threatening to intercept Assyrian raiders and messengers who have been sent into Media.[22] We discover that he is endeavoring to entice the Median city chieftain Mami-ti-arshu into plotting against Ashur[23] or joining with Dusanni of Saparda, a land long since conquered by Sargon and assigned to the Harhar province, in an attempt to plunder the cities Sandu and Kilman.[24] Finally, he stands revealed as the leader of a coalition of Medes, Cimmerians, and Manneans who are threatening to undermine the entire Assyrian provincial administration in the Zagros. Unfortunately, the texts which picture these events are fragmentary in the extreme,[25] but one well-preserved tablet yields the name of the city Kishassu, the Kishesim which

[20] In Old Persian, Hangmatana, usually interpreted as "place of assembly." Professor A. Poebel suggests that the name may rather mean something like "fortress(?) of the Medes."

[21] Klauber, *Texte*, No. 1; Knudtzon, *Gebete*, No. 6.

[22] Klauber, *Texte*, Nos. 3, 12–14; Knudtzon, *Gebete*, No. 5.

[23] Knudtzon, *Gebete*, No. 2.

[24] Klauber, *Texte*, Nos. 4 and 7.

[25] *Ibid.*, No. 8; cf. also Nos. 5 and 13; Knudtzon, *Gebete*, No. 4.

Sargon conquered in 716 B.C.[26] Doubt the kingship of Khshathrita as we may, in the light of these facts we cannot question the important rôle he played within the Zagros during the latter years of Esarhaddon, the very date which the chronology of Herodotus gives to Phraortes.

Herodotus likewise declares that Phraortes was the first Mede to bring the Persians into subjection. This statement also may be actual history, but we must first inquire into the facts concerning these same Persians. Who were they and whence did they come?

As early as 815 B.C. Indo-Iranians from Parsua, west of Lake Urmia, had descended the valleys of the Zagros toward Elam. The wanderers found a new home to the northeast of Susa not far from the Elamite land Anzan; to their new habitat they gave the name Parsamash or Parsumash in memory of the land they had left behind. By 700 their leader was Hakhamanish or Achaemenes, whom the later Persian monarchs claimed as eponymous ancestor. Presumably, he and his followers participated with Elam in the defeat of Sennacherib at Halule in 692, for the Assyrian reports that Parsu(m)ash and Anzan were among his foes.[27]

Some years later, perhaps about 675 B.C., Achaemenes yielded to his son Chishpish or Teispes. Promptly the Persian descended upon Anzan, where the influence of the Elamite kings had waned and

[26] Knudtzon, *Gebete*, No. 1.   [27] See above, p. 166.

to which Shilhak-Inshushinak II had not even laid claim. Henceforth Teispes could bear the title "king of the city Anshan," a variant spelling of the name. Had he looked about him he would have realized that danger to his newly won kingdom could scarcely come from Elam, for even Esarhaddon in Assyria knew that the Mede Khshathrita with his Cimmerian allies was far more to be feared. This coalition threatened the city Sissirtu on the border of Ellipi in the Harhar province.[28] Esarhaddon was concerned about his own territory Bit Hamban at the junction of the modern Alwand and Diyala Rivers, almost in Babylonia; he likewise knew that the Median forces, supplemented by Cimmerian and Scythian troops, were descending upon Parsumash to the southeast of Bit Hamban.[29] In the light of Herodotus' declaration that Phraortes first subdued the Persians, we might well assume that the statements of the Greek and of Esarhaddon were based on fact, and that Khshathrita about 670 B.C. reduced Teispes to the status of a vassal king.

Though successful in this direction, the Mede had still other territories of Iran to conquer before he could be declared undisputed master of the plateau. Years earlier he himself had led an attack on Sharru Iqbi in the Mannean land, but since that time a new wave of Cimmerians and Scythians had occupied this region. Under the leadership of Ahsheri the Man-

---

[28] Knudtzon, *Gebete*, No. 72.
[29] Klauber, *Texte*, No. 38; cf. *JAOS*, LII (1932), 304.

neans likewise had begun by 660 B.C. to trouble Ashurbanipal, who determined on their subjection. Before the latter's rapidly moving forces Ahsheri deserted his capital, Izertu, for Atrana and left Sharru Iqbi and other cities to the mercy of the invaders. A part of the land was garrisoned with Assyrian troops and reorganized as a province. The unfortunate Ahsheri was immediately murdered by disgruntled subjects and a pro-Assyrian ruler found in his son Ualli;[30] henceforth the Manneans were allies of Assyria against the Medes, and Khshathrita found himself debarred from their country.

While pursuing Ahsheri, Ashurbanipal appears to have entered Median territory.[31] A city chieftain, Biris-hatri, with his two sons, was captured and deported to Nineveh, a number of the near-by cities were wasted, and the power of Assyria was greatly enhanced.

Thus defied, Khshathrita may himself have decided to attack Assyria, as Herodotus relates. If this were indeed so, his ambitions far exceeded his capability as a warrior. Although no inscriptional evidence records such a blunder, the event is not in itself improbable. His death, which Herodotus would date to 653 B.C., may well have occurred as he was attacking an Assyrian border city.

[30] Cf. Harper, *ABL*, No. 1109 (Waterman, *RCAE*, II, 272 f.); Piepkorn, *Ashurbanipal*, I, 50–55.

[31] So, if *mat-a-a* be interpreted as (*mâtu*)*Mad-a-a;* the account is in Cylinder B, recently edited by Piepkorn, *Ashurbanipal*, I, 56 f.

Carefully his followers entombed his body in one of the rock-hewn graves still discernible in the mountains he had known so well. One tomb is carved from the rock in which Anubanini, king of Lullubium, had set his relief, just off the main road leading from Iran to Babylonia. Others are located near Bisitun or in the northern part of the Shehrizor or still farther north, just south of Lake Urmia.[32] Today we may be unable to decide which of these tombs is that of Khshathrita, but all appear to be pre-Achaemenian in date and may with great probability be attributed to early Median rulers.

The son of Khshathrita, Uvakhshatra or Cyaxares, was heir apparent and, had all gone well, would doubtless have succeeded to the leadership. But Scythians, whom we have already had occasion to meet within Iran, had not been sufficiently taken into consideration. Did they now turn against their erstwhile Median compatriots and prevent the accession of Cyaxares, as Herodotus tells us? The Greek's tale of Scythian devastations and plunderings may well be true; their twenty-eight-year domination of Iran (653–625), which a true Mede would almost believe to be "all of Western Asia," may therefore be historical fact.

Although we know only too little of their adminis-

---

[32] E. Herzfeld, *Am Tor von Asien* (Berlin, 1920), pp. 6–16; C. J. Edmonds, "A Tomb in Kurdistan," *Iraq*, I (1934), 190 f. A second tomb described by Edmonds, *ibid.*, pp. 185–89, is later in date.

tration, we are well informed concerning the weapons they carried and the trappings with which they equipped their horses; for the period of the Scythians and Cimmerians was roughly contemporaneous with that of the manufacture of many of the so-called "Luristan bronzes," whose rediscovery has lately challenged the attention of the artistic world.

Specimens of Babylonian workmanship had, from the dawn of history, found their way into the Zagros and Iran, there to be imitated and copied. As early as the dynasty of Agade a bronze bowl with the name of Sharkalisharri and a spear point with the legend of his contemporary *ishakku* of Susa, Puzur-Inshushinak, had reached the Zagros. Through the Third Dynasty of Ur and the reigns of Larsa and Isin, import pieces were still highly prized in the mountains, where they set the tradition for such objects and initiated a craft of bronze manufacture which continued uninterruptedly throughout the Kassite period. This native work was, however, decidedly inferior to that of the objects brought by the invaders from beyond the Caucasus in the early years of the first millennium. At that time bits for the horses and decorations for the harness, practical and votive handles for maces, and short swords with riveted grips were manufactured with great artistic and technical skill. For motives and techniques their makers were indebted to the older cultures of Babylonia and Elam, to the new world of Assyria, and, most of all, to the northern and

possibly Nordic elements from the Caucasian, Trans-
caucasian, and Transcaspian regions. The manufacture of the "Luristan bronzes," as can easily be
proved by those bearing names of kings of the Second
Isin Dynasty, was flourishing by 1000 b.c.; parallels
with objects from the north and west prove that the
technique lasted well into Achaemenian times. But
it was the period of the northern Cimmerian and
Scythian invaders which saw the highest skill of the
Iranian bronze-workers.[33]

[33] Cf. André Godard, *Les Bronzes du Luristan* ("Ars Asiatica," Vol.
XVII); R. Dussaud is preparing an elaborate study for the forthcoming
survey of Persian art. Cf. also A. U. Pope in *Illustrated London News*,
October 22, 1932, pp. 613–15; for the inscriptions see *ibid.*, October 29,
1932, pp. 666 f., and Weidner in *AOF*, VIII (1932/33), 258 f.

CHAPTER XI

THE ECLIPSE OF ELAM

TO AN Elamite living in the year 668 B.C. the division of one empire into two kingdoms, with Shamash-shum-ukin in Babylon and Ashurbanipal in Assyria, could only be interpreted as a confession of inner weakness. Consequently Urtaki, the ruler of a portion of Elam, though pro-Assyrian in his earlier years, may now have attempted to test the strength of this divided political entity on his west. Perhaps he instigated the ill-starred venture of Tandaia, a village chieftain of Kirbit, who plundered Iamutbal in the vicinity of Der.[1] A year or two later the crown prince of Elam, Huban-nugash, son of Urtaki, was mightily feared in Babylonia; this we learn from no less a personage than Shamash-shum-ukin himself.[2] It was Urtaki, however, who inspired Ashur-

[1] Babylonian Chronicle B, iv 37; Esarhaddon Chronicle, rev. 15. For the Ashurbanipal inscriptions cf. Piepkorn, *Ashurbanipal*, I, 14 ff. and 48 f.; for references to the later prisms see Streck, *Assurbanipal*, p. 791. Hereafter only the earliest reference to events mentioned in the texts of Ashurbanipal will be cited, for this is always closer to the truth; cf. Olmstead, *Assyrian Historiography*, pp. 53–59.

[2] Harper, *ABL*, No. 1385; cf. Waterman, *RCAE*, II, 466 ff. The attempt to fit letters from the royal archives into the historical picture starts with Olmstead, *History of Assyria*, pp. 431–88; cf. also the brief study of J. Schawe, "Untersuchung der Elambriefe aus dem Archiv Assurbanipals" (Inaug.-Diss., Berlin, 1927).

banipal's ire. The events leading to the outbreak of hostilities took the following course.

An Elamite general with the good Babylonian name Marduk-shum-ibni formed a conspiracy against Ashurbanipal which included a high official of Assyria and a chieftain of the Aramean tribe of the Gambuli. Ashurbanipal claimed that he himself was not hostile to Urtaki, whom he had befriended in a time of famine, but that the latter had been duped by the lies of his subordinates.[3]

This may have been close to the truth; but doubtless it would be more accurate to state that Urtaki, like his brother before him, had now come under the influence of another king of Elam, the ruler of Susa. In his brother's time this sovereign had been Shilhak-Inshushinak II; a son of the latter, Tepti-Huban-Inshushinak (*ca.* 663–653), now sat on the throne. To cement his alliance with Urtaki, a diplomatic marriage was arranged; and henceforth Te-Umman, as the Assyrians knew him, was the "brother" of Urtaki.[4] In connection with Urtaki's defection from the Assyrian cause Tepti-Huban urged the inhabitants of the Sealands to desert their elderly pro-Assyrian ruler, Naid-Marduk, established there in Esarhaddon's time, for one with Elamite leanings. Loyally

[3] Piepkorn, *Ashurbanipal*, I, 56 ff.; cf. Harper, *ABL*, No. 295 (Waterman, *RCAE*, I, 204 ff.), which recounts the Assyrian's favors to Elam.

[4] So in Harper, *ABL*, No. 576 (Waterman, *RCAE*, I, 408 ff.). The Te-Umman, bowman of the Hallalla⁾ (name supplied from Harper, *ABL*, No. 520 obv. 15), of the relief inscription in Streck, *Assurbanipal*, pp. 334 f., belongs to the time of Tammaritu.

the Sealanders refused;[5] in retaliation, one of their bridges was seized and burned,[6] and the Elamite became more insistent after Naid-Marduk's death. Already, he declared, the Chaldean tribes of the Targibatu, Nahal, Dutai, and Bananu had accepted Elamite rule, and they should prepare to do likewise.[7] This was an ultimatum, and subsequent events proved that it was not in vain. Together with Urtaki he conceived a bold attack. Urtaki was to enter Babylonia and support the rebel Gambuli chieftain Bel-iqisha; Tepti-Huban himself was to send Elamite troops to recover the Sealands.[8]

Ashurbanipal was greatly concerned. A messenger sent to his onetime ally Urtaki returned with the amazing news that the Elamites were already marching into Babylonia, covering the land of Akkad like a swarm of grasshoppers. Nevertheless, the Assyrian need not have been dismayed. Sickness and disease, or, as he interpreted it, the pest-gods Nergal and Ishum, deprived the Elamites of Urtaki; and his demise in 663 B.C. was quickly followed by the deaths of his Babylonian confrères.[9] Thus far, Assyria appeared to be in control of the situation.

---

[5] Harper, *ABL*, No. 576 (cf. Waterman, *RCAE*, I, 408 ff.).

[6] Letter from Naid-Marduk to Ashurbanipal's mother, Harper, *ABL*, No. 917 (Waterman, *RCAE*, II, 136 ff.).

[7] Harper, *ABL*, No. 1114 (Waterman, *RCAE*, II, 276 f.).

[8] On the activity in Bit Iakin see Harper, *ABL*, No. 1131 (Waterman, *RCAE*, II, 288 f.).

[9] Piepkorn, *Ashurbanipal*, I, 58 ff.

The very reverse was true. With the death of Urtaki the king of Susa, Tepti-Huban-Inshushinak, was
at once recognized as the ruler of the now united
land. Naturally his first task was the eradication of
all possible rivals. The sons of Huban-haltash II, Kudurru and Paru, together with the sons of Urtaki,
Huban-nugash, Huban-aʾpi, and Tammaritu, fled the
country to Assyria, and with them departed sixty
courtiers and numerous archers. Ashurbanipal wel-
comed them with open arms; their fathers before
them had been rulers of a part of Elam through Assyrian help, and they too might be restored. Consequently, though he received at his court Huban-tahrah and Nabu-damiq as ambassadors of the Elamite
and pictured them in relief as a fat old eunuch and a
youthful official,[10] he refused their demand for the
fugitives' extradition.

Safe on his throne, Tepti-Huban-Inshushinak erected a new temple to Inshushinak in Susa.[11] On a
stele he told how he had conquered the lands of the
Balahute and Lallari with the help of Huban and Inshushinak,[12] though another text credited his success
to the deity Pinikir.[13] An inscription on a huge stone
enumerated the high officials of court and temple together with their offerings and gifts. Those mentioned
include a high priestess of Huban, priests of Napir,

[10] Piepkorn, *Ashurbanipal*, I, 60 ff.; Layard, *Monuments of Nineveh*, 2d ser. (London, 1853), Pl. 49; Streck, *Assurbanipal*, pp. 316 ff.

[11] Scheil, *Mém.*, III, 98–99 (Nos. 60–61); cf. Jéquier, *Mém.*, I, 131.

[12] *Mém.*, III, 96 (No. 59).   [13] *Mém.*, V, 84 (No. 87).

Shuda, and Pinikir, and men of Anzan and Parashu, perhaps the very lands now controlled by descendants of the Iranian Achaemenes.[14]

Thus fortified, the Elamite once again turned to thoughts of conquest; but in July of 653 he was seized with epilepsy, doubtless induced by family intermarriage, although Ashurbanipal in Assyria attributed it to evil planned for him by the moon-god Sin. Nevertheless, the Elamite began the attack in August by encamping near Bit Imbi and threatening Der. Assyrian troops advanced in September to meet him on the Ulai, the modern Karkhah, and he retreated from Bit Imbi to Susa, then returned to offer resistance at Tell Tuba.[15] Early in the conflict one of his generals, Simburu, deserted to his enemies. The king's nephew Urtaki was wounded by an arrow and begged decapitation from his Assyrian captors, while the eunuch Ituni, but recently an Elamite ambassador at the Assyrian court, attempted to cut his own bowstring when he saw the battle turning against him, but was beheaded. Tepti-Huban and a son fled from the mêlée, but their chariot overturned and both were killed outright. The Ulai River was blocked with the corpses of the slain, wrote Ashurbanipal, and dead bodies filled the plain of Susa. Exaggerated as the Assyrian account may be—and successive editions of

[14] Scheil, *Mém.*, XI, 80 f. (No. 102).

[15] Piepkorn, *Ashurbanipal*, I, 62–69; for the dating cf. J. Mayr, *ibid.*, pp. 105–9. For inscriptions on or intended for reliefs picturing this battle cf. Streck, *Assurbanipal*, pp. 310–17 and 322–33, with references to the reliefs themselves.

the prism inscriptions added still more gruesome details—the battle appears to have been a catastrophe for Elam. Tepti-Huban-Inshushinak, king of united Elam, having been slain with his (eldest?) son, Assyria enthroned at Madaktu Huban-nugash, son of Urtaki, a refugee in Nineveh who had been brought along by the army for just such an emergency. To make matters worse, a revolt in Hidalu overthrew that city's ruler, Shutruk-Nahhunte; and another son of Urtaki, Tammaritu, likewise an Elamite refugee in Assyria, ascended the throne there.[16] The greater part of the country was now ruled by men who were at least nominally pro-Assyrian.

Susa, however, appears to have escaped the fate of other Elamite centers, and in all probability the local successor to Tepti-Huban-Inshushinak was Adda-hamiti-Inshushinak (653–648), son of an otherwise unknown Hutran-tepti. His inscriptions abound in Akkadian loan words and pseudo-ideograms, indicating a large Semitic element among his subjects. He calls himself prince of Elam and of Gisati, which may be his way of writing the Akkadian *kishshati*, "totality"; he honors the deities Huban, Kiririsha, Inshushinak, and Ruhuratir and tells of accomplishments in the lands Bessit and Shepshilak.[17] Pictured on a stele, his garment and helmet with jutting visor

[16] Piepkorn, *Ashurbanipal*, I, 70 f.; relief inscriptions: Streck, *Assurbanipal*, pp. 324 f.

[17] Scheil, *Mém.*, XI, 77 (No. 100B), and III, 92 (No. 58); cf. Pézard in *Babyloniaca*, VIII (1924), 1–26. Cf. also Scheil, *Mém.*, XI, 83, and Pézard in *Babyloniaca*, VIII, 4 and Pl. 2.

remind us of Hanni of Aiapir; his nose is short and straight, his beard hangs in long strands.[18]

For the short space of eight months Huban-nugash in Madaktu remained loyal to the monarch who had placed him on the throne. When Shamash-shum-ukin revolted from Ashurbanipal, the Elamite promptly deserted his benefactor, encouraged various Arameans to support Babylon, and sent his own generals, Attametu and Neshu, into the plain. He likewise urged Undasi,[19] another son of Tepti-Huban-In-shushinak, to avenge his father's death.

From Assyria Ashurbanipal quickly apprised other Elamites that he was aware of their defection. He pointed to the fate of the Elamite general Simburu, a deserter to Assyria at the battle of Tell Tuba, since killed for anti-Assyrian activities. Finally, he expressed his dissatisfaction with his Elamite informers, who remained inactive though they knew that Huban-nugash was now breaking his oaths of loyalty to Assyria and was taking the part of Babylon in the civil war.[20] Meantime the Elamite troops of Huban-nugash concentrated near Der, but the ensuing battle with Assyrian forces stationed near Mangisi ended in utter rout.[21]

[18] Relief and inscription: Scheil, *Mém.*, XI, 76 (No. 100*A*).

[19] Elamite hypocoristic form of Untash- . . . . ; Attametu is another Adda-hamiti- . . . . .

[20] Harper, *ABL*, No. 1380 (Waterman, *RCAE*, II, 462 ff.).

[21] Piepkorn, *Ashurbanipal*, I, 76 f. For the location of Mangisi near Der cf. the text in Nies and Keiser, *Babylonian Inscriptions in the Collection of James B. Nies*, Vol. II (New Haven, 1920), No. 33, ll. 6 f.

Revolt at once flamed in the mountains. Nabu-bel-shumate, who was making a pretense of loyalty to Assyria in the Sealands, knew that the Elamite cities had rebelled from their sovereign.[22] Hastily Huban-nugash sought alliance elsewhere, but this time he turned not to Assyria but to his brother in Hidalu. He and his son entered the city, where they met people of the land of Parsumash; with them were messengers of the land Rashi and an ambassador of Shamash-shum-ukin, who was also seeking support.[23] The revolt was nevertheless successful, and early in 651 Huban-nugash was dethroned by another Tammaritu, nephew of Huban-haltash II.[24]

The change in rulers did not result in a change in policy. Like his predecessor, Tammaritu decided to support Shamash-shum-ukin in Babylon; at his court, by March of 651, he received Nabu-bel-shumate,[25] now so openly anti-Assyrian that a year later Belibni, governor of the Sealands, was commissioned by Ashurbanipal to apprehend him.[26] Undeterred, the Elamite started his own troops on the move and threatened to overrun the Nippur region in central

[22] Harper, *ABL*, No. 839 (Waterman, *RCAE*, II, 82 ff.).

[23] Harper, *ABL*, No. 1309 (Waterman, *RCAE*, II, 410 ff.).

[24] See Table IV at the end of this volume. The genealogy is made clear by the text in Streck, *Assurbanipal*, pp. 180 f., obv. 30–34; cf. also Bauer, *Das Inschriftenwerk Assurbanipals* (Leipzig, 1933), II, 51 f., obv. 14.

[25] Klauber *Texte*, No. 105.

[26] Harper, *ABL*, Nos. 289 and 998 (Waterman, *RCAE*, I, 200 f., and II, 190 ff.).

Babylonia.[27] Ashurbanipal attempted to forestall this by sending one of his generals into Elam;[28] simultaneously he was advised to deprive Tammaritu of assistance from the region of Hidalu. The people of Parsumash, declared his informant, were not advancing to the aid of the Elamites, although Tammaritu had urged them to do so; if the Assyrian forces under Marduk-shar-usur were to advance quickly, the land of Elam would become his possession.[29]

In all probability no Assyrians entered Elam at this time. Instead, a native general, Indabigash, led an insurrection against Tammaritu early in 649. The beginning of the revolt, which found Nabu-bel-shumate in the region of Hidalu at the city Hudimiri,[30] was known even to Bel-ibni, into whose hands fell Tammaritu and his numerous retinue as they were fleeing from Indabigash.[31]

The accession of Indabigash at Madaktu gave an unexpected turn to the affair. Ashurbanipal had no means of knowing the new ruler's attitude toward Assyria; consequently, while awaiting a reply to his letter to the new sovereign,[32] he ordered Marduk-shar-

[27] Harper, *ABL*, No. 1195 (an omen); cf. Waterman, *RCAE*, II, 326 f. Cf. Piepkorn, *Ashurbanipal*, I, 78 f. and 102 f.

[28] Harper, *ABL*, No. 960 (Waterman, *RCAE*, II, 164 f.).

[29] Harper, *ABL*, No. 961 (Waterman, *RCAE*, II, 166 f.).

[30] Harper, *ABL*, No. 521 (Waterman, *RCAE*, I, 366 ff.). On Hudimiri see below, p. 204.

[31] Harper, *ABL*, No. 284 (Waterman, *RCAE*, I, 196 f.).

[32] Harper, *ABL*, No. 1151 (Waterman, *RCAE*, II, 300 ff.).

usur to bring Tammaritu and his retinue to the court. There they made abject surrender, and their lives were spared in the hope that they might prove useful to Assyria at some future time.[33] Shuma, a son of Tammaritu's sister, fled from Elam to the Tahha tribe of Arameans, from whom Bel-ibni secured him and promised to send him to Nineveh. It would be wise, continued the viceroy of the Sealands, if Ashurbanipal were to declare a trade embargo among the Puqudu against the Elamites until political matters were on a firmer footing.[34]

Indabigash appears at first to have responded favorably to the overtures of Assyria,[35] but soon he too became an ally of Nabu-bel-shumate,[36] who ventured into the alluvium, where he captured several Assyrians, including Marduk-shar-usur. At once the true state of affairs was evident, and Ashurbanipal was deluged with pleas for cavalry at Nippur and Uruk to prevent further raids.[37]

Tammaritu now saw his opportunity. Boasting his courage, he begged to be sent with Assyrian troops to Der, within easy striking distance of Madaktu; his plea was obviously a request for reinstatement as

[33] Piepkorn, *Ashurbanipal*, I, 78 ff.

[34] Harper, *ABL*, No. 282 (Waterman, *RCAE*, I, 194 f.).

[35] Piepkorn, *Ashurbanipal*, I, 80 f.

[36] Harper, *ABL*, Nos. 1323 and 1167 (Waterman, *RCAE*, II, 422 f. and 308 f.); Piepkorn, *Ashurbanipal*, I, 102 f.

[37] Harper, *ABL*, Nos. 963 and 622 (Waterman, *RCAE*, II, 166 ff., and I, 434 f.).

king of that city.[38] Ashurbanipal considered this a
good investment and moved his troops toward Der
with an ultimatum to Indabigash that unless he soon
repented of his ways he too should suffer the fate of
Tepti-Huban-Inshushinak.[39] This was not the Assyrian's only plan. By July of 648 he was in communication with an Elamite general named Huban-shibar, upon whom he urged further negotiations with
Bel-ibni.[40] The viceroy understood the situation. He
knew that Huban-shibar was stirring up a revolt in
Elam and that if the Assyrians now concentrating at
Der were to advance into the mountains Indabigash
would most certainly be dethroned. But haste was essential if all these affairs were to be brought to a successful conclusion. He himself was sending additional
troops to Der, for the king of Elam was stationed in
Bit Imbi.[41]

From the days of Tepti-Huban-Inshushinak's
death at the hands of Ashurbanipal's warriors, the
ruler of Susa had remained unrecognized in the royal
inscriptions of Assyria, although Adda-hamiti-Inshushinak was occupying the throne. By 648 the latter's
son, Huban-haltash III (648–636?), had come to

[38] Harper, *ABL*, No. 1148 (Waterman, *RCAE*, II, 298 ff.).

[39] Cylinder C, viii 47–63, in Streck, *Assurbanipal*, pp. 142 f.; cf. *LAR*,
Vol. II, § 878.

[40] Harper, *ABL*, No. 1170 (Waterman, *RCAE*, II, 310 f.).

[41] Harper, *ABL*, Nos. 460 and 1063 (Waterman, *RCAE*, I, 320 f., and
II, 238 f.).

power, and now he frustrated Assyria's attempt to make Tammaritu king again in Madaktu by becoming king of this city as well as of his own Susa.[42] He realized that Elam and Assyria need not be enemies solely on account of Nabu-bel-shumate; therefore he summoned his confederates and advised them to surrender the Chaldean, whose capture Assyria deemed so imperative. But civil war in Elam during the preceding century had brought kingship to an all-time low ebb; witness the fact that Huban-haltash could only advise, not command. Unfortunately for his own future, his advice was disregarded by his nominal subordinates. Nabu-bel-shumate continued alive and free, and nothing remained but to prolong the useless combat with Assyria.[43]

Sure of a refuge in Elam, Nabu-bel-shumate hired troops among the Hilmu, Pillatu, and Iashian tribes of Arameans on the eastern shore of the Persian Gulf and crossed the waters to harass Bel-ibni in the Sealands. Bel-ibni retaliated by sending across the Gulf four hundred bowmen, who killed several hundred oxen of the Hilmu and Pillatu; but Nabu-bel-shumate remained untouched in the city Hupapanu.[44] An Assyrian raiding party captured treasures belonging to the sheikh of the land Bananu in the land Nahal.

[42] Cylinder C, ix 89 ff.; cf. Bauer, *Das Inschriftenwerk Assurbanipals*, II, 17 f., earlier in Streck, *Assurbanipal*, pp. 144 f.; *LAR*, Vol. II, § 879.

[43] Harper, *ABL*, No. 281, obv. 23–31 (Waterman, *RCAE*, I, 192 f.).

[44] Harper, *ABL*, No. 1000 (Waterman, *RCAE*, II, 192 ff.).

Another body, one hundred and fifty in number, captured one hundred and thirty prisoners in the country
across the Takkatap River; when they tried to retrace
their steps, they were met by three hundred bowmen
of the Halat tribe, who attempted an ambush on the
river at Nahal, twenty-eight hours' marching time
from the Sealands. Fortunately only twenty were
wounded, the Elamite loss being considerably more.
Bel-ibni himself went to the rescue with six hundred
bowmen and fifty cavalrymen and secured fifteen
hundred cattle belonging to the king of Elam and the
sheikh of the Pillatu. Not all could be brought back
to Babylonia, for many were drowned in the Gulf and
others were killed on the spot; but Bel-ibni managed
to send a hundred of the best with forty drovers to
Ashurbanipal's court.[45]

The small numbers of combatants participating in
these raids and counterraids indicate that conditions
in this region were then not unlike those found by
travelers crossing southern Babylonia in the nineteenth century after Christ.[46] Yet the letters of Bel-
ibni and his fellow governors to Ashurbanipal were
retouched by Assyrian scribes to produce the cele-
brated "seventh campaign" in the so-called "Rassam
Cylinder" inscription of that monarch. This alleged
campaign is confused; it becomes clear only when we

[45] Harper, *ABL*, No. 520 (Waterman, *RCAE*, I, 364 ff.).

[46] Cf., for example, W. K. Loftus, *Travels and Researches in Chaldaea
and Susiana* (New York and London, 1857), pp. 331 and 390 ff.

realize that Assyria, after the revolt of Shamash-shum-ukin had been brought to an end, was attacking Elam from at least two bases, from the Sealands in the south and from the city of Der in the north. The objective of the southern thrust was Susa; that of the northern drive was the northern capital of Elam, Madaktu, reached through the land Rashi with its center at Bit Imbi.

The activities in the southern sector concern us first. An Assyrian garrison of five hundred men stationed in Zabdanu was ordered to raid Elam. It advanced to Irgidu, four hours' distance from Susa, killed the sheikh of the Iashian tribe and his many relatives, and with one hundred and fifty prisoners turned north to unite with the army at Der. Thus threatened, the chiefs of the Lahiru tribe pasturing southeast of this city submitted; and Ashurbanipal proudly recorded the fact, fully elaborated, in his royal inscriptions. Elamite prisoners, subsequently captured, were able to report that a son of Amedirra, Huban-nugash, had induced the district between the Hudhud River and the city Haiadanu to join him in a revolt against Huban-haltash, who had marshaled his forces on the bank of the river. A battle was imminent.[47]

The position of Huban-haltash was exceedingly precarious, but he concentrated what troops could be

[47] Harper, *ABL*, No. 280 (Waterman, *RCAE*, I, 190 ff.). This letter is obviously one of the sources from which the composer of the Rassam Cylinder drew his account of the beginning of the seventh campaign in col. iv, ll. 116–23; cf. Streck, *Assurbanipal*, pp. 42 ff.; *LAR*, Vol. II, § 800.

spared opposite Der in Bit Imbi, long since devastated by Sennacherib but now restored.[48] This was a wise move, for the Assyrians had decided to effect an entry into northern Elam. The invaders reached Bit Imbi and captured alive its commandant, Imbappi, son-in-law of the Elamite king. In his prism Ashurbanipal declared that Huban-haltash fled Madaktu for the mountains as a result of this victory, though Bel-ibni, who had simultaneously entered the southern part of the country, reported that internal revolt had brought about the Elamite's flight. Bel-ibni added that he had demanded the surrender of Nabu-bel-shumate from two Elamite leaders, Umhuluma and Undadu.[49]

Over a part of Elam centering around Bubilu,[50] not far from Susa, a rival king, Huban-habua, maintained himself for a moment after Huban-haltash turned fugitive. Then he, too, realized that the Assyrians who had entered from the north were sweeping the banks of the Karkhah River, and he fled from the scene. Madaktu fell before the invaders, and Bel-ibni, now transferred to the north, ordered all its treasures forwarded to Nineveh, though he urged that unless food were brought from Assyria the thousand prisoners he had taken would starve.[51] These same prisoners

[48] Harper, *ABL*, No. 781 (Waterman, *RCAE*, II, 46 ff.).

[49] Harper, *ABL*, No. 462 (Waterman, *RCAE*, I, 320 ff.).

[50] Bupila of the Persian documents from Susa in *Mém.*, Vol. IX.

[51] Harper, *ABL*, No. 794 (Waterman, *RCAE*, II, 56 ff.).

formed the subject matter of another letter in which Bel-ibni confessed his desire to withdraw from active command of the army. He has had word from Huban-shibar that the Elamite nobles have had a change of heart and are now willing to surrender Nabu-bel-shu-mate; their messengers have reached him in Madak-tu, protesting against the devastation of all Elam for the sake of a single Chaldean.[52]

Nothing came of this projected settlement; and from Madaktu, on sealed orders from Ashurbanipal,[53] Bel-ibni continued down the valley of the Karkhah. The list of conquered cities which found its way into the royal inscriptions includes all the most important sites in Elam which were reduced on this expedition by both bodies of invaders.[54] Most prominent are those in the land Rashi: Hamanu, Bit Imbi, Bube, Bit Bunakki, and Bit Arrabi. A second group comprises those in the valley of the Karkhah: Madaktu; Dur Undasi; Tuba and Tell Tuba, where the fateful battle with Tepti-Huban-Inshushinak had occurred; Din Sharri, where the god Ria had been worshiped in the days of Huteludush-Inshushinak; and Susa. A third group includes the cities inhabited by Aramean tribes: Haiausi,[55] Gatudu, Daeba, and others.

[52] Harper, *ABL*, No. 792 (Waterman, *RCAE*, II, 54 f.).

[53] Harper, *ABL*, No. 285 (Waterman, *RCAE*, I, 198 f.).

[54] Streck, *Assurbanipal*, pp. 46 f.; *LAR*, Vol. II, § 804.

[55] So read, instead of Haialilsi, on the prisms in the British Museum by A. C. Piepkorn.

One of those ceremonies which so rejoiced the heart of Ashurbanipal took place at Susa. There Tammaritu, son of Huban-nugash, was once more enthroned king of a part of Elam;[56] and to him, as from one sovereign to another, the absent king of Assyria inscribed a reminder of his own good treatment in the past and a promise of better things in the future, provided Tammaritu remained faithful, did not take the part of Nabu-bel-shumate, and abstained from alliance with Huban-haltash.[57]

The king of Assyria also had word for the inhabitants of Rashi. They are to recall how he sent food to Elam when there was famine in the land under Urtaki, and to act accordingly. Let them now obey the commands of their new sovereign, Tammaritu.[58] Because this advice would sound ill in the ears of a people whose capital city, Bit Imbi, had only recently been ravaged, Ashurbanipal returned to power its commander, Imbappi. Couched in all the formalities of diplomatic language, the Assyrian's words on this occasion lost none of their effectiveness: Let the people of Rashi remember the fate of Huban-haltash and obey Tammaritu, or take the consequences.[59]

Installed in his homeland where he could obtain white Nisaean horses with little difficulty, Tammaritu

[56] Streck, *Assurbanipal*, pp. 44 f.; *LAR*, Vol. II, § 802.

[57] Harper, *ABL*, No. 1022 (Waterman, *RCAE*, II, 212 ff.).

[58] Harper, *ABL*, No. 295 (Waterman, *RCAE*, I, 204 ff.).

[59] Harper, *ABL*, No. 1260 (Waterman, *RCAE*, II, 376 f.).

remembered the foreign goddess who had comforted him in a strange land and sent three of the animals to Ishtar of Uruk. From that city, after some hesitation, they were forwarded to Ashurbanipal in Nineveh, where the dedication inscribed on their harness could be read: "From the king of Elam, Tammaritu, to Ishtar of Uruk."[60]

Huban-haltash seized this moment to return from the central fastnesses, and the Assyrian nominee hastily sought refuge in Assyria. This setback was discreetly misinterpreted in the royal inscriptions; but Bel-ibni knew that Huban-haltash in Madaktu was, again to no avail, urging upon his subjects the necessity of surrendering Nabu-bel-shumate.[61] Since his advice went unheeded, the depredations of Elamites and Arameans continued. By this time the patience of Assyria was completely exhausted, and the stage was set for a final coup which once and for all should put an end to an independent Elamite kingdom. It was the turn of fate that the last successful undertaking of a decaying Assyria should be carried to completion against the land which, from the dawn of history, had been hostile to the Babylonian lowland.

Bel-ibni, who again led the invaders, first descend-

[60] Harper, *ABL*, Nos. 268 and 831 (Waterman, *RCAE*, I, 180 ff., and II, 78 f.).

[61] Harper, *ABL*, No. 281 obv. 23–31 (Waterman, *RCAE*, I, 192 f.). For the prism account cf. Streck, *Assurbanipal*, pp. 44–47; *LAR*, Vol. II, §§ 802 f.

ed upon Rashi in the north, where Imbappi had proved no more loyal than many another. Bit Imbi and Hamanu were successfully entered and utterly destroyed. Huban-haltash deserted Madaktu and crossed the Ulai with his mother, wife, and family to the city Talah. Two of his officials who had separately been in communication with Bel-ibni, Huban-shibar and Undadu, set out for the region of Hidalu intent on the gathering of allies.[62] In the prism inscription Ashurbanipal himself conducts the campaign, secures Bit Imbi, and forces the retreat of the Elamite to Dur Undasi and across the Idide.[63] It is not difficult to surmise whom we are to believe, the commander of the army in the field or the king in Nineveh.

Following the capture of Bit Imbi, the invaders ravaged the entire land of Rashi. Bit Bunakki, Hartabanu, and Tuba all fell into their hands, and they again proceeded down the Karkhah valley. Madaktu and Haltemash were secured, and the unguarded Susa and its neighboring cities Din Sharri, Sumuntunash, Pidilma, Bubilu, and Kabinak were entered. Now the campaign assumed more ambitious proportions. Huban-haltash, resigned to the life of a fugitive, gave up his position on the Idide River and withdrew to Hidalu. Thither Bel-ibni followed, for he knew that the land was already rebelling against its sovereign.

[62] Harper, *ABL*, No. 281 obv. 4–15 (Waterman, *RCAE*, I, 192 f.).

[63] Streck, *Assurbanipal*, pp. 46 ff.; *LAR*, Vol. II, § 805.

Banunu and a district of the city Bashimu fell prey
to the Assyrian, who was now at the very gateway to
the land Parsumash, over two hundred and fifty miles
—one hundred and twenty hours' march in mountainous country—from Der; and there the pursuit of
the Elamite ceased.[64]

The campaign had not been without results, including some of a totally unexpected nature. The
ruler of Parsumash, now a son of Teispes, Kurash or
Cyrus I, met the Assyrians near Hidalu, made confession of his impotence before a power greater than
himself, and as a proof of his kingly subservience offered his oldest son, Arukku, as hostage to Assyria.
The king of another near-by city-state, Pizlume of
Hudimiri, likewise sent his gifts to the ruler of Assyria.[65]

Meanwhile southern Elam had risen in rebellion
against its fugitive sovereign. The Arameans of the
Tahhasharua and Shallukea tribes accused him of
murdering Umhuluma, once in correspondence with
Bel-ibni, and of attempting to starve them into strict
obedience. Now they, too, had tired of the actions of
Nabu-bel-shumate, and Bel-ibni declared it extremely likely that Huban-haltash would surrender the

[64] The account of the campaign as here given is a composite of Streck,
Assurbanipal, pp. 46 ff. (*LAR*, Vol. II, §§ 806–8), and the fragmentary
text in Harper, *ABL*, No. 1311 (Waterman, *RCAE*, II, 412 ff.); cf. also
R. C. Thompson, *The Prisms of Esarhaddon and Ashurbanipal*, pp. 34 f.

[65] Weidner in *AOF*, VII (1931/32), 1–7; R. C. Thompson in *JRAS*,
1932, p. 239, and in *Annals of Archaeology and Anthropology* (University of Liverpool), XX (1933), 86 and 95. On Hudimiri cf. J. Schawe
in *AOF*, VIII (1932/33), 52 f.

hated desperado provided a sealed order—doubtless including an absolute pardon for the Elamite king— were sent by Ashurbanipal.[66]

While awaiting this order, the Assyrian was not in-active. Returning to Susa, he opened the city to his plundering warriors, and Ashurbanipal delighted to tell of the treasures they obtained. Silver, gold, and priceless objects accumulated by Elamite kings from Sumer and Akkad in times long past, precious stones, clothing and weapons, valuable furniture on which the kings of Elam had eaten and drunk, slept and been anointed, chariots, horses and mules with trap-pings of silver—all these and more fell into their greedy hands.

The great temple of Inshushinak, built of glazed brick with towers of shining bronze, was torn down, and Inshushinak wended his way to the plains of Babylonia for the first time in history. Other gods also whom the Elamites had revered in this degener-ate age were gathered from their shrines. Those par-ticularly noted as the gods whom the Elamite kings worshiped were Shumudu (the Assyrian transcription of the divine name known to us as Shimut), Lagamar, Partikira, Amman-kasibar (in whom some would rec-ognize Huban), Uduran (Hutran), and Sapak (per-haps the Kassite deity Shipak). Others were Ragiba, Sungursara,[67] Karsa and Kirsamas (one of whom may

[66] Harper, *ABL*, No. 281 obv. 31 ff. (Waterman, *RCAE*, I, 192 ff.).

[67] Perhaps "great king" in Elamite; cf. the city name Shuhari Sungur in Harper, *ABL*, No. 281 obv. 13 (Waterman, *RCAE*, I, 192 f.).

be Kiririsha), Shudanu, Aiapaksina, Belala, Panin-
timri (Pinikir), Napirtu (*napir*, "god"), Kindakarbu,
Silagara, and Napsa.[68] All these henceforth were to
receive worship in the land of Assyria, to which they
with their property, vessels, and priests were transported. They were splendid trophies of conquest, but
one other deity demanded and received far greater
homage—Nana of Uruk. The statue of this goddess,
which Kutir-Nahhunte had wrested from her dwelling over half a millennium before, now returned to
the lowlands with great ceremony. It mattered little
to Ashurbanipal that he added a round thousand
years to her captivity.[69]

From the temple sanctuaries of Susa, Madaktu,
and Huradi thirty-two gold, silver, bronze, and limestone statues of Elam's former sovereigns were carried out to be mutilated. Those of the first neo-Elamite ruler, Huban-nugash, son of Huban-tahrah, of his
successors Shutruk-Nahhunte II and Hallushu, and,
curiously enough, of Tammaritu, now residing in
Nineveh, were transported to Assyria. Bel-ibni
gathered together the colossi which guarded the temples, removed the fierce wild oxen which adorned
their gates, and vowed them to destruction. His soldiers trod the paths of secret groves into which no
stranger had ever been permitted to enter, and set

[68] Cf. P. Jensen, "Elamitische Eigennamen," *WZKM*, VI (1892),
47–70; De Genouillac, "Les dieux de l'Élam," *RT*, XXVII (1905), 94–119;
Hüsing in *OLZ*, VIII (1905), 385 ff.; C. Frank, "Elamische Götter," *ZA*,
XXVIII (1914), 323–29.

[69] See above, p. 111.

them on fire. Tombs of the former kings were violated; their offerings ceased.

For twenty-five days Assyrian troops marched over Elam scattering salt on the ruined fortresses. The royal families, in particular the females of the lines through whom royalty descended, were transported to Assyria along with the prefects and mayors of the conquered cities, while hundreds of captive warriors with their superior officers—bowmen, horsemen, charioteers, and footmen—were deported. Wild asses, gazelles, and all kinds of beasts, declared Ashurbanipal, henceforth should occupy the ruins; the phraseology reminds us of prophecies soon to be uttered by Hebrew captives in Babylon. Further, according to a writer in the Old Testament, Elamites, Susians, and men of the Tahha tribe of Arameans were colonized in Samaria.[70] To a people conscious of a splendid past there could be no greater sign of degradation and decay.

So much for the Assyrian royal annals. The hundreds of splintered monuments found by the excavators at Susa and the disordered condition of the mound tell much the same story.[71] There is no reason to doubt the Assyrian claim that a wealth of plunder was secured from the temple precinct of Inshushinak, but an enumeration of the objects they left behind is not without its own particular interest.[72]

The neo-Elamite kings had continued to employ

[70] Ezra 4:9.   [71] Cf. De Morgan, *Mém.*, I, 96 ff.
[72] De Mecquenem, *Mém.*, VII, 61–130; De Morgan, *Mém.*, VII, 49–59.

the foundation deposits and temple paraphernalia of their predecessors, such as inscribed gold leaves together with seals and statuettes of Shulgi of Ur. In addition to these, as their own gifts to the deity, they had vowed gold, silver, and lead pendants, threads, disks, and bracelets. Nor were these all. Serpent heads of lead, of gold-plated silver, and of bronze suggest that the snake-goddess had not ceased to hold the reverence of the Elamite worshiper.[73] Bronze statuettes of shaven men and high-coiffured women in ankle-length robes were numerous. Large bronze stamp seals, bracelets, birds, votive hatchets, chisels, and pins all sound curiously out of place for deposit in a temple, as do hundreds of stamp and cylinder seals from every period of history; but the medallions and pendants of bronze are like those of gold and silver, and the bronze leaves are identical with those of more precious metals bearing dedicatory inscriptions of former sovereigns. Ivory blocks, statuettes, disks, and plaques were perhaps more in keeping with religious usage. Such objects in ivory and an ape executed in lapis lazuli point toward undisturbed commerce with India and interior Iran, while numerous articles manufactured from shell speak of trade with or control of a shore of the Persian Gulf. Glazed bricks, plaques, and bas-reliefs best display the contemporary craftsman's skill.

The havoc wrought by the warriors of Ashurbani-

[73] Cf. Toscanne, "Études sur le serpent," *Mém.*, XII, 153–227.

pal prevents us from picturing, even cursorily, the buildings and temples which the later Elamites had adorned, though there is no reason to assume that they differed radically in appearance from those of the great Shilhak-Inshushinak. Now all were torn down, the temples wrecked, their contents plundered.

In one of his letters Bel-ibni speaks of the booty obtained from Susa, of Nana's triumphal journey to Uruk, and of Marduk-shar-usur's establishment as temporary governor of Susa. He further reports that officers have successfully been introduced into Bit Bunakki in the land of Rashi to the north, and among the Hilmu and Pillatu to the south.[74]

This was all very well from the standpoint of Assyrian administration, but few people had forgotten that Huban-haltash was still the nominal king of the land. Aware of his own weakness, Huban-haltash returned to the ruined Madaktu in a thoroughly chastened mood and communicated to Bel-ibni his desire to surrender Nabu-bel-shumate, now under guard.[75] The Assyrian general was uncertain how to act and suggested that he correspond directly with Ashurbanipal. To this Huban-haltash agreed; and nothing could more clearly indicate his subservience than his Assyrian method of dating the letter, inscribed on the twenty-sixth day of the month Tammuz, in the eponym of Nabu-shar-aheshu. He declares his willing-

[74] Harper, *ABL*, No. 1007 (Waterman, *RCAE*, II, 198 ff.).

[75] Harper, *ABL*, No. 1286 (Waterman, *RCAE*, II, 396 f.).

ness to hand over the Chaldaean and suggests a combined attack of Assyria and Elam upon the Martenai, who had broken into the city Lahiru.[76]

So graciously was this message received by Ashurbanipal that it was wonderingly declared among the Arameans, "The kings are at peace with each other."[77] Then Assyrian messengers advanced into Elam to secure Nabu-bel-shumate; but they were, after all, defeated in their purpose, for the Chaldaean in desperation committed suicide. The body could still be mutilated, and Bel-ibni preserved it in salt and forwarded it to Assyria with the news that the Elamite cities, Susa included, were completely under control.[78] In this he was slightly optimistic, for Rashi and its cities revolted from Pa'e, their Aramean ruler established by Ashurbanipal.[79] By force of arms Bit Imbi, Hamanu, Aranziashu, and the neighboring towns were again brought into subjection, and their warriors were compelled to join the military establishment of Assyria. Hereafter a large portion of Elam was a province of the Assyrian empire.

Some time later the Assyrian scribes were just putting the finishing touches to the great Rassam Cylinder when internal troubles again drove Huban-hal-

[76] Harper, *ABL*, No. 879 (Waterman, *RCAE*, II, 110 f.).

[77] Harper, *ABL*, No. 1115 (Waterman, *RCAE*, II, 276 ff.).

[78] Harper, *ABL*, No. 1284 (Waterman, *RCAE*, II, 390 f.); Streck, *Assurbanipal*, pp. 60 f.; *LAR*, Vol. II, § 815.

[79] Streck, *Assurbanipal*, pp. 62 f.; *LAR*, Vol. II, § 816.

tash from his diminished kingdom. From the city Marubishti in Ellipi partisans of Ashurbanipal brought him to Nineveh, where he joined other captive Elamites in the harness of the Assyrian's chariot.[80] Then, with the completion of this cylinder inscription, about 636 B.C., our sources cease to give continuous history. In fragmentary lists are named a mayor of the city Susanu, perhaps Susa, with the good Assyrian name Mannua-ki-Ashur; a governor of the Elamites, Pudiu; and another official of Elam.[81] They make it probable that Elam, or at least Susa, remained a province of Assyria; but thereafter our sources are silent until the neo-Babylonian period.

[80] Streck, *Assurbanipal*, pp. 82 f. and 836 f.; *LAR*, Vol. II, §§ 832 f.

[81] Johns, *Assyrian Deeds and Documents*, Vol. II (Cambridge, 1901), Nos. 904 i 4 f. and 857 iii 11 and 20; cf. Forrer, *Die Provinzeinteilung des assyrischen Reiches*, p. 102.

CHAPTER XII

MEDES AND PERSIANS

WHILE the Scythians were overrunning the kingdom which Khshathrita of Kar Kashshi had built up between 675 and 653 B.C., the king of Parsumash, Chishpish or Teispes (*ca.* 675–640), was enjoying a well-earned respite from intervention. Already in control of the Elamite Anzan and unharmed by the Scythian depradations within Media, he now moved down the valleys of the mountains to the district made famous by two of his descendants, Cyrus the Great, who built Pasargadae, and Darius, who erected the palace platform at Persepolis. At his death he was, therefore, master of two distinct regions: his original Parsumash, supplemented by Anzan, and the newly acquired Parsa, or Persian land. Nothing could be more natural than that his empire should be so divided between his two sons. Ariaramna or Ariaramnes (*ca.* 640–615), as the first son to be born after he had attained independent status, became "great king, king of kings, king of the land Parsa." Kurash or Cyrus I (*ca.* 640–600), though the elder son, became the subordinate who governed the old homeland as the "great king."

For a time the affairs of Ariaramnes prospered. On

a silver tablet he boasted that the great god Auramazda had given him the land Parsa, which possessed
good horses and virile men, and that his father Teispes before him had been king.[1] His brother in Parsumash almost immediately after his accession had
encountered difficulties. To him the invasion of Elam
by Assyria was an unparalleled achievement, which
merited some recognition. His oldest son, Arukku,
was tendered as a hostage and carried off to Nineveh,
where his presence would assure Ashurbanipal that
Parsumash had no designs on Elam.[2] For several
years thereafter our knowledge of affairs in Parsumash as in Parsa is obscured.

By 625 B.C. the son of Khshathrita, Uvakhshatra or
Cyaxares, again brought order to the Median highlands. The manner in which he accomplished this
feat is unknown. In Herodotus we read that he succeeded in making all the Scythian chieftains drunk,
whereupon he killed them;[3] but his return to power
doubtless entailed greater hardship than this. We
must likewise profess ignorance concerning most of
his subsequent conquests. Past experience had, how-

---

[1] Herzfeld in *AMI*, II (1930), 113–27. Doubts concerning the authen-
ticity of this tablet are expressed by H. H. Schaeder in *Sitzungsberichte der
Preussischen Akademie der Wissenschaften*, phil.-hist. Klasse, 1931, pp.
635–45, and by W. Brandenstein in *WZKM*, XXXIX (1932), 15–19, but
are successfully refuted by Herzfeld in *AMI*, IV (1932), 125–39, and by
E. Benveniste in Meillet, *Grammaire du vieux-Perse* (2d ed.; Paris, 1931),
pp. 1 f.

[2] See above, p. 204.   [3] Herodotus i. 106.

ever, taught him that an organized army was pre-
requisite to success; with the help of subject Scythians his people were taught the use of the bow, and
the army was separated into three classes of mobile
troops: spearmen, bowmen, and cavalry.[4] Thus
equipped, it was probably Cyaxares who brought to
an end in Parsa the reign of the "king of kings,"
Ariaramnes, and so prevented that sovereign's son
and grandson, Arshama or Arsames and Vishtaspa or
Hystaspes, from assuming even the title "king." The
silver tablet on which Ariaramnes had so proudly
boasted his descent was itself carried to Ecbatana.
Cyaxares, unhindered by Assyria, probably obtained
much of the territory south and west of Lake Urmia
also. Presumably the former Assyrian province Parsua became his at this time and the Manneans owned
him as king, although many of their number fled for
safety to Sin-shar-ishkun in Nineveh. With his capture of the Harhar province in the old Lullubi territory the way was opened by 615 to an attack upon Assyria proper.

Meanwhile a threat to the Assyrian empire had appeared in Babylonia. Nabopolassar, like Bel-ibni before him, had begun his career as Assyrian adminis-
trator of the Sealands. From this position he graduat-
ed to independent kingship. As king of the Sealands
he carried documents dealing with the temple cults of
Uruk to Susa, the control of which he had inherited

[4] Herodotus i. 103, also i. 73.

from Bel-ibni.[5] By 616 all Babylonia was under his control, and he himself attacked Assyria.[6] His invasion was met at Qablinu by Sin-shar-ishkun and Mannean fugitives. Only the arrival of an Egyptian army to the support of Assyria occasioned his retreat southward, for he had proved himself more than a match for his northern enemies. By March of 615 he had tried the line of the Tigris and secured the city of Madanu in the Arrapha province; in June he assaulted the city of Ashur, but again an Assyrian army forced his retreat.

At this point, though hardly as an ally of Nabopolassar, Cyaxares appeared on the scene, and in November of 615 assaulted a city in the Arrapha province. By August of the next year he had descended the Tigris, doubtless after a conquest of the regions north of Assyria, and surrounded Nineveh. Unable to force its walls, he was content with the capture of Tarbisu and then descended the river to Ashur, which he stormed and captured. Nabopolassar, having no desire to see the empire of Assyria the possession of an Iranian rival,[7] reached the city shortly after its

[5] Cf. Thureau-Dangin in *RA*, XI (1914), 141 f.

[6] For the subsequent conflicts see the tablet published by C. J. Gadd, *The Fall of Nineveh* (London, 1923); translation only, by the late D. D. Luckenbill in *LAR*, Vol. II, §§ 1167 ff. For the history cf. Olmstead, *History of Assyria*, pp. 634–38. For the historical interpretation of this period expressed by J. Lewy in *MVAG*, XXIX, Heft 2 (1924), 1–14, and also by König in his *Älteste Geschichte*, pp. 40–52, see the successful refutation of the former study by P. Schnabel in *ZA*, XXXVI (1925), 316–18.

[7] Cf. the greed of Belesys in the story of Ctesias in Diodorus Siculus ii. 28.

seizure. In the presence of two formidable armies the sovereigns came to terms; good will and alliance were contracted between them,[8] and Amytis, infant daughter of Astyages, Cyaxares' son, was betrothed to Nabopolassar's young son, Nebuchadnezzar.[9] Henceforth the two forces were to act as one.

Throughout 613 the Median troops were occupied elsewhere. It is at this point in his narrative that Herodotus injects the twenty-eight-year domination by Scythians; this may be merely a chronological displacement of the event or may imply still more, since Cyaxares on his return to the lowlands is called king of the Umman-Manda, "hosts of the Manda." It may suggest that during 613 the Mede obtained control over many of the Scythian wanderers in the mountain lands north of Assyria.

However that may be, by 612 both Cyaxares and Nabopolassar were ready to attack Nineveh. The three battles they fought between June and August are recorded in the chronicle and correspond with three defeats suffered by "Arbaces the Mede" and "Belesys the Babylonian" described by Ctesias,[10] but

[8] Gadd, op. cit., pp. 33 and 38; cf. LAR, Vol. II, § 1174.

[9] Berossus, frag. 43 (cf. P. Schnabel, Berossos [Berlin, 1923], p. 270), from Polyhistor, in Eusebius Chron. i. 5. 3 (ed. Schoene, pp. 29 f.); Berossus, frag. 44 (cf. Schnabel, op. cit., pp. 270 f.), from Abydenus, in Eusebius Chron. i. 9. 2 (ed. Schoene, pp. 37 f.). Ctesias Persica, exc. 2 (ed. Müller, p. 45), also witnesses to the fact that Astyages had a daughter named Amytis.

[10] In Diodorus Siculus ii. 25 f.

a final assault in August was completely successful. Late in September Cyaxares returned to Media with his share of the spoil, but the end of his participation in Babylonian affairs had not yet come. A new kingdom of Assyria had been established in northern Mesopotamia, and Nabopolassar early in 610 appealed to the Mede for assistance. By November of that year Cyaxares and his troops reached Babylonia, where they joined forces with Nabopolassar; the subsequent march of these allies to Harran was of sufficient importance to merit the attention of the Babylonian crown prince, Nebuchadnezzar.[11] The mere recollection of the destruction wrought in Harran by Cyaxares and his Medes was enough to bring fear and respect for Iranians into the heart of a Babylonian ruler fifty years later.[12] After a few more years of warfare and uncertainty the city itself remained in the possession of the Mede.

Once again, after the conquests just enumerated, Median history fades into obscurity and inference must be our guide. The original kingdom of Cyaxares may be safely delimited as including the modern city

[11] Letter in Contenau, *Contrats et lettres* (Musée du Louvre, Département des antiquités orientales, "Textes cunéiformes," Vol. IX), No. 99; cf. Thureau-Dangin in *RA*, XXII (1925), 27–29. This letter, containing the statement "the king has gone to Harran; a large force of the Medes (Madai) went with him," should alone refute the view of Gadd that Cyaxares and his Umman-Manda were Scythians.

[12] Cf. in Langdon, *Die neubabylonischen Königsinschriften*, "Nabonid" texts No. 1 i 8 ff., No. 8 ii 1 ff. and x 12 ff.

Rayy south of Teheran in the east, Isfahan in the south, and the district of Atropatene, modern Azerbaijan, in the northwest, with his capital at Ecbatana, modern Hamadan.[13] Already, it would seem, he had incorporated the land Parsa within his state, and now Parsumash acknowledged his power. The administration of both these lands was granted to Kanbujiya or Cambyses I (*ca.* 600–559), who had followed Cyrus I on the throne as "king of the city Anshan."

Much of Iran was, therefore, subservient to Cyaxares, although the Cadusians, living in the narrow hot region between the Elburz Range and the shores of the Caspian Sea, denied to him their land.[14] Ctesias alone is authority for the statement that the Parthians revolted from the Medes in the reign of Astibaras, who in the Cnidian's system was identical with Cyaxares. A treaty, concluded after numerous battles had been fought, provided that the rebels should be governed by the Medes, whose allies they were to be for all time.[15] This account is not in itself improbable, and Parthia henceforth may have been subject to Media in such a way as outlying districts were later subservient to the Arsacid rulers.[16]

[13] Cf. Herzfeld, *AMI*, VII, 17 and 22 f.

[14] The Median Artaeus of the Ctesias story (ed. Müller, p. 42 [from Diodorus ii. 33]) is to be equated with Cyaxares; see table above, p. 176. Cf. also Strabo *Geogr.* xi. 13. 3.

[15] Ctesias, ed. Müller, pp. 42 f. (from Diodorus ii. 34).

[16] Cf. Herzfeld in *AMI*, VII (1934), 29 f.; Neilson C. Debevoise, *A Political History of Parthia* (in preparation; to be published by the Oriental Institute in association with the University of Chicago Press).

Cyaxares' conquests to the northwest were even more extensive. There the territories which had once formed a part of the Haldian kingdom and now were in the possession of foreign invaders, the Armenians, became his; and Herodotus expressly declares that all Cappadocia to the Halys River (modern Kizil Irmak) was subject to the Medes before the rise of the Persian empire.[17] By 590 B.C. Cyaxares had reached the Halys, where he came into contact with Alyattes, the ruler of Lydia. Neither side gained the advantage during five years of the ensuing war; but in the sixth year, 585, a solar eclipse was understood as an evil portent and an armistice declared. Arbitration was resorted to, and Nabu-naid of Babylon, probably acting for Alyattes, agreed with Syennesis of Cilicia, the representative of Cyaxares, that the boundary between Media and Lydia should henceforth be the Halys River. To insure the perpetuity of the boundary thus defined, Aryenis, daughter of Alyattes, became the wife of Astyages, Cyaxares' son. Within the year Astyages succeeded his father.[18]

Meanwhile Nebuchadnezzar (604–562) had succeeded his father in Babylon. In addition to his extensive holdings in North Syria, he also controlled

[17] Herodotus i. 72.

[18] Herodotus i. 73 ff.; for date of the eclipse see references in Prášek, *Geschichte*, I, 164 f. Herodotus i. 103 expressly declares that the eclipse occurred in the reign of Cyaxares; Cicero *De divinatione* i. 49 and Eusebius *Chron. can.* (ed. Schoene, II, 94 f.) date the conclusion of the war to the reign of Astyages; cf. also Pliny *Hist. nat.* ii. 12 (ed. Gronovius). In Babylonian the name Astyages is written Ishtumegu.

the Sealands in the south and Susa in the east. Bricks
stamped with his name were used to erect buildings in
that city, while an alabaster vase with his inscription
and a weight with his legend are further witnesses of
his control.[19] A copy of one of his earliest inscriptions,
mentioning the Puqudu tribe of Arameans, Der, Lahiru, and Arrapha, made its way to the eastern city.[20]

The campaigns of Nebuchadnezzar in the west
have received much comment because of their interest to students of biblical history. One Greek tradition declared that he sought assistance from Astibaras or Cyaxares the Mede when he began the expedition which included the capture of Jehoiachin of
Jerusalem in 597;[21] another related that he built the
famed hanging gardens of Babylon to please his Me-
dian-born queen, the daughter of Astyages.[22] The fact
that Babylon under Nebuchadnezzar became the

[19] Bricks: Scheil in *RA*, XXIV (1927), 47 f., identical with those from
Babylon in Langdon, *Die neubabylonischen Königsinschriften*, "Nebukad-
nezar" texts Nos. 39–41. Vase: *Mém.*, VI, 56, now in Langdon, *op. cit.*,
"Nebukadnezar" No. 47. Weight: *Mém.*, Vol. IV, Pl. 18 (cf. Scheil in
Mém., V, xxiii); cf. also De Mecquenem in *RA*, XXI (1924), 109, and
Mém., XXV, 207 f.

[20] Scheil, *Mém.*, II, 123 ff., a part of the text now complete in Langdon,
op. cit., pp. 144 ff. ("Nebukadnezar" No. 17).

[21] Polyhistor (frag. 24) in Eusebius, *Evang. Praep.* ix. 39; cf. E. H.
Gifford, *Eusebii Pamphili Evangelicae praeparationis libri XV*, III,
Part 1 (Oxford, 1903), 482.

[22] Berossus, frag. 2 (cf. Schnabel, *Berossos*, pp. 271–73), from Josephus
Contra Apionem i. 19, repeated in *Antiq.* x. 11. 1; also in the Armenian
version of Eusebius *Chron.* (ed. Schoene, pp. 47 f.) in Eusebius, *Werke*.
V. *Die Chronik* (transl. by J. Karst; Leipzig, 1911), pp. 22 f.

most strongly fortified city of the ancient Orient[23] is far more indicative of the political situation and of the Babylonians' dread of their eastern neighbor.

So long as Nebuchadnezzar lived, Mede and Babylonian were too evenly matched to make a trial by battle profitable; but after his death the internal condition of Babylonia gave Astyages an unhoped-for opportunity. Amel-Marduk (562–560) broke with the policy of his father, freed the captive Jewish king, Jehoiachin, and followed the leadership of the priestly party. The militarists supplanted him with Nergal-shar-usur, who after four years fell before the pro-priestly Labashi-Marduk. In 556 the latter in turn was assassinated by militarists, who placed Nabu-naid on the tottering throne.[24]

This political crisis was aggravated by the loss of Elam and Susa, which had continued to pay enforced allegiance to Babylon throughout the brief reigns of Amel-Marduk and Nergal-shar-usur but which no longer formed a part of the kingdom by the accession of Nabu-naid.[25] Probably they became a part of the expanding empire of Astyages, while throughout

[23] Cf. Olmstead, "The Chaldaean Dynasty," *Hebrew Union College Annual*, II (1925), 42.

[24] Cf. Olmstead in *Hebrew Union College Annual*, II, 42 f., and *History of Palestine and Syria* (New York, 1931), pp. 539 f.

[25] So, if we are to judge from the archeological data. Vase of Amel-Marduk from Susa in Scheil, *Mém.*, X, 96, republished after restoration in *Mém.*, XIV, 60; cf. Thureau-Dangin in *RA*, IX (1912), 24 f. Vase of Nergal-shar-usur in Scheil, *Mém.*, X, 96.

Babylonia the belief grew that the hostile Medes would continue to advance and would hurl themselves upon the capital city.

The prophet Ezekiel had constantly encouraged his companions to accept their fate and to dwell peaceably with their new masters. Another Jew, embittered by the failure of the plan which had led to Jehoiachin's liberation, and steeped in prophecies of Jeremiah which predicted the coming of a foe from the north against Palestine,[26] saw in the threatened Median attack only the just vengeance of Yahweh upon proud Babylon. He declared that the powerful Medes, so apprehensively regarded by his captors and now supplemented by troops of Urartians or Haldians, Manneans, and Scythians, whom Cyaxares had conquered but a few years before, formed the instrument by which Yahweh would insure Babylon's destruction.[27] With keen delight he made much of the terror aroused in the heart of every Babylonian by the cruel and pitiless Medes, in whose hands the bow had become a most deadly battle weapon.[28] He recognized the internal weakness of Babylonia, where priestly and military parties in turn had set up four separate rulers in the short space of six years, and reminded his hearers that there was violence in the

[26] Jer. chaps. 4 ff.

[27] Isa. 13:17; Jer. 51:11 and 28; cf. the "Ararat, Minni, and Ashkenaz" of Jer. 51:27.

[28] Isa. 13:18; Jer. 50:14, 29, 42; 51:3 and 11.

land, with ruler turning against ruler.[29] Nor was he
unmindful of the ring of fortresses which surrounded
Babylon,[30] though he announced that the Medes
would crush them to pieces and annihilate in their
descent the Aramean Puqudu and the inhabitants of
the Sealands.[31] Finally, he declared, no Babylonian,
nor even a Jewish captive in the land, could hope that
the Medes would show mercy, for one and all would
be massacred. Rejoicing in what appeared to be the
city's imminent destruction, time and again he returned to his refrain:

> Flee from the midst of Babylon,
> Go out from the land of the Chaldeans.[32]

Unfortunately for the hopes of our would-be prophet, the threatened Median attack did not take place.
Nabu-naid (556–538) made himself secure upon the
throne, and the peril was past. Henceforth Astyages
was too much occupied with his own affairs to con-
template a conquest of the lowlands.

In Parsumash, now equated with Anzan, Cambyses I appears to have led a quiet existence. Nominally
king in his own right, he was actually subordinate to
the Medes, who had placed him over the land Parsa
after the disappearance of Ariaramnes. His marriage

[29] Jer. 51:46.   [30] Jer. 50:15; 51:12, 31 f.   [31] Jer. 50:21.

[32] Jer. 50:8, 28; 51:6, 9, 45, 50; Isa. 13:14. On this interpretation of
Isa., chapter 13, and Jer., chaps. 50 f., cf. the abstract of a paper read
before the Middle West Branch of the American Oriental Society, *JAOS*,
LI (1931), 370; cf. also Olmstead, *History of Palestine and Syria*, pp.
542–45.

with Mandane, a daughter of Astyages, considerably
raised his social status, which in Median eyes was not
high. Of this union was born Cyrus the Great.[33]
Promptly upon his accession in 559 Cyrus II began
the erection in Parsa at the site known as Pasargadae
of buildings which should mark him as being of the
true blood royal. His legend, inscribed beneath the
relief of his own personage, described him as "the
great king, the Achaemenid," a title which no less
recognized his subservience to Astyages, the "king of
kings."[34] Cyrus was, however, determined to prove
his right to the throne of the Mede. Proceeding to
gather strength within his own land by demanding allegiance from numerous Iranian tribes,[35] he accepted
at the same time an alliance with Babylon proffered
by Nabu-naid. The Babylonian hoped thus to rid his
empire of the danger from the Medes, who by their
control of Harran could at any time threaten the line
of communication between Babylonia and Syria; he

[33] Herodotus i. 107 f. This story is generally doubted, but the marriage
of a daughter of a king to a vassal is a well-known phenomenon of oriental
and Hellenistic history. There is no inherent reason for doubt. On the
other hand, the "tendency" of Ctesias in denying Median blood in the
founder of the Persian Empire (in *Persica*, exc. 2 [ed. Müller, p. 45]) is
perfectly obvious. Professor Olmstead draws my attention to the fact
that, shortly after the appearance of Ctesias at the court, Media revolted
in 410, at a time when the Persian empire was having trouble in Egypt
also; cf. Xenophon *Hellenica* i. 2. 19.

[34] Herzfeld in *AMI*, I (1929–30), 14 ff.

[35] Herodotus i. 125. Otanes and Gobryas, later conspirators with
Darius, were two leaders of such tribes; cf. Prášek, *Geschichte*, I, 203 f.

himself began to collect troops from Gaza on the border of Egypt to the Sealands along the Persian Gulf.

By 553 B.C. the plan of Cyrus was evident, and Astyages summoned him to court. Cyrus' refusal to attend constituted active rebellion[36] and was perhaps the prearranged signal for Nabu-naid to proceed against Syria. Harran was wrested from the Median garrison in this year, to the great joy of the Babylonian sovereign;[37] but Astyages was not thus diverted and ordered an army sent against his disobedient subject.

Concerning the subsequent warfare we have two variant reports by Greek historians and a dry narrative in a Babylonian chronicle. One Greek account, found in the writings of Nicolaus of Damascus, who derived his information from Ctesias, relates a story with a great deal of oriental coloring. The first battle, we read, lasted for two days and was a great victory for Astyages. Fought near the Medo-Persian frontier, the Persians, by whom we would understand the people of Parsa, fled to Pasargadae. A second battle, near this city, was also of two days' duration; although the Medes gained the advantage on the first day, the Persians, urged on by their womenfolk, obtained a

---

[36] Herodotus i. 127.

[37] Inscriptions: Langdon, *Die neubabylonischen Königsinschriften*, "Nabonid" texts Nos. 1, 8, and 9.

mighty victory on the second.[38] Astyages still remained on the offensive until a third battle[39] resulted in another complete victory for Cyrus. Astyages then fled with a remnant of his army but was captured after a slight struggle.

The second Greek account is by Herodotus, whose veracity we are seldom able to question. The Father of History knew of only two battles. In the first, at which Astyages was not present, his field commander Harpagus (from whose descendants Herodotus derived much information concerning early Media), together with a great part of the army, deserted to Cyrus. In a second battle the aged Astyages himself led the Medes and was taken prisoner.[40]

The sober Babylonian chronicle agrees with this story of Herodotus.[41] Astyages, we are told, collected his army and marched against Cyrus, the king of Anshan. The Median army revolted and handed its sovereign over to Cyrus, who at once proceeded to Ecbatana, the capital of the Median realm, and looted its treasure.

Thus ended the empire of the Medes, and thus began the sovereignty of the Persians. Elam, once great

[38] Nicolaus of Damascus in frag. 66; cf. F. Jacoby, *Die Fragmente der griechischen Historiker*, II *A* (Berlin, 1926), 365–70.

[39] Strabo *Geogr.* xv. 3. 8.

[40] Herodotus i. 127 f.

[41] Sidney Smith, *Babylonian Historical Texts*, pp. 110 ff. (col. ii, ll. 1–4).

in its own right, became the third ranking satrapy, but its custom of matrilinear succession was a baneful influence at the court of the Achaemenian sovereigns. Media, once itself the center of a mighty realm, became the second ranking satrapy, though Medes were equally honored with Persians, and foreigners spoke of them as a unity, Medes and Persians. Parsa, thenceforth considered the heart of the empire, was the satrapy par excellence, from which had come the virile successors of the Iranian Achaemenes. With the appearance of these successors the Near East entered a new phase of history.

TABLE I

AWAN	BABYLONIA
Peli (*ca.* 2670 B.C.)	
Tata	
Ukku-tahesh	
Hishur	
Shushun-tarana	
Napi-ilhush	
Kikku-sime-temti	
Luhhi-ishshan*	
	Sargon (ca. 2530 B.C.)
Hishep-ratep	
	Rimush
Helu	
	Manishtusu
Hita	
	Naram-Sin
Puzur-Inshushinak	
	Sharkalisharri
GUTI	GUTI
SIMASH	UR THIRD DYNASTY
Girnamme	Ur-Nammu (2290–2273)
Tazitta I	Shulgi (2272–2226)
Ebarti I	Bur-Sin (2225–2217)
Tazitta II	Gimil-Sin (2216–2208)
Enbiluhhan	*Ibi-Sin* (2207–2183)
Kindattu	
Idaddu I (Idadu-Inshushinak)	
Tan-Ruhuratir	
Ebarti II	
Idaddu II	Gungunum (2087–2061)

* In Tables I–III italics indicate proven contemporaneity.

TABLE II

SUKKALMAH	ELAM		BABYLONIA
	SUKKAL of Elam and Simash	SUKKAL of Susa	
Ebarti (*ca.* 2020–2001 B.C.)			
Shilhaha (Temti-Shilhak) (*ca.* 2000–1986)	Shirukduh	Shimut-wartash	Kudur-Mabuk
			Warad-Sin (1989–1978)
Shirukduh (*ca.* 1985–1966)	Shimut-wartash	Siwepalarhuppak	
	Siwepalarhuppak	Kuduzulush I	Rim-Sin (1977–1917)
Siwepalarhuppak (*ca.* 1965–1946)	Kuduzulush I	Kutir-Nahhunte	
Kuduzulush I (*ca.* 1945–1918)	Kutir-Nahhunte		Hammurabi (1947–1905)
		Addahushu	
Kutir-Nahhunte (*ca.* 1850–1841)	Tata (Atta-merra-halki)	Temti-agun	
	Temti-agun	Kutir-Shilhaha	
Temti-agun (*ca.* 1840–1826)	Kutir-Shilhaha	Kuk-Nashur I	
Kutir-Shilhaha (*ca.* 1825–1811)	Kuk-Nashur I	Shirtuh	
		Temti-raptash	
Kuk-Nashur I (*ca.* 1810–1800)	Temti-raptash	Kuduzulush II	
Temti-raptash (*ca.* 1799–1791)	Kuduzulush II	Tan-Uli	*Ammizaduga* (1801–1781)
Kuduzulush II (*ca.* 1790–1781)	Tan-Uli	Temti-halki	
Tan-Uli (*ca.* 1780–1771)	Temti-halki	Kuk-Nashur II	
Temti-halki (*ca.* 1770–1761)	Kuk-Nashur II		
	Bala-ishshan	Kuk-Kirwash	
	Kuk-Kirwash	Tem-Sanit	
		Kuk-Nahhunte	
Kuk-Kirwash	Kuk-Nahhunte	Kuk-Nashur III	
	KASSITES		KASSITES (1749 ff.)

TABLE III

ANZAN AND SUSA	BABYLONIA	ASSYRIA
Pahir-ishshan	Nazi-Maruttash	
(*ca.* 1310 B.C.)	(1319–1294)	
Attar-kittah		
(*ca.* 1295–1286)		
Huban-numena		
(*ca.* 1285–1266)		
Untash-Huban	*Kashtiliash III*	*Tukulti-Ninurta I*
(*ca.* 1265–1245)	(1249–1242)	(1255–1218)
Unpatar-Huban		
(*ca.* 1244–1243)		
Kidin-Hutran	*Enlil-nadin-shumi*	
(*ca.* 1242–1222)	(1241–1240)	
	Kadashman-Harbe	
	Adad-shum-iddina	
	(1238–1233)	
Halludush-Inshushinak		
(*ca.* 1221–1208)		
Shutruk-Nahhunte	*Zamama-shum-iddina*	*Ashur-dan I*
(*ca.* 1207–1171)	(1174)	(1189–1154)
	Enlil-nadin-ahhe	
Kutir-Nahhunte	(1173–1171)	
(*ca.* 1170–1166)	Marduk-shapik-zeri	
	(1170–1153)	
Shilhak-Inshushinak		
(*ca.* 1165–1151)		
Huteludush-Inshushinak	*Nebuchadnezzar I*	Ashur-resh-ishi
(*ca.* 1150–1140)	(1146–1123)	(1149–1117)
Shilhina-hamru-	Enlil-nadin-apli	
Lagamar		
	Marduk-nadin-ahhe	Tiglathpileser I
	(1116–1101)	(1116–1090)

TABLE IV

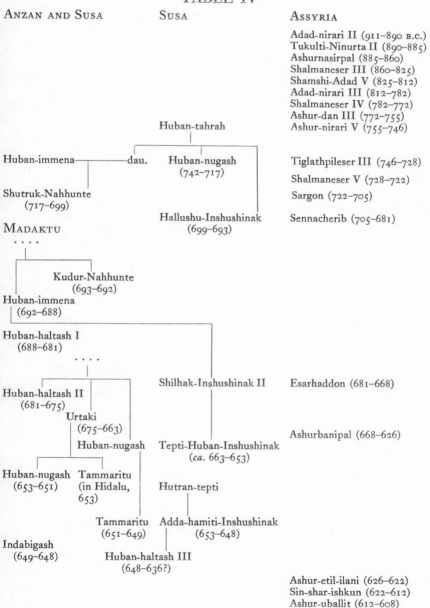

ANZAN AND SUSA   SUSA   ASSYRIA

Adad-nirari II (911–890 B.C.)
Tukulti-Ninurta II (890–885)
Ashurnasirpal (885–860)
Shalmaneser III (860–825)
Shamshi-Adad V (825–812)
Adad-nirari III (812–782)
Shalmaneser IV (782–772)
Ashur-dan III (772–755)
Ashur-nirari V (755–746)

Huban-tahrah

Huban-immena———————dau.   Huban-nugash
                                      (742–717)   Tiglathpileser III (746–728)

                                                    Shalmaneser V (728–722)
Shutruk-Nahhunte
     (717–699)   Sargon (722–705)

                         Hallushu-Inshushinak   Sennacherib (705–681)
MADAKTU   (699–693)
. . . .

          Kudur-Nahhunte
              (693–692)
Huban-immena
   (692–688)

Huban-haltash I
   (688–681)
      . . . .

Huban-haltash II   Shilhak-Inshushinak II   Esarhaddon (681–668)
   (681–675)
          Urtaki
          (675–663)   Ashurbanipal (668–626)
          Huban-nugash   Tepti-Huban-Inshushinak
                               (ca. 663–653)

Huban-nugash Tammaritu
   (653–651) (in Hidalu,   Hutran-tepti
              653)

          Tammaritu   Adda-hamiti-Inshushinak
          (651–649)   (653–648)
Indabigash
   (649–648)
          Huban-haltash III
              (648–636?)

                                      Ashur-etil-ilani (626–622)
                                      Sin-shar-ishkun (622–612)
                                      Ashur-uballit (612–608)

231

TABLE V

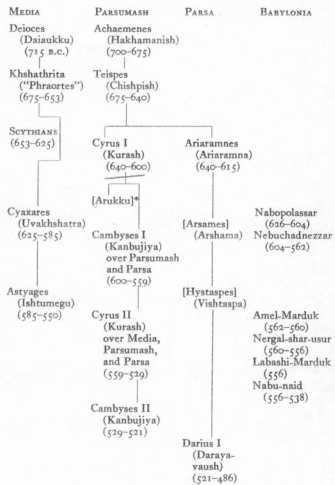

MEDIA	PARSUMASH	PARSA	BABYLONIA
Deioces (Daiaukku) (715 B.C.)	Achaemenes (Hakhamanish) (700–675)		
Khshathrita ("Phraortes") (675–653)	Teispes (Chishpish) (675–640)		
SCYTHIANS (653–625)	Cyrus I (Kurash) (640–600)	Ariaramnes (Ariaramna) (640–615)	
	[Arukku]*		
Cyaxares (Uvakhshatra) (625–585)	Cambyses I (Kanbujiya) over Parsumash and Parsa (600–559)	[Arsames] (Arshama)	Nabopolassar (626–604) Nebuchadnezzar (604–562)
Astyages (Ishtumegu) (585–550)	Cyrus II (Kurash) over Media, Parsumash, and Parsa (559–529)	[Hystaspes] (Vishtaspa)	Amel-Marduk (562–560) Nergal-shar-usur (560–556) Labashi-Marduk (556) Nabu-naid (556–538)
	Cambyses II (Kanbujiya) (529–521)		
		Darius I (Daraya-vaush) (521–486)	

* Names inclosed in [ ] are those of heirs who did not reign.

232

INDEX

With proper names the following abbreviations are used: *c.*, city name; *d.*, divine name; *l.*, land name; *p.*, personal name.

233